BOLLINGEN SERIES LXXVIII

By the same author

PREHISTORIC CAVE PAINTINGS (Tr. Norbert Guterman)
New York, Pantheon Books, 1945 (Bollingen Series IV)

PREHISTORIC POTTERY AND CIVILIZATION IN EGYPT
(Tr. Norbert Guterman)
New York, Pantheon Books, 1947 (Bollingen Series VIII)

MAX RAPHAEL

THE DEMANDS OF ART

With an Appendix

TOWARD AN EMPIRICAL THEORY OF ART

Translation by Norbert Guterman

BOLLINGEN SERIES LXXVIII

Princeton University Press

Copyright © 1968 by Bollingen Foundation, New York, N.Y.
Published for Bollingen Foundation, New York, N.Y.
by Princeton University Press, Princeton, N.J.

The translation was made from the unpublished
German manuscripts of "Wie ein Kunstwerk gesehen sein will"
and "Empirische Kunstwissenschaft."

THIS IS THE SEVENTY-EIGHTH IN A SERIES
OF WORKS SPONSORED BY AND
PUBLISHED FOR BOLLINGEN FOUNDATION

Library of Congress Catalogue Number: 65–10431

Composed and printed in the United States of America
by Clarke & Way, Inc.
Engravings by Publicity Engravers, Inc.
Bound by Russell-Rutter Company, Inc.
Designed by Bert Clarke

TABLE OF CONTENTS

LIST OF ILLUSTRATIONS

following p. 232

PREFACE

Bollingen Foundation is greatly indebted to Professor Robert S. Cohen, without whose concern and devotion this publication would not have been possible. He has given advice and assistance in many ways—in particular, with the selection of the illustrations and the provision of many of the editorial notes (in square brackets). Special thanks are due also to Professor Claude Schaefer, executor of the author's estate, Mrs. Emma Raphael, Dr. Ilse Hirschfeld, and Dr. Joachim Schumacher, who from their personal knowledge of the author's work were able to help solve many textual problems.

Thanks are also due Professor Lionetto Tintori for his help in finding the proper illustrations for Chapter III; for editorial work, to Margaret Kaplan; and for help in research, to Effi Biedrzynski, Ellen Callmann, Irene Gordon, John Rewald, Dr. Steffi Schmidt, and Gary Schwartz.

INTRODUCTION

When the author of this book died in New York in 1952, he was little known in the English speaking world. By force of historical circumstances he had lived the life of a wandering scholar, but he had nevertheless made what in my considered opinion is one of the most important contributions in our time to the philosophy of art. To understand why this was not realized during his lifetime we have only to review his nomadic existence.

Max Raphael was born in the frontier town of Schönlanke (West Prussia) on August 27, 1889. After graduating from the local high school, he studied the history of art, philosophy, and political economy at the universities of Berlin and Munich. At Berlin his principal teachers were Heinrich Wölfflin (history of art), Georg Simmel (philosophy), and Gustav von Schmoller (political economy); at Munich, Lujo Brentano (political economy). Munich at this period was in a state of creative ferment. Kandinsky had settled there in 1908 and had initiated the movement in painting that was to be known as Abstract Expressionism. In 1908 Wilhelm Worringer published in Munich a treatise, *Abstraction and Empathy*, which was to provide historical and philosophical foundations for the subsequent development of modern art. Several artists who were to become founders of Expressionism were there about this time—Jawlensky, Klee, Franz Marc, August Macke, and other artists and writers, some of whom were among the group known as "Der Blaue Reiter" (1911–12). They included Max Pechstein, with whom Raphael was to form a close personal link. From his association with these artists Raphael developed an interest in modern French painting, and probably for this reason decided to pursue his study of philosophy in Paris. There Raphael attended lectures by Bergson, then at the height of his fame. He met Rodin and the young Picasso, became familiar with the work of Matisse, and in general participated in the creative upsurge of that decisive epoch. Out of his experiences of this time came his first book—*Von Monet zu Picasso*, published in Munich in 1913.*

Raphael went back to Germany to complete his philosophical studies, but in 1912 he returned to Paris and remained there until the end of 1913. This time he worked

* For a bibliography of Raphael's published writings, see pp. 241*ff.*

principally on Poussin and on French medieval art, more particularly on the architecture, sculpture, and stained glass of Chartres. He then felt the need for a period of solitude, and went to live in Switzerland, on the shores of Lake Constance. During this phase of his life, which lasted until the outbreak of the First World War, he turned his attention to a diversity of subjects—geology, biology, botany, and the problems of sociology. He became absorbed in medieval history and made an extensive study of Shakespeare's works. A dramatic trilogy and a comedy, both of which he subsequently destroyed, were written at this time.

In the First World War, Raphael had to serve a short period in the German army. An unpublished war diary ("Geist wider Macht") he wrote during 1917 shows him confronting experiences that he later sought to resolve on a theoretical basis in a dialogue called "Ethos" (also unpublished), which deals with the moral foundations of the rights of man and anticipates the problems of his later theory of knowledge.

On his release from the army Raphael returned to Switzerland and resumed his contact with the world of art. At this period he met De Fiori, Haller, Wiegele, Schöck, and other well-known artists and published various short articles on their work. In 1919 he wrote *Idee und Gestalt*, a book with the significant subtitle "A Guide to the Nature of Art"; this was published in Munich in 1921. Here he makes his first direct analysis of the work of art, its origins and structure.

Raphael left Switzerland in 1920 and lived almost entirely in Berlin until 1932. A new phase of his work begins, which he himself described in an unpublished journal as follows: "In the first period (1902–20) judgments and condemnations were made and points of view taken up which conformed as nearly as possible to emotional longings and spiritual ideals and which for that reason were a priori. 'Should be' was prefixed to reality and a judgment was formed without objective validity." This statement, which was written later in his life and which I have translated from the original German text, continues and defines the subsequent development of his philosophy:

In the second period (1921 to 1935 or 1940) reality was registered as on a blank tablet—everything was accepted before a personal point of view had been taken up. The material of reality was assembled (and a method of thought prepared). A reaction to this multiplicity of phenomena was inevitable and was indeed implicit in such an impersonal, inactive attitude: it took shape as skepticism (self-withdrawal from judgment as a metaphysical principle) and as a devotion to the mysticism of Eckhart (which can be regarded as an emotional compensation for rational skepticism). Both attitudes implied the existence of a pure absolute (nirvana). The more abundant, particular, and concrete the reality, the more abstract, void, and functionless this absolute—though it might be said to have a function inasmuch as it was a touchstone of reality. For *philosophy* this meant that everything had to be put in doubt—hypothesis, method, system; for *art*, form, unity, objectivity, methods, and composition. Perhaps these two formulas can be reduced to one and the same.

In this second period the following stages are to be distinguished:

  I. 1921–25: the stage of the axiom
  II. 1925–32/4: the stage of empirical analysis
  III. 1932–40: the sociological-historical stage

One might say that the first period (1905/8–1918/20) was the time of *philosophical* destruction and reconstruction, of empiricism and idealism. The second (1918/21–1932/34 or 1936) was the time of *scientific* destruction and reconstruction, of the concrete manifold, of nirvana. The third period was the time of *historical* destruction and reconstruction.

Apart from his great preoccupation with Meister Eckhart, with skepticism, as well as with phenomenology and ethics, in the early 1920's Raphael wrote several articles on Newton's rules of reasoning in philosophy. In 1925, he made a long tour of the Rhineland and the region of Würzburg (Franconia) to study the architecture of medieval German churches, and this survey contained much that was new. Later he devoted himself to a period of intensive teaching at the Berlin Volkshochschule, deriving great personal satisfaction from this activity. Here are some of the themes of his seminars: analysis of a Rembrandt drawing; Aristotle; Meister Eckhart and the nature of mysticism; Thomas Aquinas; the dialectical methods of Hegel, Marx, and Lenin (1928–29); a critique of Husserl's *Logik* and Scheler's *Wertethik*; the Doric temple; the history of dialectical materialism in Greece. This last theme was suggested by Raphael for the winter semester of 1932–33 but (Nazi power was now on the rise) was rejected by the directorate of the Volkshochschule; so he resigned. From one of the above-mentioned lectures grew his book *Der dorische Tempel*. Raphael took the temple of Poseidon at Paestum as a prototype and, in preparation for this book, he had traveled to southern Italy and Sicily during the winter of 1927–28. In 1931 he published an article on the prose style of Valéry in the *Deutsch-Französische Rundschau*; a longer work, "Die pyrrhoneische Skepsis," was published in the journal *Philosophische Hefte* in Berlin.

  In the opening years of the thirties, while ominous events were accumulating in Germany, Raphael spent long summer periods in the quiet of the Swiss Alps. It was at Arosa, in 1930, that the first draft of this book was written, that is, the essays on Giotto and Rembrandt, and the two summers following found him lecturing in Davos. On his resignation from the Volkshochschule in fall 1932 Raphael left Germany, and after a short visit to Zurich, where he gave lectures and classes, he settled in Paris on December 1, 1932. He lived in France until 1941 and then in New York until his death. In Paris he first continued his empirical analyses of works of art and thereby laid the foundations for a true *Kunstwissenschaft* (theory of art). His searching analyses illuminated the whole problem of a sociological approach to art. In 1933 his monograph on the work of his friend, the architect André Lurçat, was published in the series "Architecture d'aujourd'hui" under the title *Groupe scolaire de l'Avenue Karl Marx á Villejuif*. In the same year his first book on the sociology of art appeared: *Proudhon, Marx, Picasso: trois études sur la sociologie de l'art.* One of his most important works, *Zur Erkenntnistheorie der konkreten Dialektik* was published in German in 1934 and later translated under the title *Théorie marxiste de la connaissance.* This volume contains his first philosophical and psychological analysis of the artistic process, of the creative urge in general, and is the key to the understanding of Raphael's approach to art history. A few years before his death he revised and extended this work and gave it the title "Theorie des geistigen Schaffens auf marxistischer Grundlage."

In 1935 Raphael made an extended tour of France in preparation for his unpublished book "Zur Ästhetik der romanischen Kirchen in Frankreich." His productivity, in spite of a great deal of illness, was amazing. In addition to long critical articles on the architectural theories of Auguste Perret and on the project for a Palace of the Soviets, and a critical review of a book on bourgeois tendencies in eighteenth-century German art, to which he gave the title "Marxismus und Geisteswissenschaft," he began his great unfinished work on the artistic methods of Flaubert. In 1939 he brought to a conclusion the most comprehensive of all the works of this period: "Arbeiter, Kunst und Künstler: Beiträge zu einer marxistischen Kunstwissenschaft."

The outbreak of the Second World War interrupted Raphael's literary activity. A most promising work on Racine was discontinued. But even at the concentration camps of Gurs and Les Milles, in which he was temporarily detained, he wrote a longish draft of the first half of a work planned to include a general theory of art (see Appendix), as well as further studies of Homer and Shakespeare and the philosophy of Spinoza.

In 1941, after many difficulties, he at last succeeded in leaving Occupied France and emigrated to the United States. In the remaining eleven years he concentrated on the problem of art history as a science. Hitherto he had limited himself almost exclusively to the problem of describing works of art, the "reconstruction of realities" as he called it, proceeding from the assumption that in scientific research one must know the nature of the *object* itself before its history can be written. He tackled this problem from its historical extremes, prehistoric and contemporary art.

It has been clear to me for a long time [he writes in a letter written in German and dated November 1943] that the connection between art and its "substructure," economic, social, and political, can only be presented when it can be shown what "feelings" are released by the "substructure," for, apart from the phenomenon of milieu, it is the feelings (emotions of every sort) that the artist proceeds from, so as to transmute them into aesthetic feelings, which again are determined by the world of form. I made an abstract and unsatisfactory attempt myself in this direction in 1938 which brought to consciousness all the difficulties of a situation in which neither an individual, nor a national, nor a racial psychology is of any help. One must know the general psychology of the age (feudal, capitalist, etc.) in the form special to each country and generation, and one needs a professional and, above all, a class psychology, all this convincingly derived from the historic facts.

Directly I arrived [in New York] I started off with neolithic Egyptian pottery. The first task was to show from the growing shape of the pots the growing forms of society and economy; the second was to explain the ornamentation. I proceeded on the assumption that these "ornaments" were magic symbols with an exact meaning, and, as those symbols were limited to a certain number in which mathematical observations and meaning were combined, I succeeded in translating most of them into our own language and modes of understanding. In this way I came upon a language about one or two thousand years older than hieroglyphics and which has very few models in nature (significant, for example, is the way of indicating corn). The origin of this lack of cohesion lies not so much in invasions by strange races as in the great economic, social, and political transformations that took place. I was able clearly to show how organized society, rulers and slaves, families (in the sense of workers' community), religion (as opposed to magic), arose—I was able to show the chief stages which made it essential that the real history of Egypt should begin with political domination. . . . It was the magic symbols (ornamentations) which compelled me to go farther back. Even in the paleolithic caves there were symbolic pictures. Had they any connection with the neolithic? If the latter were strictly geometric, how did this geometric magic arise from the older "naturalistic" magic? (A preliminary question to this: how and why magic religions arose.)

Such is the character of the many problems raised by Raphael in a series of highly original works, of which unfortunately only two were published in English: *Prehistoric Cave Paintings* (1945) and *Prehistoric Pottery and Civilization in Egypt* (1947).

At the time of Raphael's death several works existed in manuscript, the most important of which are:

(1) "How Should One Approach a Work of Art?" herewith published under the title *The Demands of Art*.

(2) "Classical Man in Greek Art," showing the development of Greek classical sculpture from the neolithic age and using some superb examples to demonstrate the creative methods of this particular art.

(3) A three-part series on the art of the Stone Age:

a) "Early Stone Age Hunting Culture," dealing with economics, political organizations, ancestor cults, totems, death ideology, and art.

b) "Reincarnation Magic in the Early Stone Age," an essay on the history of religions and religious symbols, examining the afterlife of the paleolithic world of thought, its art, etc. in later times in relation to the problem of reincarnation magic.

c) "Iconography of Quaternary Art: Methods and Systems." This work remained unfinished. There exist some introductory notes to the first part (methods of interpretation): (i) Method of interpretation of paleolithic art. (ii) Chronology of Quaternary art. (iii) The concept of historical progress: a treatise on the solution of the problem of paleolithic art. Also two long chapters comprising a draft of the beginning of the second part of the book. The first chapter dealt with the free animal, groups of two and three; the second, with the domesticated animal and the juxtaposition of man and animal.

It was not granted to Raphael to finish this work: he died suddenly in New York on July 14, 1952. But what he left was a complete life's work rather than unfinished fragments: he opened the way to a scientific solution of what he called "the eternal and enthralling problem of art": a theory of art founded on an analysis of the process of artistic creation.

In this attempt he was a pioneer whose seminal significance will only be realized in the future. One might say that before Max Raphael all approaches to art had been either empirical, limited to the history of artifacts or the scientific analysis of individual works of art; or theoretical, critical, or philosophical generalizations based on the writer's individual sensibility. What Raphael did, and was the first to do, was to approach empirical facts equipped with a complete understanding of the psychology of creative activity.

Some of the results of Raphael's revolutionary approach may be seen in the present work; it was not his last but the first to show his method in all its originality. It is true that in *Proudhon, Marx, Picasso* Raphael was already applying the Marxist dialectic to the sociology of art, beginning with an exposure of the latent bourgeois idealism of Proudhon and passing on to an exposition of the *scientific* method of the Marxist dialectic (then applied in the third essay to the particular case of Picasso). But Raphael, always faithful to his aesthetic sensations, was already seeking refuge in that passage in *A Contribution to the Critique of Political Economy* (1857) which has proved such a stumbling block to doctrinaire Marxists—that passage in which Marx confesses that "certain periods of highest development of art stand in no direct connection with the general development of society, nor with the material basis and the skeleton structure of its organization." All Raphael's work may be regarded as a commentary on this passage, which he calls Marx's most important declaration on the subject. But this does not exclude the dialectical method from the history and philosophy of art; on the contrary, it imposes its most rigid application. The existence of an autonomous activity (art) in society merely adds to the complexity of the problem. "The theory of art, the history and the criticism of art . . . have this in common (in opposition to any empirical sociology of art) that they isolate their subject to a degree of abstract purity and seek their proper foundation by immanent means. The sociology of art, on the contrary, is based on a material foundation exterior to art, by means of which one can explain the concrete particularity of each work, the reciprocal relations between all ideologies and the reaction of art to this foundation." In other words, the relation of these two spheres of knowledge (theory of art and sociology) are the terms of a dialectical process, a process which does not seek to deny the relative autonomy of each sphere.

Nevertheless, by the time he came to complete the present work (1947?), Raphael had learned to give ever more emphasis to the autonomy of the artistic process. Art, he now claims in a passage which strictly might have come from his earliest works, is "an ever-renewed creative act, the active dialogue between spirit and matter; the work of art holds man's creative powers in a crystalline suspension from which it can again be transformed into living energies." He distinguishes between the pragmatic and the aesthetic attitude—in the former we isolate each thing according to our needs and make it and ourselves "stones among stones," being caught up in the endless wheel of need-gratification-need. But the aesthetic attitude is very different. "It is uninterested, i.e., it pursues no purpose except this: to absorb the world through our senses—or the one inner sense—and to become one with it. It is not important how the particular part of the world looks that releases our aesthetic vision. What is important is to see it whole, in such a way that we extinguish all our momentary, individual concerns as well as the facticity of things outside us. . . . Such an experience gratifies and purges us because in it our conflicts, whether with ourselves or with the world, are resolved." The work of art is *reality enhanced* (which has so misleadingly been called "illusion"), and this is a spiritual development. Raphael's description of the artistic process that follows is the most comprehensive and eloquent that I know:

Artistic creation involves the totality of dispositions, functions, relations, facts, and values—all of these in harmonious interaction: body and soul, inwardness and outwardness, the individual and the community, the self and the cosmos, tradition and revolution, instinct and freedom, life and death, becoming and being, the self and fate, struggle and structure, the Dionysian and the Apollonian, law and accident, structure and surface, contemplation and action, education and achievement, sensuality and spirit, doubt and faith, love and duty, ugliness and perfection, the finite and the infinite. Neither one of any pair of these terms should exclude the other nor should any pair exclude any other—they must all be brought together into a higher unity.

Such is the dialectical process in art, and this is the process which Raphael delicately reveals in the analyses in this volume, affirming always that the work of art in question is "not merely communication, concretization, personal utterance; it is not merely the repetition of inner states or the imitation of the outside world, but a structure (*Gestalt*) endowed with its own life—a life at another level than that of the psyche or that of things."

Marxist philosophers must decide how heterodox, from their point of view, Raphael became in his later works. I am convinced that he considered himself always faithful to the spirit and intention of Marx. He thought that Marx believed that "the individual must realize the limits of his creative powers." Further: "Every man contributes to the shaping of human relationships according to his individual capacities and, conversely, we must demand of the political body (state, etc.) that each individual be allowed to develop his creative powers to the maximum. This is the ultimate criterion of society's value. . . . Any state which under any circumstances whatever persecutes science, art, philosophy, or religion by any sort of arbitrary measures is an immoral state and an impotent one, whose recourse to brute force camouflages its weaknesses."

Raphael believed in the vital importance of art for society—art "changes our whole attitude to life—not merely our understanding of it but also our evaluation of it, in fact, all our perspective." Art is not merely contemplation; it is an activity, and for that reason Raphael condemned our mercenary and dilettante attitude to art. In a passage not included in this volume he wrote: "Using art to decorate private houses, to display the owner's wealth or so-called culture, is a barbarism. . . . Museums . . . are morgues for the storage of works of art embalmed and shrouded with historical and national prejudices. . . . The works of art are presented in abstraction from the rest of culture, so that the essence of art is distorted. . . . If the museum is to be rescued from its present sociological predicament—and only thus can it become an institution for furthering a living relationship to art—it must be made a concern of society as a whole, must cease to be an institution of the state and become an institution of the people." Some of Raphael's criticisms of the museum have been accepted, especially in the United States where there has been a movement to make these institutions places where people are actively involved in art.

In a passage omitted from the final manuscript Raphael shows the practical nature of his intellectual enterprise, which was to make art an organic part of life. But to restore art to this condition, "a rebirth of the visual arts, beginning with architecture, is necessary, and this in turn depends on economic and social rebirth. To achieve this end, we must fight the obstacles raised against the understanding of art by entrenched theories and world views, by existing institutions and, finally, by human inertia. I hope," concludes Max Raphael, "I have made clear why this struggle must be carried on."

He had made this clear, by a life's work which he left as a legacy to the future. Now that the publication of this volume is a fact, I do not think it is likely that the considerable body of unpublished work will be left in obscurity. Raphael is exactly the kind of philosopher of art that the world most needs—a man of great scholarship and equal sensibility, a man who believed in the future but realized that the world is changing and must be changed; one who was passionately convinced that the quality of life in the new society that would emerge must depend on "the ever-renewed creative act, the active dialogue between spirit and matter," and that in this transformation of living energies, art is the most effective weapon.

*

I met Max Raphael only once, in Paris, about 1934. He was then living in a small white-washed room at the top of a tenement in the Rue des Écoles. There was little in the room except a table and two chairs, and on the wall the photograph of a piece of Greek sculpture, perhaps a head of Apollo. I was immediately captivated by a charm at once sensitive and intellectual. We became friends and corresponded a little, and when the war broke out he sent some of his manuscripts to me to take care of in the relative security of England. But I lost touch with him during the war, when he went to America. There are a few people who remain perfectly vivid and substantial in one's memory on the basis of one brief glimpse, and in my life Raphael was one of them.

I have not tried in this brief introduction to give a résumé of all his published works—indeed, there are two or three, such as *Idee und Gestalt* and *Die pyrrhoneische Skepsis*, which I have never read. The only excuse I have for intervening between the reader and the pages that follow is the conviction I formed at that brief meeting with Raphael that I was in the presence of one who shared the angelic nature of his mentor, Meister Eckhart. I have found that this impression was shared by all who knew him.

The writing of this Introduction would not have been possible without the collaboration of Max Raphael's disciple and legal executor, Professor Claude Schaefer, who provided me with all the details of the author's life, and without the assistance of Professor Robert S. Cohen, who has followed every stage of the preparation of the text and its translation with a devotion inspired by his admiration for Raphael's genius.

HERBERT READ

THE DEMANDS OF ART

PREFACE TO THE FIRST DRAFT (1930)

THIS WORK is addressed to all who aspire to culture in the broadest sense, and especially to young people who must work for a living. My aim is to teach them to understand art through the work of art itself; i.e., my approach is scientific. No branch of knowledge, surely, should be denied the right to make art an object of study—not even art history, although it neither retraces history nor deals with art. So far none of the disciplines indispensable for preliminary study (iconography, psychology, ethnology, aesthetics, etc.) has brought art itself closer to us. None of them enables us to retrace the essential constitutive stages of the process of artistic creation, as distinct from its accessory features, such as the artist's technical preparation and his manipulation of various mediums. Our purpose, therefore, is to discover the method by which a specific work of art has been created. To this end we start with the work of art itself—with its actual appearance to the eye, which we first describe by constitutive concepts and then interpret in terms of the philosophy underlying it. Thus we combine the language of forms—i.e., the means of representing the world—with the language of various world views, treating the work of art as one element in the history of ideas and, more than that, in history pure and simple.

Our method requires, first of all, a word about how we "see." Seeing is a psychic activity—not merely of the eyes, but of the person as a whole; it is not an abstract activity, the same for everyone everywhere in every age, but a highly concrete one which is determined, among other ways, by the cultural attitudes both of the individual and of the given historical epoch. Looking or seeing is a two-way activity. First, there are factual data whose mode of reality lies outside us, but which impinge upon us, and which are gradually assimilated by the whole and concrete man. Second, to look or to see is at the same time to project inner feelings, visions, dreams, ideas, etc., gradually assimilating them to individual objects or to the world in general. The two processes may diverge or they may converge, and in highly varying degrees.

In every case looking or seeing is thus the inception of a productive act. In art this act is performed by another person, whose productive forces are superior to our own. The contemplation of a work of art can be fruitful only if we renounce our personal attitudes and prejudices, our desire for emotional excitement, and wholly submit to the artist's

will; only then can we first re-experience with our senses and then reconstruct intellectually the specific creative method that had produced the given work—not to be confused
with the artist's own psychological experience of the creative act.

     This way of stating our purpose requires a methodological clarification. Do we start
from the general historical conditions and deduce the work of art from them or, conversely, do we first analyze the work of art and then link it with the general historical situation?
It might be argued in favor of the second approach that the work of art is the most direct
datum for the spectator and, when it comes to us from prehistoric times, is the principal
or only datum; that it is impossible to deduce the specificity of art (as distinct from other
creative domains) from general historical conditions; and, finally, that correlation between an individual work of art and the given historical situation must remain vague and
undemonstrated until the work of art itself has been grasped in all its specificity. On the
other hand it can be argued that without studying and taking into account the general
historical conditions and the creative methods prevalent in each epoch, analysis of the
work of art leads to a formalism that makes it impossible to link art to the history of ideas
—let alone political and economic history.[1] The alternative is, however, a false one. It is
only by taking account of both aspects that we can arrive at a history of the methods and
problems of art. In this book we deal with one part of the task only—that of grasping the
work of art *as* a work of art. Thus we are obliged to take the work of art as our point
of departure. But this does not mean that we should isolate the artist's accomplishment
from its various contexts—those which helped to influence its creation (the individual,
social, and metaphysical contexts) or those toward which the artist himself deliberately
oriented his work.

     Concerning external influences upon the artist the concluding essay will have a
number of things to say. As for the artist's own intentions, we may make the following
observation. If every activity of the human spirit involves three aims—to grasp and master
the material, to develop and test a method, and to transform the world in the light of
that mastery and that method—then this last aim must be particularly stressed in the
study of art. In saying all this I am aware of the limitations of the conceptual approach.
To begin with, we are dealing with an object that is not entirely accessible to our understanding (but this does not exempt us from the duty of mastering it intellectually as far
as we can). Furthermore, conceptual analysis and reconstruction of the homogeneous
whole which is the work of art cannot replace direct experience of it. Only when a living
contact, however vague or unconscious, has been established with the work of art can
explanation be meaningful. For this reason the reader should first quietly contemplate

1. [The author elucidates his method of understanding
relations between historical conditions and works of art
in *Prehistoric Pottery and Civilization in Egypt*; in *Proudhon,*
Marx, Picasso: Trois études sur la sociologie de l'art; and
in his unpublished "Corot: Kunst unter dem Liberalismus—Monographie eines Bildes."]

the reproductions in this book, putting aside everything he knows (especially art history), all his doubts and private preoccupations and any premature urge to arrive at conclusions. Then the text will cast light upon the work under consideration and will also purify and enlarge the reader's ability to understand other works of art. But he must never look for sloganlike formulas or labels or be satisfied with "explanatory" definitions—only the methodological explication itself, in its fullest scope, can bring understanding.

Finally, no text can tell the reader how to apply the understanding of art he has gained, how to transform his life or that of his community in the light of this new source of energy. Only a different act, a fresh contemplation of human life and society, can do this. Every work of art is a storehouse of creative energies. The text will try to set them free and, in so doing, to release spiritual forces in the viewer of art. However, what use the reader makes of them, and to what end, is something the individual must decide for himself if a people is not to cease being a cultural community.

I have tried to stimulate this activity by not writing down to my readers. These essays were conceived within a study group which demanded intensive co-operation and concentration on the part of every member.[2] The same demands are made upon the reader, and this in several senses. Only a few concepts and points of view are presented at a time, but thereafter they are expected to form part of the reader's equipment—they continue to apply. Gradually, according to a sequence growing out of the nature of the problems discussed, the system of concepts is completed. It is left to the reader to apply the concepts presented later to the works of art discussed earlier and vice versa. No one of these essays can lead the reader to an understanding of art: only the series as a whole (together with another series, "How to Evaluate a Work of Art"[3]), if studied thoroughly, might help to do that.

Arosa, Switzerland, March 1930   M. R.

---

2. [The author originally delivered the contents of most of this book—an early draft of chapters I–IV—as lectures at a Swiss school for adult education. He had also delivered lectures with somewhat similar intentions when he was teaching at an evening high school for adults in Berlin during the late 1920's.]

3. [This work was never written.]

I. THE WORK OF ART AND THE MODEL IN NATURE

Cézanne: *Mont Sainte-Victoire*

(PLATE I)

Here is my motif. (He put his hands together . . . drew them apart, the ten fingers open, slowly, very slowly brought them together again, clasped them, squeezed them tighter and tighter, as though meshing them into one.) That's what you have to try to do. If one is higher or lower than the other, all goes to pieces. Everything has to so mesh with everything else that there is no way for the feeling, for the light, for the truth to escape. You must try to understand that I work on the whole canvas, on everything in it at once. With one impulse, with undivided faith, I bring all the bits and pieces together. Everything we see falls apart, vanishes, doesn't it? Nature is always the same, but nothing in her, nothing that appears to us, lasts. Our art must render the thrill of nature's permanence along with her elements, the appearance of all her changes. It must give us a taste of her eternity. What is there underneath? Maybe nothing. Maybe everything. Everything, you understand. So I bring together her wandering hands. From here, from there, on this side and that, everywhere, I take her tones, her colors, her shadings, I set them down, I bring them closer together. They form lines. They become objects, rocks, trees, without my planning. They take on volume, value. If these volumes, these values, correspond on my canvas, in my sensibility, to the planes, to the spots which I have, which are there before our eyes, then my canvas has brought its hands together. It does not waver. It is neither too high nor too low. It is true, compact, full. But if there is the slightest distraction, if I fail just a little bit, especially if I interpret too much one day, if today I am carried off by a theory which runs counter to that of yesterday, if I think while I paint, if I meddle, whoosh! everything has gone to pieces. . . .

The artist is no more than a receptacle for sensations, a brain, a recording apparatus. . . . But if he sticks his nose in, if, poor feeble creature that he is, he dares deliberately intervene in what he should be translating, his own pettiness gets into the picture. The work becomes inferior. . . .

Art is a harmony paralleling nature's. What can we say about the fools who tell us: The painter is always inferior to nature! He is parallel to her. Provided he does not intervene deliberately. Don't misunderstand me—his only aspiration must be to silence. He must stifle within himself the voices of prejudice, he must forget, and keep on forgetting, he must make silence all about him, he must be a perfect echo. Then the landscape will be inscribed on his sensitive tablet. When he records it on the canvas, when he externalizes it, technique will certainly come in, but respectfully: for it, too, must be ready to obey, to translate unconsciously, so well does it know its language, the text it is deciphering, the two parallel texts, nature as seen, nature as felt, the one which is there (he pointed at the green and blue plain), the one which is here (he tapped his forehead), both of which must merge in order to endure, to live a life half human and half divine, the life of art, I tell you—the life of God.

CÉZANNE, *quoted by Gasquet*

I sat for him only five or six times. I believed that he had given up the picture. I learned later that he had devoted to it about sixty sessions, and that during our conversations, whenever he looked at me closely, he was thinking about the painting, and went back to work on it when I had gone. What he was trying to bring out was life itself, the way it looks, the way it feels, the way it speaks, and without my ever suspecting it, he was making me expand to where he could catch my very soul when discussion carried us away and anger or enthusiasm exposed that inner eloquence of which the least of us is capable. He often worked that way, especially on portraits, going back to them when his model had gone. . . . I insist on this because it has often been alleged that Cézanne would not paint, and even that he never painted, without the model in front of him. He had a perhaps unmatched memory for line and color. Like Flaubert, he forced himself to "contemplate the humblest realities," with his tremendous power of will he constrained himself to make a direct copy in which his own lyricism was imprisoned. "The reading of the model and its realization," he wrote, "are sometimes very slow to come."

GASQUET

We must be in perfect harmony at all times, my model, my colors, and I, together to capture the moment as it passes . . .

CÉZANNE *to Gasquet*

II Mont Sainte-Victoire seen from Les Lauves (Photo: John Rewald)

I CÉZANNE. *Mont Sainte-Victoire*. 1904–6. 29½ × 37 in.

Anyone who travels in Provence will often feel that the landscapes between Aix and Marseilles are like a gallery of Cézannes (whereas one may spend time in Arles without for a moment being reminded of Van Gogh). But as soon as any specific part of the region is compared with a picture Cézanne painted of it, the painted work, for all its faithfulness of detail, turns out to be fundamentally different from the "original." The longer we contrast the two, the less marked the external likeness, the profounder and more crucial the difference. And yet two generations of painters have been unable to free themselves from the compulsion to see Provence as Cézanne—and only Cézanne—has shown it to us: it is as though he had said everything there is to say about its appearance and essence.

The complex relationship between art and nature cannot be defined as one of imitation of a model given once and for all—whether the model be a portion of nature or a religious or socio-political dogma. Even when "imitation" is defined in the classical sense, as a mimetic representation of living nature, the term still does not tell us what is meant by "living nature" or what "mimetic representation" consists of in a specific art medium. A similar question arises with respect to a third interpretation, namely, that "imitation" bears upon the ideas and the laws of nature and that the task of the artist is to discover and reproduce these ideas and laws that lie hidden under outward appearances. What is the path that links outward appearance to law and to the artistic rendering of the law? In each of these definitions two things are opposed in all their diversity and vitality—the human mind and nature. The concept of imitation obscures the gap and even the contrast which exists between these two fundamental factors; it discourages us from discovering and analyzing the historically conditioned ways in which they are connected, merge, and come into unity. It also does away with the specificity and autonomy of the new object that results from their dialectical interaction—the work of art.

Just as nature alone does not determine the mind, so the mind, conversely, cannot dictate its laws to nature (Kant). Either theory overweights one factor at the expense of the other, and they are both subject to the same criticism. Man's active, creative mind is never identical with itself for any length of time; whatever the sphere of its activity, it is determined, among other things, by the total historical conditions of a specific and complex class society. A great many different methods and spiritual attitudes are to be found at successive stages of historical development and also contemporaneously at any given stage. Whenever man attempts to free his mind from these historical conditions, he runs into the fact that he cannot know himself a priori, purely on the basis of his categories, but only through the results he achieves intellectually and practically in his shaping of nature and society. In other words, he can know himself only *post festum*, as it were, as a being subjected to historical conditions. For this reason we must speak of society imposing its laws on the mind before we can speak of the mind imposing its laws on nature. Even in what seems the most "abstract" instance, where the sole content of the mind is its own working processes (as in the theory of knowledge), the categories of the mind contain only as much reality as they have absorbed from the facts and processes of nature, society, and the mind (art, religion, etc.). The Kantian theory accounts neither for the connection between historical conditions in society and the mind of the artist nor for that between the artist's mind and the work of art he creates.

For the very reason that in art the human mind neither imitates nature nor imposes its own laws on it, the work of art possesses specific reality and is governed by laws of its own. Even though there is no such thing as a single, uniquely beautiful proportion of the human body or a single scientifically correct method of representing space, or one method only of artistic figuration, whatever form art may assume in the course of history, it is always a synthesis between nature (or history) and the mind, and as such it acquires a certain autonomy vis-à-vis both these elements. This independence seems to be created by man and hence to possess a psychic reality; but in point of fact the process of creation can become an existent only because it is embodied in some concrete material (which varies with the area of activity). This material, though a product of the practical action of society upon nature, at the same time makes possible a record of the gratification of our intellectual and emotional needs in a form characterized by inner necessity. Each time the mind comes to grips with nature (or history), the result is an art possessing its own reality and laws—or else the result has nothing to do with art.[1]

Before proceeding to our analysis of Cézanne's *Mont Sainte-Victoire*, we must draw a few general conclusions from the foregoing considerations:

(1) Even though one of the three elements in question—nature, mind, artistic form —may preponderate in a theory of art concerning a specific epoch or a specific social class, both general theory and individual analysis must allow for the possibility that all three basic elements are equally significant and that they develop simultaneously and re-

1. [A detailed exposition of this conception of art is contained in the author's *Zur Erkenntnistheorie der konkreten Dialektik*.]

latedly. This is especially true of Cézanne and particularly of the painting we shall deal with. To interpret his work as intellectual constructivism is to overlook the tremendous significance nature had for Cézanne and to understand his slogan "aller au motif" as imaginative deficiency, whereas the artist himself was concerned with gaining insight into the essence and laws of being and the processes of nature in "God's laboratory." And to interpret his work naturalistically is to overlook the fundamental difference between Cézanne and the impressionists, the fact that he was interested not in the problem of perception but in that of pictorial figuration (which is, of course, not to be confused with the problem of decoration, symbolically or formalistically understood). Moreover, both interpretations overlook the emotional element, which, though present in all Cézanne's works, emerged fully only at the end of his life, as if his demon had visited him (as it visited Socrates shortly before his death) and ordered him to drop all rationalist aspirations and realize his inner struggle in form and color as immediately as possible. If we hope to understand his art we must take into account the extreme tensions—between spirit and nature and between each of these and art—with which Cézanne had continually to live.

(2) We must beware of language, of the tendency in our words to endow with distinct and fixed meanings the things around us. Language presses us, even against our will, to compare the finished work of art with its model in nature, and thus diverts us from the fundamental fact that the work of art has come about through a dialectical interaction between the creative, forming spirit and a situation that is given to begin with. Therefore we must sharply distinguish between the given situation (nature), the methodical process (the mind), and the total configuration[2] (the work of art). The given situation is itself highly complex, for in addition to being a component of nature it contains a personal psychic experience and a sociohistorical condition; nature, history, and the individual do not tend to coincide, to be harmonious, but conflict with each other and so accentuate their differences. The artist seizes upon this conflict and thereby divests it of its factual character, transforms it into a problem—a task which consists in bringing these three factors into a new relatedness, merging or fusing them into a new unity with a new, internally necessary form. Mere existence is thus made into a process, and the result of this process is another existent, an existent of a special kind, founded upon a new unity of the conflicting elements as perceived by man and embodied in matter. To the viewer of the work of art this man-made yet "autonomous" (i.e., self-sufficient) reality is immediately accessible. When he tries to analyze it into its components in order to gain insight into the process that brought it into being, it is not enough for him to note the differences between the finished work of art and the given model. He must also know how the respective data of nature, history, and the artist's personality were creatively combined, as a problem to be

2. [For "total configuration" (*Werkgestalt*), see the Appendix, pp. 225–234.]

solved—and how, thus, the work of art came about—in so far as this creative process was not a mere matter of psychological accident but was governed by laws. This is what we shall try to do here.

Keeping all this in mind when we compare the landscape to the work of art, the first difference we discover is material. In the painting we find one substance only—paint (applied to canvas)—whereas in nature we find a number of diverse substances. Each substance belongs necessarily to an object—stone to the mountain, wood to the tree; they are the substances of which actual objects are composed. In painting the object (the "picture") is composed of paint, but the objects in the picture are not composed of paint; through paint they are being evoked for the senses. At the same time that it calls forth objects and spatial relationships, paint also evokes emotions and ideas, so that each spot of pigment simultaneously performs various, necessarily interrelated, functions. Furthermore, each spot has the tendency to go beyond its mere local function, to become an autonomous form with its own relative significance, such that the smallest part not only serves the whole but also, in a limited sense, is a whole. In nature, each individual substance contains embedded in its matter the presence, the vitality, and the structure of the thing, but the human eye cannot discover any necessary relationship between these three factors and their material vehicle; nor can it discover such relationships among the various substances of several objects or between the substances of things and their distribution in space, let alone between the various materials and human perceptions, feelings, acts of will, or thoughts. In other words, with every stroke of the brush the artist sets out to perform a number of highly dissimilar acts:

(1) He translates the various component substances of things into a single pictorial substance; the same is true of psychic life, which is seemingly nonmaterial as we experience it but which now appears in paint, as paint.

(2) He translates the pictorial substance into an evocative substance.

(3) He differentiates each spot of color, giving it a specific local value in relation to the whole, which he builds up from an articulated variety of such spots (whereby each of them acquires a third function).

(4) He transforms the functional spot of color into a form, a whole within a whole.

Cézanne was clearly aware of the fact that the natural (or artificial) pigment acquires a representational, evocative, and compositional function, and that this function in turn becomes form. "Nature must not be reproduced, it must be represented. By what? By shape and color equivalents."[3] (Similar equivalents are stones for the architect, concepts for the philosopher, sounds for the composer, vowels and consonants for the poet.) And what goes for nature also goes for emotions, ideas, etc., which are evoked by the

---

3. Quoted by John Rewald in *Cézanne, sa vie, son œuvre, son amitié pour Zola* (Paris, 1939), p. 275.

artist. Cézanne noted that Balzac described a dinner table as "white as a layer of freshly fallen snow, on which napkins crowned with wheat-colored rolls were placed symmetrically." Cézanne reflected: "As a young man I used to want to paint it, this tablecloth of freshly fallen snow. I know now that 'the napkins placed symmetrically' and 'the wheat-colored rolls' are the only things that can be painted. When it comes to the 'crowned,' I have to give up. Don't you see? If I really could balance and vary my napkins and rolls as I find them in nature, you may be sure that the crowns, the snow, and the shimmer of light would all be there."[4] The moment the painter conveys his feeling directly or portrays objects for their own sake, he degrades color to a mere means and ceases to be a painter. Now Cézanne did not want to go beyond painting; his aim was to bring it to perfection within its own boundaries. That is why color, and color alone, can serve as "the place where our brain and the universe meet. That is why color seems so dramatic to true painters."[5] Feeling is not to be expressed through the intermediary of color, but color itself is to be feeling, idea. "To be a painter by the very qualities of painting."[6] "Poetry comes into the picture spontaneously. When it is dragged in it becomes literature."[7]

This is the crucial point, without which neither this painting by Cézanne nor painting in general can be understood: what is not made visible in color does not exist at all. "There is only one way to render everything, to translate everything: color."[8] The artist who will not sacrifice everything to this—his ideas and feelings about himself and the world—cannot attain the state of grace of the painter's condition. However, this sacrifice is only the beginning of the test to which he will be put, for only *post factum* can he know for sure whether everything he has sacrificed can be regained in terms of the one material. The artist is no ascetic, either of the intellect or of the heart; he renounces direct methods in order to gain through indirect ones more than he sacrificed. "In order to paint [the world] in its essence one must have a painter's eyes, capable of seeing the object in terms of color alone, of taking possession of it, and of relating it to the other objects."[9] Color contains everything, is everything. "Colors . . . are ideas and God made visible flesh. Through them, mystery is revealed."[10] The painter can achieve this revelation when each spot of color fulfills a number of conditions simultaneously: he must give us "light, air, objects, composition, character, drawing, style."[11] By this the painter does not mean that he creates a world of illusion, but reality itself as opposed to any kind of abstraction or fantasy. How did Cézanne set out to attain his goal?

4. Joachim Gasquet, *Cézanne* (Paris, 1926), pp. 204.*f.*

5. Ibid., p. 135.

6. Quoted by Émile Bernard in *Souvenirs sur Paul Cézanne, et lettres* (Paris, 1920), p. 39.

7. [Quoted by Heimo Kuchling in *Paul Cézanne: Eine Auswahl von Briefen und Aussprüchen* (Klagenfurt, 1948), p. 46.]

8. Quoted by Gasquet, p. 145.

9. Ibid., p. 146.

10. Ibid., p. 153.

11. Bernard, "Souvenirs sur Paul Cézanne et lettres inédites," *Mercure de France* (Paris), CXXXVIII (1920), p. 298. All subsequent Bernard references are to the volume cited in n. 6.

He worked out a system of "color equivalents" and formed a working material according to his own personal method.

This system resulted in the creation of a specific palette. According to Émile Bernard it included the following:[12]

YELLOWS	REDS
Brilliant yellow	Vermilion
Naples yellow	Red ocher
Chrome yellow	Burnt sienna
Yellow ocher	Madder lake
Raw sienna	Carmine lake
	Burnt lake

GREENS	BLUES
Veronese green	Cobalt blue
Emerald	Ultramarine
Terre-verte	Prussian blue
	Peach black

This list has often been reprinted since it was first published, but it has rarely been analyzed in detail. It shows that, unlike the impressionists, Cézanne did not want primarily to paint the medium of air. He also differed from them in considering the opposite of air to be not merely the object, but earth, water, and sky in their structural unity as landscape. Cézanne wanted to paint the substance of things, not their relations alone—that which is in and for itself, not that which is only by virtue of its relations to other things. His is the palette of a peasant who takes long walks over the land, every natural object pressing against him, one who feels the world in terms of the resistant bodies and heavy masses around him. He was a man who spent long days alone with earth and sky. His was not the palette of the city dweller, for whom walls are not substantial realities but merely occasions for the refraction of light. Furthermore, to Cézanne color itself was mass, body, weight, resistance; and light does not make these qualities more evanescent, but on the contrary solidifies them, endows them with maximum substantial reality. Because of this emphasis on the primary qualities of matter, color becomes the boundary between that which lives within things and that which acts on them from without. Color defined as such a boundary asserts its own existence against both the dissolving action of light and the painter's obligation to render the surface features of things. Both this imitative function of color and its function of mediation between the inner and the outer worlds are reduced to a minimum in favor of the autonomy of color as a boundary. Every color is endowed with energy—a feature it has in common with every other color—and each possesses a life of its own. These two features, one general and the other individual, are implied in and transcend each other.

Cézanne's palette encompasses the whole range of the rainbow; for him the world

12. Bernard, pp. 63*f.*

was polychromatic, indeed "panchromatic." On the other hand, he regarded each separate color as a concrete, specific individuality, and individuals as intrinsically unrelated to other individuals. This conception of individual color is particularly evident in his emphasis on local color—in disregard of the rules that prescribe the use of specific quantities and tones of complementary colors. Cézanne thought that local color was the requisite means to pure painting. "All painting consists in this: either we yield to the influence of the atmosphere or we resist it. To yield to it means to deny the importance of local color; to resist it means to endow local color with strength and variety. Titian and all the other Venetians worked with local color. This is the way of the true colorist."[13] Toward the end of his life Cézanne would cite the example of other colorists as well—the late Romanesque and early Gothic painters on glass, whose intensity and transparency he tried to equal in oils. One day, passing the basin of holy water in a church, he said: "I'm going to have my slice of the Middle Ages."[14] This influence on Cézanne has been less often remarked than that of Poussin and the classical painters. His striving for local color in a world he conceived of as panchromatic raised the following problem for him: What are the principles for linking local colors so that they neither exclude each other as incompatible nor merge into a uniform gray? Cézanne's solution, of which more later, was to intensify their contrasts to the point where they repel each other, and to introduce between them such a wealth of mediating differentiations that, through the combination of discontinuity and continuity, a self-contained network is formed, a network in which each spot of color is both sharply distinguished from its neighbor and most closely related to it. "Objects interpenetrate each other. They never cease to live. Imperceptibly they spread intimate reflections around them."[15] Thus every individual spot of color is in communication with all the others, together constituting the colored surface which separates the inner life of things from the air surrounding them. Cézanne's view of the world is essentially dualistic, but its unity is postulated by the artist as the result of his step-by-step creation (and not as a metaphysical datum). The artist is thus the mediator between things that are alienated from each other and their common metaphysical sources, which have been lost.

Cézanne's pursuit of a substantial panchromatism prevented him from endowing the range of light and shadow with as independent an existence as that of color. This does not mean that a conflict between local color and light does not take place, or that the range of light and shadow denies a space-building role to local colors or ties them to specific places. Rather, Cézanne renders light through color—he does not give us colored light, like the impressionists, but color in light, the light of color. "Shadow is a color as light is, but less luminous. Light or shadow is merely a relation between two color tones."[16]

Thereby light loses its significance as universal immaterial substance, a direct emana-

13. [Kuchling, p. 43.]   14. Bernard, p. 42.   15. Gasquet, p. 203.   16. [Kuchling, p. 44.]

tion from God or the cosmos. Now it is earthbound; even in opposition to the earth it becomes earthly and heavy. Color is not, for Cézanne, the reflection of a higher reality, but the whole of actual reality in its concreteness and plenitude. "Things and creatures alike, we are only a little bit of solar heat. . . . The diffuse moral energies of the world may be the effort it is making to become sun again. . . . We are an iridescent chaos."[17] The original sin of the sun, followed by the emergence of the world as a colored chaos—such is Cézanne's cosmogony, the myth with which he would justify the artist's task: to order the chaos here below, where sun and earth are struggling against each other.

For Cézanne, therefore, painting goes beyond the *peinture claire* of the impressionists, beyond the baroque contrasts of light and shadow, beyond Poussin's dialectical development of shadow into light.[18] He aimed at a greater diversification, stronger tensions, a richer orchestration, and in his last works achieved a kind of chiaroscuro based on color (in contrast to Rembrandt, who arrived at color starting from chiaroscuro). He used dark and light colors together and in co-ordination, giving shadow and light equal accents. Recognizing nothing beyond nature, nothing from which nature could derive, he had to reject every deductive method.

In the version of *Mont Sainte-Victoire* painted just before his death Cézanne restricted his palette to four main colors—violet, green, ocher, and blue—which he used in sharply contrasting ways. In the foreground we see a triad whose components—violet, ocher, and green—do not show the slightest inner connection, for although the red in the violet is complementary to the green and the blue in the violet is complementary to the ocher, the two greens he chose are not complementary to *this* red and the ocher is not complementary to *this* blue in the violet. The mutual exclusion of color qualities is not overcome by any external means of connection or mediation; the three colors in the foreground do not form a harmonious chord, but a shrill dissonance of tremendous force. As early as 1884 Cézanne had written to Zola: "However . . . the external appearance of art is undergoing a terrible transformation, taking paltry forms. At the same time, ignorance of harmony is becoming more and more apparent in a discordant use of color and, worse still, in a tone deafness."[19]

Cézanne's palette was that of a peasant, but of a peasant who was at odds with the world. In his day the earth had yielded its primacy as a means of production to the machine. The fruits of production were no longer goods (i.e., substances) but commodities (i.e., factors of exchange). The typically peasant ideology of transcendence had become socially obsolete. In short, Cézanne the peasant lived under industrial capitalism, but at a time when agriculture was not yet industrialized. In consequence the act of painting, to

17. Gasquet, pp. 134 *ff.* [Tr. Jackson Mathews.]   18. [The author first treated this in *Von Monet zu Picasso*, p. 119.]
19. Letter to Émile Zola, November 27, 1884, in *Paul Cézanne: Correspondance*, ed. John Rewald (Paris, 1937), p. 198.

the very extent that it was instinctively and unconsciously pursued, inevitably transformed—even against the artist's will and to his own surprise—an intended harmony into a disharmony, whose own inner contradictions, at least in their artistic quality, would have destroyed one another had Cézanne not deliberately staved off destruction by creating transitions and connections through analyzing nature and integrating the results of his analysis into a compositional whole.

Cézanne's capacity for differentiation is extraordinary: the abundance of color gradations to be found in his works could be created, recorded, and mastered only by an exceptionally strong artistic temperament, a superior intellect, a stubborn will, and an uncommonly sharp eye. His general principles of differentiation, in addition to light and shadow, involve contrasts between warm and cold, opacity and transparency, brilliance and dullness, thickness and thinness, smoothness and roughness, structure and absence of structure; degrees of intensity and magnitude, and relative position. There are brighter and darker greens, violets, etc., warm and cold ochers, greens, blues; all the main directions—the vertical, the horizontal, and many slanted ones; all tendencies to movement—reclining, standing, and extending; every sort of positioning on the surface and opening up in depth, and every kind of transition from rest to movement. The thicker layers of paint are more opaque, more structural, and rougher, whereas the thinner layers are less opaque and smoother; the result is a play of textures, with transparency in depth and relief in the foreground.

In terms of quantity the color element tends neither to the infinitely small (in the manner of Monet's "commas" or the postimpressionists' dots) nor to broad color areas; what we find are color areas extended in all ways yet limited, reminiscent of the sections of a stained-glass window. These technical resources favor the development of relatively independent, individual formal elements comparable to organic cells or physical atoms. Every step in a color gradation is accomplished by a particular color tone which acquires independence in relation to every other tone to such an extent that it produces the effect of a single hewn stone as in a wall. The picture is built up, so to speak, of such individual stones of color and possesses an inner massiveness at odds equally with its dimensions as an easel painting and with its function as interior decoration.

But however great Cézanne's capacity for differentiation may seem to us, he himself complained a few weeks before his death: "I cannot express the intensity that my senses perceive ever more fully; I lack the magnificent richness of color that animates nature."[20] He had a dangerous tendency to regard his achievements as worthless, while the realm of the unattained seemed to grow ever larger.

How the color equivalents look all together depends upon our distance from the picture. As we move away, what at first seemed a disorderly confusion of spots of color comes

20. Letter to his son, Paul, September 8, 1906, in *Correspondance*, ed. Rewald, p. 288.

alive as a landscape and, as we continue, finally ceases to be perceptible as clearly formed; the reverse takes place as we approach it. When the viewer is close up, all the spots of color seem to lie on the same plane; they vary in size and movement, and the weft they form seems to possess no definite decorative pattern. The spots of color seem to be in a process of fermentation, each seeking its definitive place in a self-ordering chaos. One is struck above all by the large number of self-contained spots clearly distinguished from one another; for the most part they seem to lack firmly outlined limits, but their inner structure is extraordinarily clear. Other spots are defined less by their inner structure than by their surroundings; some, thick and opaque, have no structure at all and some are structured to a varying extent. From this derives a certain contrast between openness and closeness, precision and vagueness, a play between created and creating. Every detail *is*, but the whole surges with life in the manner of a richly orchestrated melody of many voices, played on the "great organ."[21] A strong will holds everything together—there is no relaxation, no thinning out, no stretching or dwindling away. Nor does this will ever manifest itself independently of the material, indulging in the play of ornament or being simply carried away by its own freedom. The differences in intensity of brush stroke are gradual, with no abrupt fall from one contrast to another. We have here a kind of chiseled lettering in color, with the values but not the appearance of a personal handwriting. It is characterized by uniform barlike strokes with space left between them; it is not a species of calligraphy but blocklike in structure, each unit being distinct in its support of the others and the total effect full of character and order. Cézanne's brush strokes are a peasant's footprints impressed into the soil, like the furrow made by a plow.

The artist and his art are immediately known, thanks to this quality of handwriting— "known" in the Biblical sense of the word, with its connotation of the sexual act. Not only does the painter paint bodies, the paint itself is a body and must first be apprehended with the body. It was in this way that Cézanne comprehended Veronese: "One is only aware of a great waviness of color, wouldn't you say? An iridescence, colors, a wealth of colors. That is what the painting ought to give us first, a harmonious warmth, an abyss into which the eye plunges, a mute ripening of the seed. A colored state of grace. All those tones enter into your bloodstream, flow with it, don't they? You feel exhilarated. You come into the true world at last. You become yourself, you become painting. To love a picture you must first have drunk it in like that, in long draughts. Lose consciousness. Go down with the painter to the dark, tangled roots of things, and come up to the surface again with colors, bursting into bloom with them in the light."[22] The difference between Cézanne and Veronese is not merely one of temperaments but one of principles. Veronese's script dissolves in the things painted, the personal is fused with the impersonal, and the result is a well-bred man's vision of the world. For all that Cézanne tried to be impersonal, the effect

21. Gasquet quoting Gauguin, *Cézanne*, p. 101.   22. Ibid., p. 166.

of his work is nonetheless highly personal: his script exists as color-form and not as things. It lacks urbanity and reveals the hermit in too direct communication with the cosmos.

Up to this point we have been dealing only with what Cézanne called the color equivalents. But it should be clear by now that these are not new sense perceptions discovered by the artist in nature alone. They originate neither in Cézanne's personal optical vision nor in the landscape of Provence; they reflect, rather, his view of the world (always particularized as a specific conception), his ideas on pictorial figuration and, finally, a study of nature aimed at realizing his conception of the world and of pictorial figuration. The color equivalents are the points where these three factors come together, and each factor is both cause and effect, for all three develop together and in interaction with one another. This becomes clearer when we pass from the material constituents of the individual form to its spatial characteristics, which Cézanne designated as plastic equivalents. Within the complex process of interaction between the elements we receive from the outside world (nature *and* history) and the additional elements taken from the inner world of human consciousness and the unconscious, of thought and feeling, in order to create and evolve a total world picture, modeling is a creative act. It is not something that can be learned or imitated. Every original conception of the world requires its own kind of modeling, and as a part of his method the creative artist has to invent it. But whatever the type of modeling may be, it serves the "main purpose of the picture: to achieve depth in space."[23]

In nature there is no necessary connection between the substance of things and their shape—at least no such connection is perceived by the senses. Not even analytical reason, which investigates the manifold inner and outer conditions, to which organic and inorganic substances are subjected, will succeed in explaining the individual appearance of an object beyond its abstract outline—the roundness of a tree trunk, for example. This accounts for the many various and contradictory speculations about the relations between matter and form in the history of philosophy. Nor can we establish a necessary relationship between the position of an object in space and its substance or shape (or both). When we deal with nature we can always imagine that a given object does not exist or exists at another place; we can also look at it from different angles and at varying distances. The artist's task consists in bringing about such a twofold necessary relationship— that between matter and form and that between form and space. This implies that to comprehend a work of art it must be viewed from a particular angle or angles. Two conditions must be fulfilled. First, the shape of the individual form must be developed at the same time as, and on the basis of, its material constituents, not independently of them. Second, the modeling of the individual form must follow the method used for creating the pictorial space in the work as a whole. Thus, modeling is a further step in the formation of

23. Rewald, *Cézanne*, p. 394.

color and space is a further stage in the shaping of form. Like Baudelaire, like Flaubert, Cézanne was fully aware of his methodological problems: "I should like . . . to paint space and time so that they become the forms of color sensibility, for I sometimes imagine colors as great noumenal entities, living ideas, beings of pure reason, beings with which we might be in communication. Nature is not on the surface, it is in depth. The colors are the expression of this depth on this surface. They arise out of the roots of the world. They are its life, the life of ideas. Drawing is entirely abstract. Therefore it must never be divorced from color. It is as though you tried to think without words, in pure numbers, pure symbols."[24] Modeling is not a formalistic process; to create pictorial space is to penetrate not only into the depths of the picture but also into the depths of our intellectual system of co-ordinates (which matches that of the world). Depth of space is depth of essence or else it is nothing but appearance and illusion.

In using the term "modeling" for the spatial structuring of the spot of color we seem to contradict Cézanne who, as early as 1876 (he was then in L'Estaque, Provence), wrote to Pissarro: "The sun is so frightening that it seems to me that the silhouettes of the objects rise not only in white or black, but also in blue, in red, in brown, in violet. I may be mistaken, but this is the direct opposite of modeling."[25] The term "modeling" (*modelé*) is here obviously used by Cézanne in the classical academic sense—the body described in outline and then later tied in with pictorial space by means of shading to suggest depth. This technique has two basic presuppositions: that the actual purpose of the picture is to represent a three-dimensional body, and that space is empty. According to Cézanne, this technique is utterly inappropriate to the landscape of Provence (similarly, the impressionists had maintained that it could not be brought into accord with the vibrant atmosphere of the Île-de-France). But whereas the impressionists stopped drawing the outlines of things in contrasts of black and white at the same time that they abandoned modeling by means of shading, and thereby abandoned geometric form, Cézanne asserted as late as 1904: "Treat nature in terms of the cylinder, the sphere, the cone; put everything in proper perspective, so that each side of an object or a plane is directed toward a central point. Lines parallel to the horizon give breadth, that is, a section of nature or, if you prefer, of the spectacle that the *Pater omnipotens aeternus Deus* spreads out before your eyes. Lines perpendicular to this horizon give depth. But to human beings like ourselves, nature is more depth than surface, hence the need of introducing into our light vibrations, represented by reds and yellows, a sufficient amount of blues to suggest air."[26]

Unsuccessful attempts have been made to deny the importance, in Cézanne's art, of geometric figures (with their frontal high lights) and of perspective (single vanishing point and gradual decrease in size and intensity). There is no contradiction between Cézanne's

24. Gasquet, pp. 150*f.*   25. Letter to Camille Pissarro, July 2, 1876, in *Correspondance*, ed. Rewald, p. 127.
26. Gasquet, p. 147.

practice and theory on this point, though it is true that throughout his life he had recourse to two alternatives. The first was rooted in the view of space as empty, needing to be filled with objects and air—and the foregoing quotation reflects this view. The second was rooted in the idea of a filled space and is reflected in other pronouncements: "Drawing is entirely abstract. Therefore it must never be divorced from color."[27] "Drawing and color are not really distinct: as we paint, we draw; the more harmonious the colors, the more precise the drawing. . . . When color is at its richest, form is at its most accomplished."[28] Cézanne called this method of obtaining form from color *moduler* (to modulate) as distinguished from *modeler* (to model). It replaces the a priori method of outline drawing with a method of inner definition. Form no longer arises out of delimitation, out of the contrast between the filled volume and void, but out of self-delimitation, self-determination, which results in setting filled volumes beside filled volumes. This conception of form also accounts for Cézanne's method of work: "In still-life painting . . . he advised me to begin lightly, using almost neutral tones. Then I had to go on, further and further up the scale, and concentrating the intermediary tones more strongly." "His method was singular . . . and extraordinarily complicated. He would begin with the shaded parts and with one spot of color; this would be painted over with a second . . . then with a third, until all these tints, overlapping, had modeled the object and at the same time colored it."[29]

After these general considerations, let us return to the *Mont Sainte-Victoire*, which so far we have analyzed only in terms of spots of color. At a relatively small distance from the canvas each of our color equivalents seems three-dimensional, i.e., it forms something like a solid body located in space. This effect is achieved by color alone. The various colors perform various spatial functions which can be accentuated more or less strongly by differentiation and by variation in the combination of nuances. A color (or combination of colors) may appear in several distinct layers, or several layers may be linked together. Thus, by continuous or discontinuous steps, Cézanne achieves the impression of depth and the three-dimensionality of the spots of color. "The planes within color! . . . I make planes with tones. . . . One must see the planes. . . . But they must be organized, fused."[30]

To begin with, let us consider the nearest plane: a dark area made up of various violets and greens. One color (violet) is decomposed into a warm (reddish) tone and a cold (bluish) tone; the first comes forward, the second recedes. This creates a tension which sets these tones apart yet relates them to each other, so that they seem to belong to distinct layers although there is no perceptible space between them. The number of layers employing the same color varies, but whether the contrast involves two or more layers, our actual perception is one not of movement but of tension. In consequence, perception of time is eliminated from our perception of three-dimensionality; or, to be more exact, we

27. Ibid., p. 151.   28. Ibid., p. 204.   29. Bernard, p. 65; pp. 29*f.*   30. Gasquet, p. 152.

do not perceive time as elapsing while we become aware of a multiplicity of layers. Contributing to this effect, in addition to the differences between the warm and cold violets, are the differentiations into opaque and porous, different directions of the brush strokes, and different degrees of structure or lack of structure. Among the various violets we find various greens. Since these have different degrees of vibration, they separate the various layers of the basic color, violet, and occupy a layer of their own between them. Variants of this basic color, green, are behind the successive layers of violet, thus completing the modeling function of green.

Since the differentiations are achieved by several means, the result is a number of variants; moreover, these can be combined in different ways. The colors may be sharply delimited, the violet may be painted over the green or the green over the violet, or a darker violet may be painted over a lighter violet. Differences between thick and thin or rough and smooth play an important part where tones overlap, because they afford various degrees of transparency in depth, opacity, and relief, and hence localization. Despite the variety of possibilities the range of each spot of color is limited. Each spot shows three tones—two extremes (for instance, the extremes of warm and cold) and one intermediary —the three being qualitatively combined in one local color. There are very similar effects in early stained-glass windows, where local color takes on an extra vibration because of the leads. As a result, each spot of color becomes a point in space, both in the two- and the three-dimensional sense.

These differentiations and combinations together make up the nearest dark plane, which pushes back all the other planes. In this first plane the dimension of height and the dimension of width part company, while height and depth are continually placed in tension all across the painting. Thus the plane is built up by dimensions which in turn are formed by spots. It seems to be created before the viewer's eye, so that the method of creation, the spiritual process, takes precedence over the plastic presence which it produces. And finally: even the closely related tones, such as the warm violets, do not lie in a single plane but either come forward or recede, i.e., the flat surface is transformed into a concave or convex surface; as a result the form of this whole group of spots of color extending in depth is related to its boundary on the flat surface. One might say that the elements of figuration of space help transform the spot of color into a three-dimensional body and, conversely, that the elements of this transformation contribute to figuration of space. The formation of successive layers through gradations of a single color (by the various means mentioned above) is nothing but the extension of modeling from within each spot of color, however small.

In the middle and upper parts of the picture the modeling follows the same principles but the colors are less intense and the modulations less abrupt. The mountain shows two sharply contrasting parts—one in shadow, the other in light. The dark-blue and violet area is divided from the reddish-gray area by a ridge where two surfaces come together: one upright, slightly turned back toward the diagonal, the other reclining, and ascending as an inclined plane rather than receding into the picture depth. What we are dealing with is the principle of the arris; however, the edge here is not vertical but slanting, and the sides (of unequal length), instead of receding, form inclined planes. Seen from a distance, against the over-all form of the mountain, the reclining plane in shadow seems blue; from closer up, various greens and violets outweigh the blue. Furthermore, from a distance the contour of the mountain appears as an almost unbroken line, whereas a closer view reveals several interruptions, angular projections, and slight curvatures. Finally, we may note that some brush strokes run parallel to the contour, others at various angles to it. Occasionally variations of one color have been applied at different angles simultaneously. At some distance these differences merge in a more or less uniform surface which projects forward. Above it is the sky, another surface which vibrates in itself and yet presses forward. Thus modeled form exists only as effective form; what is actually on the surface is less form than an element in the process that leads to form. In this way modeling becomes the transition from formlessness or merely potential form to the actual form[31] as perceived by the viewer, the bridge between chaos and organization; it is becoming and being in one. However, the plastic form is never identical with the thing or the object.

On the upright plane of the mountain the light is delimited by blue shadows below and on the sides, that is to say, it is concentrated in the middle and at the height. Here the warm tones employed are reddish-brown, the cold ones gray-blue: the hovering lights and shadows are rendered by shifting warm and cold tones within a fixed range of differentiation quite unlike the sharp contrasts between highly intense local colors such as those at the bottom of the picture—between violet (and green) and ocher (and red). That the intensity of the individual colors is weakened, and consequently the contrasts between them, shows within what limits Cézanne observes the laws of aerial perspective. He does not make things in the distance smaller; and instead of continuous recessive movement into depth we find the reverse, a forward movement. Rather than infinite depth, Cézanne gives us a space which is tightly closed at the back. But between the enclosing walls of foreground and background the colors are nevertheless graduated in the double sense just analyzed. The reason for this lies in Cézanne's conception of space as filled rather than empty; only in the latter can perspective, and especially linear perspective, exist.

There is an essential difference between these two kinds of space. Filled substantial space is composed of corporeal points, whose origin and nature as color and plastic equivalents we have already analyzed in detail. Empty space, on the other hand, is defined by its external boundaries, within which the bodies are assigned positions largely independent of those boundaries; or else it is defined by movements through it in each of

31. [For "effective form" (*Wirkungsform*) and "actual form" (*Daseinsform*), see the Appendix, pp. 210, 217, 222.]

its dimensions—in either case the point in space is much less important than the boundary or the movement conceived a priori. In filled, substantial space there is no continuous movement from point to point, but there is the double movement of attraction and repulsion between points of space. The repulsion is effected by means of contrast, and the simultaneous attraction by means of intermediate tones situated between the contrasting ones. The individual and relatively independent points of space are thus transformed into groups of points both continuously and discontinuously. The simultaneity of the movements in opposite directions at each individual point makes all points simultaneously perceptible (despite the logical development), and space is perceived as timeless. Since each point (or group of points) has an internal limit, the external limit loses all significance, i.e., filled space is not constructed within outer boundaries from which fixed pathways lead inward, but is of internal origin and extends from a central point outward. The limit of each point is transcended only to find a new limit, which no longer tends to move away from the first but to move back toward it. It is possible that by this continual self-transcendence of each point of space a limit of artistic reality is reached beyond which the whole transcends itself and becomes a symbol of a transcendent world. Assuming that Cézanne was led to the conception of filled space by recollections of medieval stained-glass windows or some of the later works of Tintoretto, he did not, like them, carry this transcendence as far as the Absolute; he never used art for nonartistic purposes—religious, scientific, political, or literary. In this sense he subscribed to the doctrine of art for art's sake. Finally, the corporeal-substantial point of space implies that space can no longer be conceived of as a medium (air, atmosphere) in the manner of the impressionists. This does not mean that the picture as a whole is devoid of air (or mood), but that form determines the air (and not the other way round). Air is subordinate to form and never extends beyond the point of space to which it is attached.

We have already mentioned that, close up, the picture appears as a flat surface covered with spots of color. As the viewer moves farther away, the surface appears articulated in planes. Three such planes emerge, not as abstract and formal components of space as such, but as structural differences, as geological strata. They denote levels of emotion at the same time that they denote elements in the composition of space. Space possesses a "stone skeleton" of geological origin; Cézanne thought that an essential task of painting was to lay bare the anatomy of the earth. The foremost plane is composed of a dark area (violet and green), which rises parallel to the picture surface and pushes back everything behind it, and a lighter area (ocher and red), which lies flat and whose forms press backward while the colors, on the contrary, tend to come forward. The second plane inclines upward and departs somewhat from the horizontal, so that it seems to move forward from left to right. The third and topmost plane comes forward from a farthest—vibrating yet enclosing—limit and is stopped short. We thus have, between the planes, a contrast be-

III   CÉZANNE. *Three Skulls*. ca. 1900. 13⅜ × 23⅝ in.

IV CÉZANNE. *The Quarry at Bibémus.* 1898–1900. 25⅝ × 31⅞ in.

tween inward and outward movement, a contrast mediated by the articulated middle plane, which balances it out. Although they are differentiated, the planes so strongly press one on the other that the total effect of a single surface is preserved. This is why we have used the term "planes" rather than "foreground, middle ground, and background." The latter terms convey measurable distances, to be traversed by the eye separately and successively; they are not simultaneous in terms either of space or of time. But the planes exist simultaneously: in so far as the eye can be said to move from one to the other it does so in a stepwise motion, up and down. In this way motion through a dimension is transformed into a tension within that dimension, and this tension is not between successive stages but rather between simultaneously existing points in space.

This is possible because Cézanne recognized only two independent dimensions—the horizontal and the vertical; depth is developed not along an axis of its own but vertically, by means of plastic equivalents. But for this very reason depth becomes the primal, all-determining dimension, and the two others, for all their linear and axial independence, merely serve as resistances to movement in depth. This is a consequence of the nature of filled space. Because such a space consists of substantial-corporeal points, the system of dimensional co-ordinates loses its a priori character and the dimensions can be developed only to the extent permitted by the substantial and resisting nature of the points of space. The fact that the basic dimension of depth is precisely the one that does not manifest itself independently will seem paradoxical only to those who measure the magnitude of freedom by the absence of resistance it encounters, i.e., those who in the last analysis interpret freedom negatively as arbitrary choice within the full range of possibilities rather than as a positive force that asserts itself against specific resistances and gives necessary form to specific realities.

The horizontal dimension runs along an axis from an indefinite beginning to an indefinite end, from left to right, from one form to another; it has the character of a "spurious" and hence self-abolishing infinity.[32] The depth dimension (represented in the vertical axis) is shorter, finite, closed. It involves two opposite directions of movement in centripetal tension with each other and, thanks to stoppages, gaps, and changes of direction that occur along it, it contains a number of interrelated contrasts; it has the structure of an internally contradictory and hence self-abolishing finitude. These essential differences transform a purely external intersection into an action: the horizontal axis (light) breaks

32. [The author uses the conception of a "spurious" infinity which first appears in Hegel's *Jenenser Logik*. By this Hegel means that the attempt to define an entity completely by using an endless number of finite terms is, by the finite nature of the terms (each cut off from and limited by the others), bound to fail. To this Hegel opposes "genuine" infinity as the characteristic of that self-determination by which an object becomes itself through its differences from everything outside itself; not the false infinity of "unlimited" but the true infinity of "self-delimited." The elucidation of true being through the relation between finite existence and this real infinity may be taken as the central task of Hegel's logic.]

through the vertical axis and as a result is somewhat bent back toward depth; and the
vertical axis, after this collision, resumes its movement along the depth axis but in an inverse direction, i.e., forward. The axes thus reciprocally activated maintain tension with
each other by the force of an attraction exerted upon them by the point of intersection.
This point, a triad of violet, green, and ocher, is, as it were, the heart of the picture, the
point of crystallization of the composition: everything starts there and everything leads
back to it. This is what holds the pictorial space together; it is the reason for measuring
it from the center outward. Like all life processes the pictorial space is quantitatively
finite, but qualitatively infinite. This is the opposite of Monet's and Pissarro's diffuse,
atmospheric space. More than that, it is the opposite of naturalistic space.

The fact that Cézanne's *Mont Sainte-Victoire* shows a view slightly different from that
of the photograph (Plate II) is not very important, but the fact that he did not confine
himself to any one viewing point is important. To be sure, he anchored a high-lying line of
vision[33] at the foot of the mountain so that the inclined plane in front of it is seen from
above; but we do not know whether the trees in the foreground are actually seen from
above or from a point somewhat lower. Moreover, Cézanne must have placed himself
facing the center of the picture or a little to the right of center; but if so, he could not have
seen the left wall of the red-roofed house at the right of the ocher farmstead. In either case,
he combined various views not out of pure arbitrariness or to substitute a more complete
and effective imaginary view for the actual view. Rather, his will to pictorial figuration
compelled him to subordinate visual perception to idea, motif, and composition. According to Cézanne, for the artist "to see is to conceive and to conceive is to compose." To
him, however, sensory perception, emotional experience, and the idea of the picture or,
in his own words, "the confused sensations with which we are born,"[34] "the reading of
the model" ("la lecture du modèle"),[35] and "realization," are in conflict with each other.
He found his point of departure too remote from his goal,[36] which was the representation
of nature, and the causes for this were social and economic, as Cézanne clearly recognized
on occasion. He once observed: "You have no idea how presumptuous this ferocious
population [of Marseilles] is: it has only one instinct, that of money; they are said to make
plenty of it, but they are an ugly lot—modern methods of communication wipe out the
salient typical features as seen from outside. In several hundred years there will be no
point in living, everything will be leveled. But the little that is left is still dear to our eyes
and to our hearts."[37] In order to solve this conflict, Cézanne asserted the requirements of
the motif and of the pictorial idea against the assumption of a single point of view and a
single intellectually calculable vanishing point. He was neither pure sensualist nor pure

33. [For "line of vision" (*Blicklinie*), see Pl. XXV and
the Appendix, p. 222.]

34. From an undated fragment of a letter to Gasquet,
in *Correspondance*, ed. Rewald, p. 227.

35. Gasquet, p. 91.

36. Letter to Émile Zola, May 8, 1878, in *Correspondance*,
ed. Rewald, No. XLIV.

37. Letter to Zola, September 24, 1878, ibid., p. 150.

rationalist (in terms of linear perspective); he always sought to combine a maximum of pictorial logic with an optimum of verisimilitude.

This concludes our analysis of the plastic equivalent with respect to both its corporeal and its spatial features. We have seen time and again that the two are closely interwoven and condition each other. But Cézanne's peculiar conception of the *Mont Sainte-Victoire* led to a contradiction: while the pictorial space swells and expands vitally, only to be compressed by the iron brackets of the nearest and farthest planes toward the heart of the picture, corporeality retreats from the stereometric volume to the spots of color. Spatiality comes into being as corporeality fades. As a result, life and death are brought into closest interpenetration. In the middle plane, which is the most extensive area of space, corporeality is at a minimum; where the movement of space into depth comes to a definitive stop and reverses its direction, corporeality is at a maximum. This antagonism is absent from Cézanne's earlier works; in them, bodies and space had an equal coefficient of plastic expansion, whether this coefficient was stereometric or planimetric. The emergence of this antagonism attests that a new tension had entered Cézanne's life (or become dominant in it), namely, the tension between being and nonbeing. It is only through this tension that filled substantial space acquires its spiritual depth.

Thus it turns out that the three terms—"to see," "to conceive," "to compose"—are not successive, but are present simultaneously and are interdependent. It is no accident that Cézanne thought of "to conceive" as the middle term: the conception contains, on the one hand, the whole complex inner world coming to grips with the outer world (nature and history) and, on the other hand, the material and formal unity which is developed and summed up in the composition.[38] Neither something isolated nor something ready-made, the conception is a more or less definite feeling which guides the entire process of creation, although it becomes itself an existing form only in the course of this process. This feeling is rooted both in man (including the historical conditions of his life) and in nature (including the economic means of production which transform nature). Any aspect of nature or history can arouse feeling in the artist and the nonartist alike; the former is distinguished from the latter less by the overwhelming force of his feelings than by their originality, total comprehensiveness, and durability. The artist perceives in himself and in nature untold things that lie beyond the confines of accepted cultural conventions. He goes back to the "Mothers," to the region where man and the cosmos have their common origin, and he brings both together between points of depth and height, center and periphery, where they never before had met. In the artist's feeling, all of man and the cosmos is alive and thus enters into the concrete work, making it a vehicle or symbol of the whole, at once subjective and objective. The artist, in fine, is capable of preserving this new feeling in its striving toward totality instead of permitting it to congeal

38. [For "composition," see below, p. 53, and the Appendix, pp. 234–238.]

and freeze until such time as he has found an adequate inner and outer form for it. Compared with this spontaneously developing aesthetic feeling,[39] the "natural" nature which had served either as starting point for the experience or point of support for the realization seems banal, superficial, meaningless, in contrast with the revelation of the hidden to be found in "painted" nature. From the purely psychological viewpoint of the creative artist the feeling will always contain more than the created form, and the created form more than what the artist put in it consciously. From the point of view of a theory of artistic creation that recognizes the reality only of what the artist has put on the canvas consciously or subconsciously, what matters is the degree of originality and the comprehensiveness of the feeling, as well as the adequacy and completeness of the form that realizes the feeling. We find nothing of all this in "natural" nature, not in the landscape alone nor in man alone. The two factors are brought into reciprocal interaction only through the artist's creative power. Hence, there are two aspects to every aesthetic feeling—a qualitative one and a methodological one, depending upon whether the viewer concentrates on the subject matter or on the process by which the subject was conceived and composed.

We have given a partial analysis of Cézanne's method without going into the feeling of elation that is generally present in the creator (or the re-creator)—a feeling that Cézanne called "le plaisir de l'étude." We shall go on to examine the concrete feelings relating to the content of *Mont Sainte-Victoire*. The painting discloses a highly dramatic emotion, an inner tumult expressed with emphasis but without rhetoric, the heavy torrent of feeling which is laboriously controlled. This feeling pervades the picture as a whole, right down to every individual spot of color. "I am in such a state of cerebral agitation, in an agitation so great, that at one point I was afraid it would engulf my frail reason," Cézanne wrote when he was working on this painting.[40] In his late works we find clues to the anxiety that disturbed him: the still life *Three Skulls* (Plate III); the landscape *Quarry at Bibémus* (where the very rocks sway drunkenly and fall apart like a disintegrating corpse; Plate IV); the two portraits of elderly people, *Woman with Rosary* (Plate V) and *Self-Portrait of the Artist in a Cap* (Plate VI), which follow the *Boy in a Red Vest* (Plate VII), portraying a youth in the throes of puberty. It is as though the artist wanted to contrast the awakening and the decline of spiritual forces, somewhat as, in the landscape *Lake at Annecy* (Plate VIII), he had set off the extremes of mountain height and the deep waters of the lake to express what Lionello Venturi so aptly called "sentiment panique." It is the fear of death, the anxiety as to whether he would achieve the goal he had conceived in youth. He had devoted, even sacrificed, the whole of his life to it, and it seemed farther from realization

---

39. [For "aesthetic feeling" (*aesthetisches Gefühl*), see the Appendix, pp. 217–219.]

40. Letter to Émile Bernard, September 21, 1906, in *Correspondance*, ed. Rewald, p. 290.

with every picture he completed. This mounting fear at the approach of death, at the failure of self-realization through his art, violently burst open the floodgates of customarily repressed feeling.

At this ultimate moment, when Cézanne was faced with the question of whether his life had been one of fulfillment or failure, the familiar landscape of Mont Sainte-Victoire seems to have assumed for him a new and higher significance—that of an autobiographical symbol. "I should like to mix melancholy with sunshine. . . . There is a sadness in Provence that no one has expressed."[41] We have seven versions of this painting; each is like a confession before nature in which one man accounts for his creative power and his weakness. In all the versions the landscape is inhuman, uninhabitable, uncivilized—it suggests some titanic elemental conflict going on outside society. The artist (or, if you will, the earth) is alone in a solitude where no human footstep ever fell. But with each version the relation between the lower part of the picture and the mountain, as well as the form of the mountain itself and its position, vary. In certain versions Cézanne emphasized the breadth of the plain which extends beyond the flanks of the mountain, so that the level, passive part of the landscape is emphasized at the expense of the rising part. In one version the lower part is drawn into this rising movement, so that the vertical preponderates over the horizontal. In the version under study, however, such emphatic one-sidedness is avoided. The vertical and the horizontal movements clash dramatically, they interpenetrate, they are balanced in their contest, until finally the contrast between them is resolved in the two slanting ridges of the angular contour of the mountain.

Similar observations apply to the two ridges themselves. In some versions the rising (left-hand) ridge extends far beyond the center of the picture; in one version, where it does not reach the center, the other ridge preponderates as it descends and fades away. In our version, however, the distance across the peak is almost equal to the difference in length between the two ridges. As a result, the ascending and descending movements are perceived at once: the laboriously gradual rise is always seen in relation to the more abrupt, broken fall, although the movements may also be perceived successively. To enhance the contrast between the two opposed movements every formal analogy between the ridges has been eliminated or toned down: the left side minimizes the humps, while on the right side the stages of the decline are emphasized and contracted. The two ridges seem to embody a feeling which Cézanne a few years earlier had expressed as follows: "I work on stubbornly, for I am beginning to see the promised land. Will my fate be that of the great Hebrew leader, or will I be able to enter?"[42]

This latter-day Moses does not gaze at the future from some alien Sinai, but from his own Provence; not as a wanderer in the desert, but as a spirit breaking itself against the weight and inertia of a native matter, just as this breaks itself against the will of a restless

---

41. Gasquet, p. 193.   42. Letter to Ambroise Vollard, January 9, 1903, in *Correspondance*, ed. Rewald, p. 252.

spirit. The basic elements of the painting—the interplay of weight and upsurge, of rising and falling movements, and the figuration of this conflict—are now identified with the creative process of the earth itself, its coming into being and passing away. These are not conceived of as a cycle of life-death and death-rebirth, but as simultaneous and interlocked, such as we encounter them in nature during twilight or during the seasons of transition between summer and winter. Cézanne sees the earth as the peasant sees it, at work, in the process of giving birth, without sexual connotations: it is a *hierosgamos*, a rebirth in man's consciousness. Cézanne identifies himself with *terra creatrix* in the state of *creare*, in its travail; he postulates and experiences himself as the basically adequate representative of the *Creator mundi omnipotens*. Thereby, however, the artist has left the peasant ideology behind him, for he no longer recognizes the absolute transcendence of the powers upon which successful tilling of the earth is thought to depend. Instead, Cézanne is both the humble slave of the entire creative process of nature and the master of every present moment. As a result he is in a state of extreme tension marked by utmost concentration and sense of responsibility. "One minute in the life of the world is going by. Paint it in its reality!"[43] This has now become the crucial task: to capture a transitional moment in which two contrasting movements—that of the earth and that of light—separate from each other and yet remain in tension and interaction. Cézanne does not set down this moment as completed; he gives it life within universal movement. As a result, the general and the particular are not related as genus to individual, but as a permanently identical process is related to a unique manifestation—the latter thus acquiring the character of an essence. Concept and development do not exclude each other, they constitute together the plenitude of the form which is in and for itself.

It is clear what Cézanne achieves by this identification of his own inner conflicts with the earth's birth pangs, his own struggle to achieve form with his experience of how the world is formed: the drama does not lead to tragedy, the titanic hero is not destroyed; for the number of "minutes passing by" is infinitely great and to fashion them into full reality is an unending task. But the continually renewed struggle between earth and light is no comfort to the artist. Even though he can see the transitional moments between life and death and between death and life, he does not see, in this twofold interplay, the redeeming promise of rebirth without death, the promise of beatitude. On the other hand, the artist does raise the earth by stages from its subterranean unconscious servitude into the realm of consciousness. Cézanne, however, views this process as one who is earthbound—the earth being one particular spot, isolated from the cosmos and passively enduring the cosmic element of light. The soil of Provence does not become the cosmos for him, as the Dutch seacoast became the cosmos for Jacob van Ruisdael. The fragment of nature does not stand for the universe; Cézanne and his earth are Titans who struggle and evolve in

43. Gasquet, p. 137.

a hermetically closed world. No path leads from it to God or to the cosmos; the only path leads to aesthetic consciousness, the only way out is the artist's transformation of the land-scape into a logically developed, structured entity. He achieves this without transcending the principle of art for art's sake or removing the corruption of regional and topical art. This is not to deny that Cézanne had cosmic sensibility, that he was "consumed by a cosmic obsession." But his "heroic sense of reality" involved two things—"the torrent of the world in a little bit of matter"[44]—an infinite in movement and process, and a finite fixed existent as well. Cézanne sought to fuse the two, but the infinite did not always achieve form and the finite did not always become torrent. There remained a gap be-tween them; his will forced a "first approximation" while his superior understanding demanded: "We must live in harmony—my model, my colors, and myself."[45] But some-where in the course of the long way of creative activity the unity between spirit and world or between the self and the colors was broken.

The discord between earth and cosmos is paralleled by the isolation of the individual from society. We have seen that each plastic and color equivalent, the solid material point of space, though endowed with its own individual form, has no radiation, does not associ-ate freely with the whole, but only with its immediate neighbors. Although each part of the painting is relatively independent in a superficial sense, the relations between the parts remain external, have no essential effect on the parts themselves. The points do form groups, but these higher units, too, remain isolated from each other. All they have in com-mon is that they play a functional role in a purely aesthetic whole. The sole mediator be-tween them is the pictorial idea, a purely formal element which contrasts with the sub-stantiality of each point of space. We have seen that each point of space—each individual member of the pictorial society—is set against more or less unstructured spots of color and that the form is ripped out, as it were, from the formlessness of the mass, so that individual and mass are in varying degrees linked to and isolated from each other. Thereby the configuration[46] acquires the form of a process rather than that of an existent, and the fact that the inner form cannot completely separate itself from the process of its emergence limits the autonomy of the total configuration. The work results from compulsion as much as from freedom. We further recall that the horizontal axis, situated in the sphere of the earthly and, by the same token, in the sphere of social action (whereas Cézanne emphasizes only its landscape function as a horizon), is least limited, and that its parts are conceived of as successive in time and hence are scarcely interrelated internally. In the vertical axis consciousness is in tension with the force of gravity; into this self-contained contest between spirit and nature, social action erupts as a higher and unlimited power, as something alien. This is because the individual strives to assert himself as a structured personality in a society whose movement is unstructured or circular, i.e., defined by re-

44. Ibid., p. 156.   45. Ibid., p. 195.   46. [For "configuration" (*Werkgestalt*), see the Appendix, pp. 225–234.]

current cycles of construction and destruction. (Degas, with his pessimistic *ressentiment*, took this cycle as the main form of his compositions.)

In striving to become a person, the isolated individual counteracts the tendency to separate the various faculties from one another and to use them in isolation; he tries, on the contrary, to integrate them in order to achieve plenitude, to make the emotions, the senses, the understanding, the body, and the will share in the creative work. What matters here is how the faculties are linked together: this is determined by the qualitative nature of each individual factor. We have just dealt with the emotional factor. In the *Mont Sainte-Victoire* the rational factor—we shall later deal with its main features—is no longer, as in Cézanne's earlier works, dissociated from the emotional one in order to control it by means of the pictorial construction. Here reason is the unfolding method of emotion itself, the logic of feeling; the emotion is organized by it and made to run coherently along a path with a beginning and an end; moreover, sensuality is limited by it in a manner we shall presently describe. By doing these two things, reason ceases to be formalistic and aprioristic and acquires a substantial character to which the purely formal elements (which create a system out of relationships) remain subordinated.

Regarding sensuality, we have already mentioned that Cézanne's capacity for subtle differentiations does not aim at plurality pure and simple, but at diversity of related elements and separation of all that is hostile to fusion and uniformity. He divests sensations of the absolute metaphysical character they had for the impressionists and firmly situates them between emotion and reason, between the irrational and the rational. They become a central piece in a more than merely sensory whole after modeling had gone beyond perception variously in two directions, that of volume and that of idea and conception. The sense perceptions possess plenitude inasmuch as visual, tactile, and even olfactory elements have been welded in a monolithic complex. Yet this indissoluble unity of sensations lacks erotic, sexual elements, lacks anything that might be called tender or voluptuous (as in Renoir, Watteau, or Rubens). Nevertheless, it would be entirely erroneous to regard Cézanne's sensuality as abstract. Even when he strove to be classical, he was worlds apart from Ingres or David, i.e., intellectual sensuality of any kind was foreign to him. His own sensuality, though it was ideational, was at the same time emotional, physical, material—i.e., it comprised many antithetical elements. The term "ideational" here denotes that the initial conception is rooted in feeling, not in transcendental consciousness (as it was with Leonardo da Vinci); "material" in this usage denotes a tendency toward the physical reality of color.

Thus we see that feeling, reason, and the senses co-operate to build a bridge between the pictorial idea and the world of things—a bridge which has a reality of its own. In Cézanne's case this does not come about as a result of free co-operation among the various creative functions working together out of an instinctive need to complement each other.

V   CÉZANNE. *Woman with Rosary.* 1900–1904. 31¾ × 25¾ in.

VI   Cézanne. *Self-Portrait of the Artist in a Cap.* 1898–1900. 25⅝ × 21¼ in.

VII   CÉZANNE. *Boy in a Red Vest.* 1890–95. 35 × 27⅞ in.

VIII   CÉZANNE. *Lake at Annecy*. 1896. 25½ × 32 in.

It is an iron, all-controlling but not omnipotent will that forces them to work together. This voluntarism in method and synthesis is the more marked in that it foregoes any animistic interpretation of objects, any anthropomorphic rendition of nature, any identification of spirit with nature, any form of monism. The artist's will must intervene because there is an antinomy between the subject's aspiration to exercise all his faculties and the world of things which had become fragmentary and specialized in Cézanne's period—the antinomy between a mind that resists its historically determined self-alienation and a world of objects which has already become alienated. One effect of this antinomy in Cézanne's work is that his northern French landscapes rarely attain the profundity and plenitude of his southern French landscapes. And yet, throughout his life, the artist sought to compare and to encompass the different features of landscapes north and south of the Loire. The narrow world of objects forced Cézanne to choose between two possible attitudes: either to content himself with a single spiritual faculty or to fuse all his capacities together in an undifferentiated unity, a kind of lyrical pantheism. But neither sober single-mindedness nor indulgence in fancy was compatible with Cézanne's temperament, which drove him to differentiation and analysis as a preliminary to synthesis. This led to a profound conflict between subject and object, with the result that, on the objective side, the link between permanent process and momentary phenomenon was too direct to make it possible to arrest the transitory and give it determinate form, while on the subjective side, emotion, sensuality, and reason operated in closest interrelation without arriving at dialectical interplay. At this point the will intervened to bring about by force what could not take place freely, and thus found itself checked in its striving for perfect expression. The will cannot abolish the isolation of the individual from society, or of the soil of Provence from the cosmos, nor can it realize the surface qualities of things. For this reason, ideality and reality are kept in extreme tension: the ideality of the conception does not completely permeate the concrete things and vanish, although they are radically reconstructed in their essential features, as though Cézanne were at once geologist, architect, biologist, etc. Nor, conversely, is the generality of things incorporated without loss in the specific content of the conception.

In resolving this antinomy—one of many in Cézanne's character and art—both within the individual form and the total configuration, Cézanne keeps clear of two extremes. He does not conceive the world as a still life devoid of spirit, nor does he force meaning upon a world that is in itself meaningless. Cézanne once said: "L'esprit m'emmerde" ("I am sick and tired of spirit"). Here he was referring to the kind of theory that would dictate formal laws to the world or ascribe meanings to it. His own theory—taking this term in the broadest sense, as a systematic view of the world—did not try to make statements about things, but to make the things themselves speak. Cézanne was convinced that if things could be made to speak, they would disclose more "spirit" than the most imaginative artist could ever dream of. He had a deep, healthy distrust of the facile games of unconscious subjectivism and conscious system-building. The only theory he respected was that which proves its worth experimentally—for example, in a picture which has mastered the innumerable difficulties that nature presents to the mind and which has transcended them intuitively. "Everything, and particularly in art, is theory developed and applied in contact with nature."[47] Cézanne fought a war on two fronts: in alliance with nature against the pure spirit, and in alliance with the pictorial idea against empirical nature devoid of spirit. The pictorial idea was entirely his own: "Only the initial impetus, i.e., temperament, can lead a man to the goal he wants to attain."[48] But at the same time: "When we respect nature sufficiently, she always finds a way to say what she means."[49] The divorce between nature and spirit (as that between spirit and power) was a historical fact which Cézanne sought to raise to the heights of the timeless in his art.

Our analysis of the process of conception has shown that the "nature" to which Cézanne turns has two components, one relating to the inner world and one to the outer world (both historically conditioned). In the work of art the two must be brought into a necessary relationship. It should be clear that the unity of the two can lie neither in the mind nor in the objects, and that the artist must create a new type of reality, equally founded in both yet independent of either; this new reality is not an illusion, but a reality of a special kind. And just as the aesthetic feeling contains a general factor and a concrete factor, more or less unified according to the method and degree of artistic figuration, so artistic reality has, in addition to the general factor of its formal existence, a concrete form, namely, the motif. The motif is the sum total of line, color, and light by means of which the conception is realized, developed, and comprehended in terms of the so-called composition. The motif embodies the concentrated content, the nucleus from which the total configuration is developed. The two functions of the motif are not present in natural appearances, but arise out of the artist's interpretation and figuration of them. The motif serves as a common denominator for the qualitative and structural features of things, which in nature are found as a juxtaposition of separate elements. When this leads to formalism the object becomes entirely secondary. When art aims at knowledge of nature rather than at formalistic speculation about nature, the motif is controlled by the subject in nature. Ideally, the motif is the idea of the subject and the creative act tends to a synthesis of subject and motif. In the extreme case the motif is lost in the subject.

The (linear) motif of *Mont Sainte-Victoire* is the angle formed by the outline of the mountain. Similar triangles are discernible in the jagged outlines of the mass of vertical shadows in the nearest plane of the painting—a first statement, as it were, of the motif

47. Gasquet, pp. 170*f*.   48. Ibid., p. 134.   49. Ibid., p. 144.

of the mountain mass at the top. Behind these vertical bushes a similar form is projected into depth by the ocher farmstead, but it is interrupted by a horizontal band. The tip of this triangle, a triad of violet, green, and ocher, is again directed upward. Here is the point of intersection of the vertical and horizontal axes (both are slightly tilted), which is the heart or point of crystallization of the picture. It can be interpreted as the point where two diagonally intersecting (adjacent) angles meet. The mountain surmounts the group of diverging sides and binds them together. Thus, the mountain is constituted as the motif, which is developed by stages, through various dimensions, layers of space, and colors to its greatest clarity and completeness. Into this continuous development a second, contrasting factor is introduced: Cézanne situates the line of vision very high (at the foot of the mountain) and emphasizes it strongly, so that the hilly landscape appears at a lower elevation than it really is. But from our viewing point in front of the dark area at the bottom the eye is led upward, and this upward movement continues on the inclined plane as far as the line of vision. This twofold movement in opposite directions isolates the mountain, raising it above the rest of the landscape, upon which it sits heavily, as a crown. Here, as everywhere in Cézanne, we have both sharp contrasts and mediating transitions, gulfs and bridges, tearing apart and joining together, polarity and continuity, violence and gentleness. There remains, however, the question as to how these contrasts are related—are they to be found in nature or has the artist imposed them upon the landscape?

Photographs give a distorted impression of the painting, overemphasizing the linear element of the motif and at the same time making it almost impossible to discern the diagonals in the middle plane. In the original the motif is a color chord of definite timbre and form based on the violent contrasts mentioned above. Color, light, and the disposition of volume and space are so intimately blended that the development of the motif in the composition can be described with equal justification in terms of each of the three. It is always effected on a pictorial surface whose sides are roughly in the ratio of $5 : 6 +$ (or $3 : 4-$)—in close relationship to the ratio (already discussed in detail) between the horizontal and vertical axes. This format is in three parts both horizontally and vertically. In the vertical dimension we have three bands of varying median heights: the middle band at a height denoted by a is smaller by about two units ($2x$) than the lower one and by about three units ($3x$) smaller than the upper one. We thus obtain the succession (from bottom to top) of $a + 2x$, a, and $a + 3x$, where a and x seem to be in some sort of relationship. However, the heights vary from place to place, so that the bands dovetail at many points, although their boundaries, and by the same token the rhythm of the over-all structure, are emphasized by lines of color. In the horizontal dimension the middle part has the form of a tapering wedge which runs obliquely across the plane (and into depth), so that all the heavy masses and more vehement movements lie to the left of the vertical middle axis (which remains imaginary), whereas to the right there are inclined planes without masses flowing into the open. These unequally filled sides are not balanced; rather, Cézanne wanted to hold the tremendous dynamism in absolute repose by stressing the inner oppositions, a repose that contains the whole impact of the energy charges and concentrates them in their point of crystallization. It is not reason which, from outside as it were, calculates, weighs, and balances the emotions, thus transforming the dynamism into an unstable equilibrium; it is, rather, the fermenting emotions themselves which, by being related to their own center, achieve the form of repose, as though they were suddenly frozen at their climactic point: the most intense life becomes or is the point of death in life. (There is a similar effect in the *kouros* of Sounion.[50]) This was doubtless what Cézanne meant when he said: "I swore I would die painting"[51]—words that literally came true.

As for the role of light in the composition, we can scarcely assume a naturalistic source of light; at all events, the source is not at the top of the picture whence the light would be directed downward. Rather, it runs across the picture like a river of warm ochers, in emphatic contrast to the movement into depth on the vertical axis. Cézanne thus renounces not only any kind of naturalism but also any rationalization of nature in terms of perspective. The horizontal direction of the light denotes a path between two widely separated areas of dark—the sky and the earth. The light does not originate in the sky as a source, nor in the earth as reflection. In another, probably somewhat earlier version, Cézanne had a bright foreground which he later abandoned in favor of a more dramatic effect: the light presses upon the rising earth where it achieves great compact mass, but in the process it loses the greater part of its warmth; at the top, where it becomes narrower, it is less intense but warmer. In the vertical dimension a warm dark area changes into a colder dark area and, between them, cold light is transformed into a warm half-light. This compositional development of the motif of light contributes to the resolution of color dissonances by helping to muffle them. The introduction of cold light into warm dark areas produces a dissociation in the lower part of the picture, indeed, a gulf, between consciousness and unconsciousness. At the top, however, the two converge to produce a half-twilight state, a very slight relaxation of the active will. With the light distributed in this manner the landscape expresses a process of consciousness rather than a fact of nature, but it does not symbolize a state of mind (permanent or temporary); it realizes a conflict of the mind with itself and with nature, a battle that the imperious will brings to a climax within clearly set boundaries.

Mont Sainte-Victoire is not painted in consistently clear tones; light and dark colors alternate continually in an austere rhythmic structure. At the bottom plane of the painting a darkness of violets and greens is used throughout. The middle plane can be divided

50. [National Museum, Athens, no. 2720; see also G. M. A. Richter, *Archaic Greek Youth*, Catalogue, No. 2 (figs. 233–39).]   51. Gasquet, p. 201.

into three bands, each showing three articulations: in the lowest the values are disposed horizontally as light-light-dark; in the middle one the disposition is reversed (dark-dark-light); in the upper reigns symmetry (dark-light-dark), preparing the bipartite division of the sky into a cold and a warm dark. The distribution of light may also be described as follows: the painting is divided by a line which runs from the lower left corner to the center top; to the right of this line a shadow falls dramatically across the path of light; to the left a light and half-light area falls across the shadow, producing a contrast which gives way to symmetry at the top. But this distribution is nevertheless only the external, regulative aspect of the composition of light. It must also be noted that the lower part shows a number of violent contrasts both in depth and horizontally. In the upper part, however, the contrasts penetrate and pass into one another; the middle part is transitional in the sense that many small lights and shadows are concentrated in a small space in the form of external contrasts which begin to interpenetrate in a hovering manner, but are not yet as clearly outlined as in the mountain. But in studying this rich compositional development we must not overlook the presence of conflict—the fact that the light is merely a path which runs horizontally between two different kinds of dark, trying to penetrate them, but without brightening them. It is as though light were an image of life flowing between the eternal darkness that precedes birth and the eternal darkness that follows death: on the one hand a terrestrial darkness coming from the depths of the earth, and on the other, a celestial darkness produced by the blinding power of light itself.

As for the role of color in the composition, the division of the painting into three horizontal bands is again of crucial significance. At the bottom the principal colors are violet, green, and ocher; they are strongly concentrated in relatively large masses which together form a kind of oval. The lower section of this oval consists of rising violet tones pressing into depth, rhythmically interrupted by dark greens. The upper section of the oval consists of various greens which check the movement in depth. The warm dark green at the right has a heavy downward movement; the brighter, cooler green at the left, a slightly upward movement. The two parts of the oval are linked by the ocher of the farmstead (with the red roofs), whose linear boundaries extend into depth, while the intense cold color seems to be immobilized between the two opposed movements, forward and backward.

Unlike this self-contained oval with its relatively large, strongly contrasting, very intense color masses, the color areas of the middle band are smaller. The ochers, violets, greens, and reds vary constantly, so that the band has articulation rather than form. The articulation is determined essentially by the position of the violet tones. At the left they are found midway between the lower and upper edges; at the middle, close to the lower edge; and at the right, close to the upper edge. In this way there are, above each other in the middle plane, the following colors:

Left side: ocher-green and violet-ocher. (Consequently, the relation between top and bottom is symmetrical.)

Right side: green-ocher and red-violet. (The green and violet which are together at the left side thus appear separately, concentrated at the upper and lower edges.)

Center: violet-green-ocher. (This marks a transition, since symmetry is abandoned, and the central group at the left [green and violet] is taken apart, though its components have not yet been moved to the edges.) The center of the middle plane has an accent in so far as the violet is situated at the beginning of the development, thus seeming to resume the development of the lower plane (violet-ocher-green). The difference between the planes, then, consists not only in the reversal of the order ocher-green into green-ocher, but above all in the fact that the strongly concentrated ocher of the lower plane, massed and directed diagonally into depth, is broken up into small differentiated parts and scattered over the entire breadth, with equally scattered, differentiated greens punctuating it.

In the top layer (third plane) there are two large masses, finite mountain and limitless sky, the former towering against the latter. Each is divided into a darker and lighter part. Here blue predominates, accented partly with green and brown tones and partly with reddish-violet ones. These colors flow into one another, in contrast to the lowest plane, where colors and forms are delimited and fixed, though only in an external sense, so that the vehemence of the contrasts threatens total disintegration. As a whole, the development of the top plane tends to resolve the dissonances as the ocher—the contrasting color—is eliminated and the blue, a component of violet that so far has not appeared in isolation, becomes predominant. Furthermore, the contrasts that were external are being reconciled in fluid transitions which serve to perform two opposite spatial functions —to differentiate the planes in the direction of depth by a gradual weakening of color intensities, and to close their succession so as to cause the most distant ones to press forward again.

Cézanne chose his palette to fit his conception of the picture, once he had devised a color motif. Then he tried to discover all the possibilities for variation and combination immanent in the fundamental harmony of this motif and to construct these logically. To this extent the colors possess both internal unity and external continuity. But the dominant color rhythm is also determined by the dramatic character of the oppositions, as can be seen from analysis of one detail. The ocher of the farmstead in the lowest plane, which is dissonant with the dark violet at the lower edge, is checked by green on both sides and at the top. It is checked most energetically at the center (for the dark green is followed by a dark vertical violet, a somewhat lighter green, and a very subdued ocher); on both sides, however, the ocher pushes through the green boundary. At the left the light and dark greens are followed by an obliquely rising strip of ocher which grows darker and warmer, thus weakening the initial thrust. At the right the breakthrough gains momentum, since the limiting green is followed by an ocher-red and then by a repeated alternation of green and ocher which finally ends with a green at the broadest spot.

Our analysis of light and color in the composition (both closely linked to the composition of space and, though artificially separated, actually aspects of one and the same material—the plastic color equivalent) has not been undertaken for its own sake, but with a view to illustrating Cézanne's creative method and actual way of working. Usually, neither layman nor philosopher tries to discover a method in sensory perceptions or emotions; method is taken to be purely a product of thought which the mind, conceived of as an a priori entity, imposes on inner and outer nature. Cézanne would never have agreed with such a definition. He was convinced that his method was neither invented nor revealed, but that it is contained in nature or in the sensory impressions nature releases and hence was merely to be discovered and developed. Like others of his generation he believed in induction as firmly as previous epochs had believed in deduction. But he differed from his contemporaries in that his inductive method aimed at synthesis as well as analysis. He realized that pure analysis must remain superficial and arbitrary, and that it must be complemented—if it is to acquire a character of necessity—by synthesis. But synthesis does not simply follow from induction; even in science induction serves merely to provide data for theory, and theory in turn leans on hypotheses that the understanding evolves following a method different from induction.

Cézanne at a very early date realized the existence of a leap from analytical induction to synthesizing theory. He discovered—and it was a painful discovery to him—that a predetermined element in the self stands in the way of objectivity or the realization of a work of art as an objective reality. He sought to bridge this gap between the raw data and the desired solution in and through work, with the help of the pictorial idea. The term "idea" is here to be taken in the Platonic sense, as an entity with a reality of its own, situated apart from concrete things and also from the thinking mind in such a way that the things "participate" in it and that the mind can "recollect" this participation. Anyone who endows the "idea" with a content specified once and for all—such as the idea of classical composition—fails to understand it in its true relation to created form. Actually, every subject has its own pictorial form and every pictorial form is only a potentiality— though a highly active potentiality—which is to be discovered and realized by the imagination. Had Cézanne merely grafted historical compositional form on modern (impressionist) modes of seeing, he would have been a mere eclectic, an academician. But his saying "refaire Poussin sur la nature" ("to do Poussin over from nature")[52] means the exact opposite: to refashion the classical in a completely new way and at the same time to give nature classical solidity. He did not want to imitate Poussin, but invoked that

52. Gasquet, p. 192.

great name to indicate the bent of his labors: to build the sensory perceptions into the picture with perfect logic, to realize the pictorial idea in terms of sensory perceptions of nature.

Thus Cézanne's method has two unlike components—one empirical-experimental, and the other theoretical-ideational. And just as analysis cannot arrive at a synthesis of "sensations" by induction alone, so theory cannot arrive at nature and reality by deduction alone. Rather, both tasks must be pursued simultaneously, each recognized as dependent upon and in constant interaction with the other. Every empirical nuance must refer back to "theory"—i.e., to the pictorial idea—and every function of the pictorial idea must bear upon the analysis of nature. The pictorial idea separates usable from unusable elements of natural appearances and, conversely, study of natural appearances chooses from among all possible manifestations of the pictorial idea the one that is most adequate. The difficulty of the method comes down to "proving what one believes"—"proof" here consisting in this, that the opposed methodological starting points (experience and theory) are unified, brought together in a reality of a special kind, different from either, and that this reality owes its pictorial life to a motif adequate to the conception and developed compositionally. The solution of the problem is determined by the type of conflict that constitutes the motif.

For this reason we shall give only passing mention to Cézanne's occasional failures. Sometimes he is one-sidedly objective, as when he fails to develop the natural subject in terms of an adequate motif, and sometimes one-sidedly subjective, as at times his constructive intellect, at other times his dynamism of feeling prevails. As soon as synthetic unity is replaced by a state of tension that only tends toward unity, the artist's spontaneity is restricted, his will to free creation made finite and material, because the conflict is willed and forced rather than self-positing. There is just such a limitation in the painting under study, with respect both to total configuration and to method, particularly if the latter is compared with the dialectical method. To be sure, the painting depicts a central conflict; but this conflict is resolved by the artist's individual fiat, not independently of him through the concretion of internal oppositions. The oppositions lack a fundamental unity out of which they might grow and become a totality. For this reason the dynamism that pervades the oppositions leads not so much to synthesis as to crystallization around a central point, Or, to express this inevitable process from the subjective point of view: the total configuration suggests an architectural structure which, unlike that in some earlier works, is built not by means of a scaffolding but through a process of accretion, one stone set upon another—produced by an act of will, which imperils the constitutive element and emphasizes construction; the result has a systematic character, but it is an inorganic rather than a spiritual system, which does not succeed in giving the segment of nature a universal status while the plastic color-equivalent is logically developed into pictorial totality. It is as though too strong a concretion of the universal working process of nature had been "organized" intellectually: this deprives the painting of that spontaneous quality which would make it possible for the viewer to return to it time and again with a fresh eye and which is the essence of organic artistic form. The work exemplifies "art for art's sake" in the sense that everything Cézanne has succeeded in expressing about nature and his own inner life remains at the level of representational means. This criticism is not to be interpreted as a demand that Cézanne should have transcended the sphere of art; it merely states that he could not go beyond certain limits within his art.

It would be erroneous, however, to look upon Cézanne, because of these limitations, as an artist who was prevented from realizing his talent by some pathological inner conflict. It was not Cézanne who was sick but the society of his period, torn by the absolute contradiction between material power and spirit under the impact of industrial capitalism. Cézanne heroically resisted this unfavorable effect of industrial capitalism on art and carried art as complete as was possible through an epoch which was bound to destroy art and then itself—a development which affected him all the more, sometimes depressing and sometimes exalting him, because he did not understand it, though he felt its consequences and hated them. It is evidence of Cézanne's essential sanity that his work does not disclose the slightest *ressentiment*, either as contempt for people (Degas) or as arrogance of genius (Van Gogh, Nietzsche); rather, his work endeavors, with the greatest naturalness, to be nothing but an absolutely faithful hymn of praise to the glory of God's creation.

As a result, Cézanne's work, in addition to its artistic value, possesses a moral significance, an exemplary value for the life of creative men. The generation that followed him felt this at once, and Gasquet gave expression to this fact by contrasting the truth of Cézanne's painting with the untruthfulness of the age of "Napoleon the Little," in opposition to which the artist's view of the world had been formed. "Throughout the frenzied years of the Second Empire, France was consumed by a delusive ardor. It laughed at Flaubert, Courbet, Renan. It condemned Baudelaire. It knew nothing about Taine or Claude Bernard. Its licentious taste, its frivolity, greeted with hatred all those whose vision was clear, straightforward, solid, profound. This way leads only downward. While Wagner was being hissed, the Bearded Lady was being applauded. While Manet was being looked upon as a madman, Thérésa or Émile Ollivier were the fads in vogue. There was a general breakdown in values: artificiality, falsehood, degradation."[53] What was behind the banality and the dubiousness was the degradation and dehumanization of labor; in order to survive, Cézanne was driven to look upon work as the highest value. "Could art be a kind of priesthood, in effect, requiring pure men capable of giving them-

53. Ibid., p. 63. [Thérésa (pseud. of Emma Valadon) was the most popular humorous singer of the day.   As head of the Government, Ollivier led France into the Franco-Prussian War.]

selves wholly to it?"[54] Thus a social theme was introduced into the artist's dialogue with nature, and even though it was not dominant in his consciousness—smuggled in, as it were, through the back door—it was of crucial importance in determining the essence of his art. In the creative act itself Cézanne was to feel the alienating dual character of labor in modern times. While he drove himself to infinitely painstaking efforts, at sitting after sitting, and more than once despaired of ever attaining his goal, believing his hand inadequate to realize his vision and his eye inadequate to analyze nature, he wanted to believe that "an artist . . . should create his work as an almond tree produces its blossoms, as a snail produces its slime."[55] But the very possibility of such a harmony between nature's and man's creativity had disappeared forever when capitalism destroyed the artisan, industrialized agriculture, and alienated man from himself. Cézanne had to make of work a morality, a metaphysics, a religion, because it had lost its auxiliary function in man's self-fulfillment. "Happiness lies in work"[56] is the postulate of an epoch which proves the contrary every day; but Cézanne made this postulate come true day after day in spite of his epoch. "To be a good worker, to practice one's trade well, was for him the *sine qua non*, the foundation of everything. To him, to paint well was to live the good life. He put himself entirely into every one of his brush strokes. You had to see it to believe what painful tension possessed him when he worked, his expression a silent prayer, to realize how much of his spirit went into his labors. He would tremble all over. He was not sure of his next step, his forehead would get hot and would seem to bulge with the effort of thought, his neck would be retracted between his shoulder blades, and his hands would shake; then suddenly the moment would come when his hands would stop shaking and with as much deliberation as delicacy he would lift the brush and apply it with great sureness, and always from right to left. Then he would draw back a bit to judge of what he had done, once again turn his eyes from the picture to whatever it was he was painting; slowly he would go over every facet of the objects, making combinations among them, looking inside them, seizing hold of them. When his eyes stared at some fixed point he was terrible to see. 'I can't tear my eyes away,' he told me one day. 'They are so glued to one place that it seems to me they are going to bleed.' Whole minutes would go by like this, sometimes as long as a quarter of an hour. It would be almost as though he were asleep. What he was doing was digging down to the ultimate roots of reason and the world, at some level where the human will encounters the will of things and is either regenerated by them or submerged by them. Shaking all over he would wrench himself free and turn back to his canvas, to its life, where he would now record in a single tone the mysterious emotion, the ecstasy, the secret he had stumbled upon. . . . No wonder that Renoir said

54. Letter to Ambroise Vollard, January 9, 1903, in *Correspondance*, ed. Rewald, p. 252.
55. Gasquet, p. 98.

56. Ibid., p. 45. [Cézanne chalked this motto on the wall of his studio.]

of him: 'How does he do it? He can't make two brush strokes on a canvas without producing something good.' "[57]

But to Cézanne it was never really good—not for him the satisfaction of Jehovah at the sight of His creation. Even finished, the picture was to him no more than a promise to himself and to the future. "The day will come when one carrot painted with originality will be pregnant with revolution."[58] Yes, the revolution occurred in the paintbox and on canvas, but it was of interest to none save a few recently wealthy snobs, who looked upon the most revolutionary art as the only commodity of permanent value. Cézanne hated the newly arrived bourgeois; his passionate affection went to the common people, the worker, the peasant, the day laborer. The people, however, did not understand him. That was the price he paid for his political neutrality while realizing his theory in the face of nature—a price that had to be paid if he was to remain an artist. For his age was up in arms against art and artists. Cézanne was well aware of it, too. "I paint my still lifes, these *natures mortes*, for my coachman who does not want them, I paint them so that children on the knees of their grandfathers may look at them while they eat their soup and chatter. I do not paint them for the pride of the Emperor of Germany or the vanity of the oil merchants of Chicago. I may get ten thousand francs for one of these dirty things, but I'd rather have the wall of a church, a hospital, or a municipal building."[59] Neither his curses nor his desires were realized, and the painter was thrown back on one last maxim: "One must be a good worker. . . . The ideal of earthly happiness—to have a beautiful formula."[60]

57. Gasquet, pp. 100*f.*   58. Ibid., p. 46.   59. Ibid., pp. 206*f.*   60. Ibid., p. 177.

II. THE WORK OF THE ARTISTIC IMAGINATION

Degas: *Leaving the Bath*

(PLATE IX)

You work? I bloom.

ELSE LASKER-SCHÜLER

A picture is something that requires as much cunning, trickery, and deceit as the perpetration of a crime.

DEGAS

My paintings are the result of a series of calculations and an unlimited number of studies.

DEGAS

Only when he no longer knows what he is doing does the painter produce valuable work.

DEGAS

State 1

State 5

State 14

IX DEGAS. *Leaving the Bath* (states 1, 5, 14). ca. 1882. Etching, 5×5 in.

According to Delteil,[1] this work came into being under the following circumstances. One day Degas dined at the home of his friend Alexis Rouart. Because the streets were slippery, he stayed the night. On awakening in the morning he asked for a copper plate. "I'd like to make an etching," he said. He traced the first state of *Leaving the Bath* on the plate and said: "This is how our friend, Madame X, must look when she gets out of her bath."

A layman might suppose that this lady is the principal subject of the etching, but to his surprise he will discover that this is not so. During the night Degas had undressed the lady in imagination: she is shown in surroundings he had often painted before—a bathroom. But the lady and the setting are only a pretext: the kind of body portrayed, in a gesture revealing her state of mind, is completely subordinated to a play of light and shadow, to a spatial organization on the flat copper plate, and to a specific composition. The female body is only sketchily outlined in this first state and plays no more important role than the other objects represented—the bathtub, the chair, the vases, the rug, the peignoir, etc. The artistic means of representation determine the natural impression; the whole determines its parts, including the starting point of inspiration. Accordingly, in studying this work we shall begin not with the subject but with the working material.

The use of light and shadow stresses extreme contrasts. They set each other off: broad masses of unbroken light areas (the water in the tub, the female body, the door, and the bath towel) form an almost unified luminous surface which is contrasted with the dark areas—the floor, the chair, and the wall. Only here and there do we find small patches where dark areas are set against lighter ones (for instance, the woman's hair against the door, the back of the chair against the floor), dark areas against dark areas (part of the hair against the wall, the fringes of the chair against the rug), and—in larger planes—light areas against light areas (the vases at the right edge, the female body against the door, and the bath towel).

These distinctions of light and shadow are highly significant in determining the expressive values of a drawing. To understand this fundamental fact, take a blank sheet of

---

1. Loys Delteil, *Le Peintre-graveur illustré* (Paris, 1919), IX, no. 39.

white paper, outline any figure on it, and make everything else black; then draw the same figure on another sheet of paper, making it black and everything else white. In the former case the otherwise unbounded white has been enclosed by the black and the whole of its radiating force operates only in the depth dimension. In the latter case the black is bounded and asserts itself against the radiant white all around it. In both cases white and black are sharply set off against each other, whereas light against light and dark against dark tend to be resolved and to merge. We rarely see these simple properties in their purity; for differences between warm and cold and in the position of hatchings at once complicate matters.

We have seen that the first state of Degas' etching is characterized by a very light white and a very dark black. Besides this external contrast there are internal contrasts: each of the extremes, taken in itself, is devoid of porosity and vibration—there is no slightest suggestion of shadows in the light areas nor light in the dark areas. The two are set against, beside, or behind each other, but the relationships between them are all external; the few middle tones that might serve as links or transitions are not developed one from the other or from the extremes of black and white, but are merely juxtaposed. They all start below at the tub, leading in two different directions: upward, over the female body to the wall, and to the right, over the back of the armchair, across the strip of the floor, to the vases.

The polarity of the oppositions and the external character of the links between them are emphasized by the coldness of both lights and shadows; the few intermediate tones are for the most part cold light muffled by cold shadows (the wall behind the bath towel; the back of the armchair in the foreground) rather than intermediate tones in a warm-cold scale. Thus the contrasting elements enhance each other to the point of fanatical sobriety, sharpness, and bite, which unmask not only Madame X but even more so Monsieur Degas.

It is the shadows that have been created. Throughout we feel the sharp scratch of the etching needle that formed them; only rarely (on the towel) do softer passages occur. Many strokes begin at independent points and fade out in isolation, but between the ends the hatching melts into dark masses where only tiny chinks of light reveal the original separation. This induces a shifting tension between single and massed lines which here and there leads to painterly overlapping of various hatchings or, occasionally, to an ornamental play of isolated lines (for example, in the fringes on the chair).

Besides the lines that make up dark areas there are lines that indicate the shape of objects—the back of the armchair, for instance. But these contour lines have no internal relation to the areas of dark or light they define; they are added. The forms thus defined and delimited seem to be there only for the sake of contrast with forms less clearly defined, which merge with their surroundings. Furthermore, there are space-articulating lines, like the horizon line of the room; but for the most part the limits of the space remain indistinct, though the space is clearly hollowed out within these limits.

However different may be the tasks to be performed by a single line or by a mass of lines, they have in common a certain energy and lack of ambiguity. Take the foreground, for example, viewing it from left to right. At the corner there is a small light area followed by a mass of lines drawn obliquely upward. These are delimited as a triangle by two lines which, although they are attached to different objects and start at different edges of the plate, yet converge into depth. The three slanting lines of this triangle are the exposition of the whole, as we shall demonstrate. Next to this triangular figure in the corner is a rectangular one (the back of the armchair) which is tilted upward toward the viewer (i.e., in a direction opposite to that of the triangle) and filled with thickly crowded horizontal lines. Its horizontal extension is interrupted by a mass of deeply slanting lines at the right of the armchair; it forms a dark area between two others, but different from either in direction and structure. It constitutes a boundary, formless in itself, between the object it helps to define and another one to which it does not belong. The characteristic *ductus*, the temperament that guides the artist's hand, related as it must be to the artistic function, is particularly evident here, where the artist has hesitated between straight and curving line.

Next in order—we are still at the bottom of the picture—we see a rounded light area and then a dark mass of lines (the rug) in which level and slanted hatchings interpenetrate for the first time. As a result both are relieved of their one-sided function, and instead of directional tension and movement they produce a local vibration indicating the texture of the rug. This crosshatched area ends at an area of cold light which contrasts with the warm darkness. It extends to the right edge of the picture and some vertical, slightly curved lines fall down into it.

We have now examined the narrow strip along the bottom of the entire picture and found that line is used to perform very different tasks—hollowing out space, composition, characterization of material qualities, constitutive formation of the means of representation, etc.—and that it varies in structure and ductus as well. It is now uncertain, now violent; now limited to function, and now determined by the artist's will, energy, and temperament. We have also noted a characteristic tension between the single line and the mass. What we have here is a richly varied, vigorously emphatic *handwriting*.

When we examine the relationship between the two components of the means of representation so far analyzed—light and line—we find that light and dark are the end and line the means; and that the means have not yet proved adequate to the end. The broader areas of light are not internally organized; there is no logical connection between the boundaries and the areas they delimit. Moreover, individual lines are often treated as ends in themselves rather than as means, for they do not merge into light and darkness.

At first glance we note a dualism which is not resolved in any higher unity. This is in keeping with the absence of intermediate tones between strongly contrasting light and dark areas and with the disparate, frequently unrelated functions of the lines.

Just as the subject yields precedence to the means of representation, so it yields precedence to the pictorial space into which the basically flat copper plate is being transformed. The means for constituting pictorial space are not the representational boundaries of the bathroom—such as the demarcation between floor and wall by the horizon line, which is placed quite high, or the dimly indicated corner of the room. Essentially the means consist in strongly stressed diagonal planes extending across the bathroom. The artist proceeds from both lower corners of the picture simultaneously, but the slanting planes which extend into depth are different in character: the shrill white of the water in the tub at the left is deeper, higher, and wider than the flower shelf at the right. The difference between these accents is balanced by the fact that the other slanting planes receding in depth (rug and armchair) run parallel to the less accentuated slant of the flower shelf but are kept closer to the floor; and their movement is arrested more promptly, the rug by the vertical and horizontal planes of the fringed chair, the back of the armchair by the horizontal light band at its top. The planes of resistance that break off the movement into depth are so shaped and placed that they lead the eye forward from the far end of the flower shelf, linking the end of the one marginal slant to the beginning of the other. Thus the movement into depth has its greatest extension and its fastest pace along these two slants near the edges. Between them, length and impetus decrease, and the entire movement into depth is led back to one of its starting points (the ideal point of intersection being sought elsewhere). This indicates that the movements of the diagonals are held between parallel planes, of which the front one is not tied to any object, while the back one is embodied in a solid object.

The mode and magnitude of the checking movements have a definite purpose: they justify the visual transition from the movement (running parallel to the floor) leading directly into depth to the movement leading there indirectly (i.e., dependent on verticals). We see this transition in the two legs (light areas), one of which is in, the other out of the bathtub; the area formed by the angle between them is divided into a light portion which stands upright and a dark portion which recedes. The woman's back, though still unclear as to volume and contour, clearly discloses its twofold function in the figuration of space: it arrests the rising movement of the legs and continues the slanting movement of the bathtub into depth simultaneously in both the original slanting directions. The bath towel forms a still steeper slanted plane independent of the nude figure, and thereby nearly eliminates the differences of left and right which lie on the horizontal. Where the female body and the towel meet, the widely divergent contrasts

X   DEGAS. *Place de la Concorde, Paris (Viscount Lepic and His Daughters)*. ca. 1873. 31¾ × 47⅜ in.

of movements in space and of space-dimensions are gathered in one point, a kind of point of reversal (peripeteia) in the figuration of depth.

Before carrying our analysis beyond this point of reversal, we must observe that more than linear directions are involved. Depth is also created by the contrasts between light and dark. Whereas the cold white (e.g., behind the head) and the cool dark areas lead the eye, in various ways, into depth, the warmer lights and shadows press forward (e.g., the warmer dark areas of the wall). Occasionally the spatial functions of light thus expressed contradict those expressed by line; for instance, the relatively warm dark area of the rug presses forward in contradiction to its diagonal outline.

The movement into depth, which starts at the two lower corners, is centripetal, although the outermost slants never intersect at any point of the picture surface. The left edge of the bathtub (in so far as it can be made out) would, were it extended, pass through the upper left corner of the towel, and the line of the flower shelf, similarly extended, would pass through the upper right corner. Consequently, the span between the two corners—stressed by a sag in the towel and the upper portion of a female head behind it—is the measure of the distance maintained between the converging centripetal trends, this time expressed in terms of the width of the picture. This distance is definitive in as much as the meeting point of the slanted lines, if extended beyond the corners of the towel, lies outside the picture. Within the picture it is not even ideally effective. In terms of classical perspective, this means that the vanishing lines of the floor have no common vanishing point: first, because the picture is not built around a middle axis, and second, because the depth dimension is succeeded by the dimension of height. A perspective is strongly suggested but is broken off; instead of a vanishing point we have a meeting point lying on the vertical plane of the white bath towel, where the movement into depth is reversed (peripeteia). It is situated at the place where one of the woman's buttocks touches the towel. This point divides the width in the proportion of 4 : 5 and the height in the proportion of 3 : 5. It is not accentuated in any way; the shadow in which it lies serves only to set off the white body against the white towel.

From this point of reversal the figuration of depth discloses a striking contrast. One slanting movement, starting from the right foreground, is continued over the woman's back across the white door, curving from depth to width. The opposite, initially stronger slanting movement (which starts from the left foreground) stops at the towel; behind it is only a dark wall approximately parallel to the picture surface. The bath towel, together with the back of the fringed chair, separates the pictorial space into two qualitatively different areas: one is crowded, wide in front and narrow in back (centripetal); the other is empty, narrow in front and wide in back (centrifugal). In consequence, we may look upon the bath towel as indicating the diagonal axis of the picture space.

The third factor, stressed more strongly than the representational and the emotional elements, is composition. To begin with, there is the disposition of the areas of light and dark. In the lower part of the picture we have a wedgelike dark area (the rug) in the middle, flanked by two differentiated light areas; in the upper part we have, on the contrary, a light area (the door) flanked by two dark areas of different widths; thus we have light-dark-light below, and dark-light-dark above. In the lower part the dark area is drawn into itself, while the light areas open outward; both the light and the dark areas are defined as triangular, rectangular, or curved, thus becoming a series of definite shapes. In the upper part the dark areas at the sides frame a strongly outlined rectangular light area but are themselves unstructured. Thus the relations between light and dark areas are reversed as between floor and wall. Between the two lies the central motif, the light against light of woman and towel. Only this part is fully structured in triangles and rectangles; the rectangle of the woman's back looms above the vertical triangle of the legs, while the upright rectangle of the towel ends in two triangular points (thus the upper edge of the towel forms three different angles). In this respect, too, the composition stresses woman and towel as central motif, although they occupy only a small part of the picture surface.

Now, this central motif is not situated at the center of the picture: to have stressed the axis would have weakened the reversal of contrasts, and such an effect had to be avoided. While the arrangement of the lower part of the picture is symmetrical, that of the upper part is strongly asymmetrical; the woman's movement mediates this contrast and at the same time underlines its violence. The picture itself has the form of a square, a static form. But Degas makes no use of the structurally accentuated lines of the square: he avoids the middle axes as well as most of the possible divisions by the golden section. The horizon line is broken off abruptly and is to be interpreted as a paradoxical play upon the basic structural exigencies of visual perception. Nor does Degas fix the subjectively distinguished points of perception: the line of vision is absent, and the meeting line[2] is reduced to a single point. Within the square, itself a restful form, the viewer's eye finds no point of repose anywhere. This renunciation of compositional potentialities is of course based on the nature of the motif itself, which is developed in the clash between two diagonal planes—the vertical one of the bath towel and the level one of the water surface and the woman's back. Since these are variants of the diagonals of the picture square, this stresses once more that the point of reversal has been shifted from the point where the plane diagonals meet to a point above it and slightly to the right. This in turn stresses the contradiction between the lower and upper pairs of slants: in the lower, larger part the slants converge as energetically as they diverge in the upper, smaller part. The motif does not respect the format but shatters it.

2. [For "line of vision" (*Blicklinie*) and "meeting line" (*Trefflinie*), see Pl. XXV and the Appendix, p. 222.]

Composition involves more than distributing masses and centering them on a single motif; it also involves development of the motif, the unfolding of its contradictions in the various dimensions of space. Let us begin with the dimension of width. One arm of the woman reaches out so far to the left that the accent is almost transferred to the left edge of the picture. This effect has been prepared on the opposite side, first through the receding slant of the flower shelf, then by the curved back of the fringed chair, which has been slightly turned from the parallel plane for this purpose, and, finally, by the more open variant of this same curve realized in the lines of the woman's back, shoulder, and arm. At this terminal point of the horizontal development the opposition of width and depth are side by side; their later connection occurs neither on the horizontal nor within the picture. If the woman were moving in this compositional direction, i.e., to the left, she would be entering the bathtub; but as she is shown, she is leaving it—i.e., moving to the right and toward the viewer. Although the relationship between the two horizontal directions is not yet clarified here, it is evident that the one-way movement from right to left has been abolished and that the accent at the left edge is matched by a stronger accent at the right edge. The development in width is distorted by centrifugal forces which push the accents to the edges. (This can be seen most clearly in Degas' portrait of Viscount Lepic and his daughters, Plate X.)

The dimension of height is also broken up into its opposite directions: the ascending movement leads into depth, the descending one up from depth; they meet where the woman's thighs come together. Each movement has several components, refracted into angles; hence all suggestion either of upsurge or of support and weight is eliminated. The two movements meet and clash in the woman's body, but it is not possible to see how it receives them and asserts itself against them. Whereas in the horizontal dimension we found two accents at the far edges, in the dimension of height there is only *one* accent and it is near the middle: the woman's sexual parts, suggested from behind. This point lies so close to the one we have designated as the point of reversal (where buttock and bath towel meet) that the distance and the competition between the two become measurable, as though Degas had wanted to emphasize the independence of the vertical development from the horizontal development, as well as a certain gap between them.

The development of the depth dimensions begins loosely, immaterially, without objects, i.e., in abstract planes which recede from the viewer. But the more the eye is drawn into depth, the more stubborn the resistance becomes, until the eye is definitively blocked by the wall. Degas opens a perspective view from front to back, and the movement of the bath towel forward serves only to enhance the movement into depth. But contrary to the customary system of perspective, which opens a view into the distance, Degas confines the viewer, so to speak; indeed, the development into depth does not lead farther back than the point of reversal: rather it spills sideways. Instead of the view into infinity we have been led to expect, paradoxically we find finitude made as it were absolute.

To sum up the compositional development in the three dimensions: we are in a world that is seemingly open but actually closed, without exit, in which every movement has been turned away from its original goal. Despite their qualitative contradictions, the movements are gathered up either at one point or in the space between two adjacent points—the sexual parts suggested from the rear, and the edge of the right buttock. The implication is that of a cynical, pessimistic devaluation of love, a view that is in sharp contrast to the central and metaphysical role of love in the nineteenth century. Moreover, this work reveals a pessimistic attitude toward an artistic shaping of the world. For the forces set in motion are co-ordinated in such a way that any dramatic conflict, any internal resolution of their contradictions, is avoided. From the formal point of view the masses are thrown off balance by diagonal forces and rebalanced at that point at which they destroy themselves. This new balance is not informed by any universal, let alone absolute, principle; for the middle axis system is so completely eliminated that it is not even possible to measure the extent of deviation from it. Nor does this balance result from any internal development of self-positing conflict. It is an order imposed on self-destructive contradictions, revealing the artist at the calm center of the conflict of forces of which he experiences no more than their relativity, purposelessness, and nullity.

Only now—after the means of representation, the development of the plane into depth, and the composition—can concrete factors become significant: space, bodies, surface textures, and emotional expression.

In studying the picture space we are struck by the fact that it has neither a unified shape nor a unified atmosphere; it is broken up into individual objects and compositional lines or, more accurately, it has not yet gone beyond them to become a coherent entity. All we have is its dimensions, not its inner structure; individual things rather than an atmosphere. Nor are most of the objects made more concrete than an indication of their function. A few suggestions of texture are discernible: the porcelain of the vase, the plush of the chair, the linen of the towel; but such suggestions are completely absent on the left side of the etching. As for expression, the bearish clumsiness of the woman's broad and heavy body is unmistakable, although we cannot discern the exact position of her foot, what she is doing with her arms, the proportions of the torso, the breadth of her hips, or the relations of firmness and slackness of the flesh. In some areas, the psychological aspects are even less clear than the representational ones. The space as a whole lacks unified texture. Cool analytic understanding and a fanatically concentrated will are far more prominent than sensibility, let alone emotion. The woman represented is an animal pure and simple; her movement has an instantaneous, instinctual, and subconscious character which contrasts with the deliberateness of the artist's creative will.

Why did Degas take the subject that inspired him, and the situation which he chose as suited to its presentation, and subordinate them to the means of representation, the figuration of space, and composition? First of all, for objective reasons—because these are the elements and the grammar of the artist's language: to create a work of art is to translate inspiration and situation into this language or, more accurately, to reshape them in it. Second, for subjective reasons: Degas' analytical comprehension of art and his will to artistic integration were stronger than his capacity for sensuous enjoyment and intuitive sympathy. Or—what is more likely—the reality that presented itself to his senses and emotions placed a negative accent on his sensibility and emotion. For this reason—for the very reason perhaps that he was oversensitive—his senses and feelings withdrew and his conscious intellect was free to organize a composition based on diagonals, using a dimensional frame of reference, by means of which bodies and space are set down without being given form. Degas looked upon the sensory world as unformed; to be able to give it form the artist must not enter it, must not become intimate with it but, on the contrary, keep aloof, deny it in a spirit of asceticism. In this way he can impose on it a schematic first principle such as is expressed here in the intersecting diagonal planes, which at first contract the "spurious" infinity[3] and then release it, transformed. Intelligence and will can play with things which the artist's senses and feelings, more directly and more violently affected, must reject. In so far as the impressionists' point of departure was the sensory atmosphere, Degas was their diametrical opposite. They began with sensations which were a lyrical fusion of visual impressions and emotional reactions; Degas begins with the assertion of intelligence (burdened with repressed emotions) and (like Leonardo da Vinci) attempts to arrive at sensibility. From this it is to be inferred—and this is of crucial importance—that the first state of the etching does not render the first working stage of the artist's imagination. Rather, we must assume that it was preceded by a long process which led from the original multiplicity of sensations to the schematic construction of movement and space. We can analyze this process only in reverse order, for from the first to the last state of the etching Degas, as it were, pursues the earliest impact, hoping to recapture its original unconscious plenitude through conscious effort. The first state does not render the shock of the first impression, but rather an abstraction of the first impression, a provisional negation of it which nevertheless makes the positive representation possible.

If we now compare the fifth state of the etching with the first, the changes to be noted seem both minor and major. Minor, because the format of course remains the same square, the essential objects are in the same positions in space, and only two new objects have been added: a picture on the wall and flowers in the vases. Major because both ob-

---

3. See above, p. 25, n. 32.

jects and space—and particularly the woman's body—have acquired structure; moreover, changes have occurred in the constitution of the form and in its compositional development. Many a viewer will be pleased to see, at last, a bathtub, a woman, and a towel, instead of a single white surface. But it is not because of this increased clarity of subject matter that we shall begin our analysis of the fifth state with problems of realistic portrayal. We do so only to learn whether and to what extent the changes have depended upon modifications of means of representation and of composition.

The white surface, which in the first state suggested a woman's body by a sketchy leg, a black blot suggesting hair, and an indefinable something else, is now unmistakably a woman's body. Its volume is defined by a heavy line, revealing its anatomical structure and position. The outline has an incisive quality at certain places, a cold definiteness, an intensity, and these almost brutally create a boundary that is threatened with bursting from within. Here and there it is less intense, weaker, looser; the cool glaring sharpness becomes duller and softer. At still other places the outline has been crossed out, as it were, or consists of tiny oblique strokes to suggest modeling (where the thigh meets the bathtub). Elsewhere the brightness is set off against the surrounding darkness without an outline (as in the right foot). All these variations change nothing in the over-all function of the line, which serves to create so narrow a boundary that the flesh seems pent up within it, ready to burst out but for the almost poreless density of the skin, its leathery firmness. It also serves to articulate the joints: the ankle and the straightened knee of the right leg, the left hip and, by other means, the spine, which is the axis of the movement of the upper body. The flesh is inseparable from the skeleton beneath it and possesses fullness without being slack.

Just as clearly delineated is the body's stance: the weight is supported by one heel only; the strain on the knee is evident, the torso turns slightly to the right, as casually as an animal turning in the sun. It is not only the back we see, but now also a bit of the stomach and one breast; the shoulder blade is drawn to the left by the outstretched arm, though only the elbow touches the bathtub; and, finally, the hand in shadow grips the edge of the tub, though the support so given is inadequate. The position is transitional —the woman is half standing on the floor and half standing in the water. It is a momentary gesture, a movement which is and already is no more, recorded in the moment split between these poles, arresting the infinitesimal nuance between them. The body performing the gesture is squat and broad, unresilient, clumsy, without trained grace, but with the naturalness of an animal—a combination so paradoxical that it would be caricature save for the artist's aloof penetration and cool fanaticism, expressing objective irony as much as personal enjoyment.

The sharply outlined body is at every point set off from its surroundings—from the bath towel by the shadow, from the bathtub and the water by the modeling of the left leg. The contours of breast and arm are traced with deliberate care to avoid collision with the edges of the bathtub. This detachment of the body at the same time clarifies the connection between the various spatial positions and layers. This can be seen most distinctly in the woman's back at the borderline between the darker and lighter areas, which does not quite coincide with the line of the spinal column; the lighter areas seem to curve forward more unmistakably than the dark areas recede along an inclined plane. Thus, the decisive thing is not the articulation of the body but the creation of spatial tensions. That is why the back is broken up into two areas, one of which is merged with the side and front of the body. Similarly, the left arm prolongs the shoulder line to create a movement counter to the rightward twist of the body, while the right pelvis is brought directly into the leg, setting off the body on that side from the towel.

Much the same could be said about all the objects. The bathtub has acquired a sharp outline: in front by the white rim, at the back through sharp contrast between the dark wall and the slanted middle tones of the bathtub, and, finally, at the curving end by a black contour line; only the shadows of the towel and the rug blur the sharpness of the form, where they run together at the dark side of the tub. The inside of the tub is clearly distinguished from the outside; differences of both texture and color seem observable. Inside the tub the same is true of water and wall.

The tendency dominant now is to define and articulate forms. We see this especially in the picture frame, which has been added in this stage of the etching. Actual line drawing reserved for the door is not employed in it, but differentiations between light and dark distinguish rounds from hollows, and the smooth stretches from the ornamental corners. The dark wall has acquired a definite material character. The volume, shape, and texture of the vase have been strengthened; the white of the porcelain vase is no longer the same as the enamel of the bathtub, the linen of the towel, or the flesh—the differentiations are incomparably stronger than in the first version. In the fringed chair, the plush has a texture different from the fringes; at the same time, it is brought into relation with the textures of the rug in front of it, the wall behind it, and the cloth on the flower shelf.

Thus the new treatment of the objects aims at self-contained volumes and richer surface textures. Volumes are particularly well defined on the left, textures on the right. The largest volumes have unsensual, hard textures, as though intended not to reproduce the life of the objects but to hinder it or to arouse analogies with other objects; conversely, where the textures are most developed, volumes are slightest. The same effect is arrived at by favoring cold light and dark areas on the left and warm half tones and dark areas on the right; their division more or less coincides with the vertical middle axis of the print, otherwise not emphasized. Thus the work seems to fall into two parts: on the left, objects and their movements constitute the picture space—as they did in the first state, but here to a far greater extent. On the right, a homogeneous spatial atmosphere pre-dominates, and the objects stand within it, are surrounded by it, dissolve in it. On the back wall, in the door and in the picture, this duality is so clear that we must assume Degas struggled with two different principles of figuration—one of bodies, the other atmospheric. In this state of the work they remain entirely distinct. The former is classi-cistic and derives from Ingres; the latter is impressionist. The fact that both are merely set side by side shows how deep a discord was anchored in Degas, whether we think of it as between traditional and contemporary or between rational and sensual. This is why the things represented have no radiance: not only is the woman holding her breath, but the pores of her skin seem to have closed; all warmth has departed—her blood, as it were, has yet to circulate. At the right, to the contrary, even such materials as the plush, the porcelain, or the rug seem to breathe. And this is why, at the left, the woman's head seems to knock against the door and the tips of the bath towel against the picture frame on the wall—although we should expect considerable empty space between them in both cases. On the right, however, the much smaller distance between the flower shelf and the chair is clearly indicated.

Just as the individual objects have acquired structure and self-contained volume, so, to a certain extent, has the whole picture space. The side walls are indicated more clearly, in different foreshortenings; on the edges of the etching open and closed places lie catercorner. Floor and wall are no longer so crudely set off from each other at the horizon because the contrast between light and dark has been weakened in favor of intermediate tones. The objects in the foreground up to the fringed chair are more clearly placed upon the floor and thus accentuate its horizontal extension in contrast to the verticals of the back wall. In general, the horizontal—as a static element of spatial structure—is more strongly emphasized than the slanting lines. For one thing, the lower part of the etching has greater homogeneity and the differences between light and dark have been subdued. It is more obvious in the fringed chair, which has lost its slightly slanted position and acquired the function of an axial plane parallel to the picture surface. As such it separates a foreground filled with objects from an empty background, the middle ground having shrunk to zero. This, in conjunction with the introduction of an ideal verti-cal middle axis, constitutes, to be sure, a very minimal connection between space and plane, yet it is essentially new within the persisting diagonals leading into depth. In the first version the only planes parallel to the picture surface were in the extreme foreground and the extreme background. Now, however, these two planes have been brought into relation to a common axial plane and thereby to each other. Recessive and forward movements are no longer unrelated; the pictorial space has acquired the beginning of an inner structure now that depth has been brought into relation with plane.

Precisely because the pictorial space is more structured, the previously mentioned contrasts between warmth and cold, atmosphere and absence of atmosphere, are all the more striking: the etching has no *unified* spatial atmosphere of its own. This means that there are two spaces: in the warm part vibration and movement predominate at every point, while in the cold part each point is rigidly fixed. In the former the rate of directed movements is alien to the space traversed, but in the latter it frees the points from their fixedness, gathering them into one movement through space. Between these juxtaposed— indeed, divergent—contrasts of warm vibrance and cold rigidity the female body moves from the empty space above the bathtub toward the waiting towel. At this central point body and towel are connected like two interlocking contrary movements by means of the new broader shadow and suggest the impending act of being swathed. This contrast creates a balance between the left and the right side of the etching and weakens the diagonal effect of the bath towel. The same purpose has also been served by narrowing and muffling the cold white area between the rug and the cloth on the flower shelf, as well as by shifting the fringed chair to face squarely front, etc. In other words, the atmospheric contrast is used in order to link more firmly the inherently discordant figuration of space to the picture surface, a need which is not recognizable in the first version.

The changes in the figuration of objects and space are accompanied by changes in the means of representation. Sharp contrasts of light and dark have been eliminated. The homogeneous light area at the left, which in the first version extends above the tub to the door and the bath towel, has been greatly reduced and has lost its harsh glare. The back edge of the armchair, the water in the tub, the towel above and below the woman, the right side of the woman's back, and the doorframe are all more or less in half tone. That is, the left part of the etching shows more frequent variations—between dark and middle tones, middle tones and light, light and light, light and middle tones, middle tones and dark, dark and dark. This rhythm of brightness and darkness appears most clearly in the servant's head: the relationship of face to forehead, hair, and bonnet is that of medium dark to light, dark, and medium light, and the head as a whole stands between the white linen and the dark picture on the wall. Moreover, this passage is not so much a new formation as a development of possibilities suggested in the first sketch. The prevailing coldness of the first version is preserved on the left but the light effect has been reduced in scale, eliminating glare, and the extremes of light and dark are connected by middle tones.

On the right, Degas has made the greatest depths more numerous and warmer; for instance, the flower shelf has become an unporous dark. But at the same time he has multiplied the intermediate tones here too, whether to brighten previously dark areas (as in the fringed chair) or to subdue former light areas. The flower shelf and the rug, for example, are no longer separated by a shrill white but are connected by a dull, medium-warm intermediate tone. Now almost all the light areas are cold, all the deep shadows warm, and there are more intermediate tones oscillating between these extremes. Crude contrasts have been replaced with nuances and transitions save in a few places where warm dark areas bring out the intervening coldness. In consequence of these changes the subjective, arbitrary effect of the contrast of light and dark in the first version has been superseded by a more objective one.

Accordingly, the technical treatment of line has become depersonalized. The putting down and lifting of the hand, its pressure, the temperament of the personal handwriting, are to be discerned only in a few places, as on the back of the armchair. The isolated beginnings and endings of the strokes, and the twists in the fringe below the flower shelf have gone. The tension between individual line and mass, characteristic of the first version, has been reduced to a minimum; where it has been preserved it has lost its icy harshness because the extreme lights and darks have been subdued and brought closer to half-tone effects. Masses that cannot be broken down into elements (flower shelf) and smudges (bath water) have been added; in conjunction with closely hatched or cross-hatched areas such masses predominate in the total effect. This means a greater variety of techniques and more independent, calmer treatment. It is true that now some of the transitions seem superfluous, but the treatment has acquired inner structure and objectivity even though it cannot always completely merge in the objects.

The newly introduced half tones do not affect the dualism between light and line which prevailed in the first version. It is true that outlines have been eliminated at several places or replaced with sharper or softer light contrasts, e.g., in the flower shelf, in the fringed chair, etc. At a few significant points, however, outlines have been added: on the woman's body, the doorframe, etc. We described these outlines in detail above. Here it is important only to note that the dualistic principle in the means of representation has not been changed.

The compositional scheme, too, seems to have remained unchanged. Small alterations have been made, however, and these are interesting. The shadowed fold that falls vertically from the upper right corner of the towel toward the chair no longer reaches the horizon of the room (as it did in the first version); instead, it has been prolonged upward by the vertical border of the picture on the wall. As a result, the horizontal border of the picture stresses and bridges the distance between the two corners of the towel (i.e., the fact that the centripetal energies cannot meet). Such bridging of distances is one of the new tendencies in the composition. Thus, the upper left corner of the picture on the wall is situated on a line with the woman's upper arm; the upper left corner of the towel is now more precisely on a line with the edge of the rug; and the parting of the servant's hair is now on a linear extension of the bottom edge of the cloth on the flower shelf. What this means is that the figurative compositional scheme has been consolidated to emphasize several important motifs, e.g., the triangle formed by the woman's legs. Reversals of this motif are particularly frequent: divergent lines opening from a real or ideal point (the latter outside the picture) occur, for instance, in the edges of the bathtub or in the narrow light area on the floor, both of which form angles opening toward the back. Thus a special variation on the motif is introduced, combining position on the surface with position in pictorial space.

While the over-all compositional scheme has been tightened, some elements of it have been loosened. These are best seen in the new treatment of the fringed chair, whose rounded back—a variation on the other curves—mediates between the two centripetal slants (the curve formed by the woman's back and arm performs a similar function). Formal structure is now brought into agreement with formal function, whereas in the first version they violently contradicted each other. Similarly, the top edge of the arm-chair is darker—this links it more effectively with the dark areas of tub and rug; also, the shading which has been added on the back of the chair is related to the new shading on the door.

The picture on the wall shows how closely connected are the tendencies to tighten and to loosen the composition. The contrasts between light and dark on the wall have been weakened and the four variations of the rectangle related to one another. Despite interruptions they now encircle the figurative motif. The flowers which have been added to the vases serve the same compositional purpose: they fill the area between the right border of the etching and the towel, and at the same time decrease the distance in depth between the flower shelf and the picture on the wall, i.e., they close the spatial motif and connect it with the central figurative motif. This is done tentatively, but it sets off the essential feature of the new composition: whereas the first version showed no clear relationship between the diagonal pattern and the rectangles, these have now been connected by a movement consisting of leaps, and this movement is placed concentrically around the diagonal scheme so that the figurative motif and the spatial motif are each developed separately and at the same time make contact across the distance. As a result, the geometric figures that lie between the extremes of triangle and rectangle serve as mediating elements; the lines, like the light and dark areas, create transitions. Judging by this, the development of the imagination seems not arbitrary but determined by certain tendencies which the artist conceives as interrelated and represents in the whole of this version.

Comparing the fifth with the first version, we see that the duality of the compositional motifs was implicit in the first version, and little more was required to make it explicit. But only with the complete realization of this duality could the various geometric figures of the two types of motifs be multiplied, combined, and even merged. This is one method for progressing from the play of forces which dominated the first version to a figuration of pictorial space.

The picture on the wall contributes to this goal in still another way. The figurative motif shifts the accent (as in the first version) increasingly to the extreme left, while the concentric spatial motif is displaced to the right, the accent falling on the vases. Similarly, in the foreground the centrifugal movement has been more strongly stressed to balance it with the centripetal movement. The same tendency to create balance also operates in the centripetal movement, for the modeling of the objects (particularly the bathtub) shows that the centripetal movement into depth is expressed in widening centrifugal forms (flower shelf, strip of light on the floor, bathtub). These tendencies not only interpenetrate in the foreground but also in the background. The centripetal tendencies are no longer broken off at the point of reversal (peripeteia), but are carried beyond it and concentrated in the picture on the wall, the upper edge of which—as mentioned above—is equal to the distance remaining between the converging diagonals. To be sure, this is not sufficient to achieve a balance of the opposing forces, but the principle is established: thus, whereas in the first version the centripetal tendency of the foreground was contrasted with the centrifugal tendency of the background in a purely external manner, here the two tendencies interpenetrate in both parts of the picture space. They do so in different ways, and as a result the peripeteia still serves to mark a violent reversal.

In addition to changes in the external composition there are changes in the internal composition, which we shall analyze for each of the three dimensions. With reference to the width dimension there is nothing new to be said. With reference to the dimension of height, the crucial change has been the strengthening of the horizontality of the floor, mentioned above, and of the upper part of the etching. Because of this the movement and force of the intersecting diagonals have everywhere been defined and harnessed and the difference in height between the lower and upper parts has been emphasized. As a result, the woman's broad back does not rise as is her intention but seems to receive a heavy burden. This effect is deliberate. Her upward effort is countered by a heavy pressure from above: by its volume and by its yielding turn Degas makes the human body seem capable of holding its own in the indefinite, hopeless suspension between will and necessity. The human being is capable of resistance, but he cannot help himself nor can he be helped by others. What comes from without—in this case the towel—imposes effort: it is expecting rather than helping. If the towel were to fall upon the woman, in this position, the pressure upon her would be still greater. If we recall those works of art in which the development from bottom to top symbolized development from unawareness to consciousness, from servitude to freedom, from the earthbound to the world of thought, we will realize that Degas' world is a prison out of which no consciousness can lead, and in which each man is thrown back upon his own resources, a force among forces, alone, with anguished joy that he has not yet been crushed.

As for the depth dimension, we notice a strong increase in three-dimensionality from the foreground into the middle ground, although the treatment is different at the left and at the right. The middle ground itself shrinks to a merely ideal layer with almost no depth. This fact, which characterized the first state, is here further stressed by an intensification of the compactness and mass of the back wall, which presses forward. There is no dematerialization as we go from front to back, as would be required by the principles of aerial perspective, which opens a vista into the cosmos (and which supplanted Christian transcendence); nor as we go from back to front, as might be required by metaphysical-pantheistic principles. Degas recognizes no absolute or even continuous development from his own finitude toward the cosmos, nor from cosmic infinity to his imprisoned self. What he intends is a collision between two different forces simultaneously moving from front to back and vice versa and reducing all that lies between to nothingness. To this end the objects up to the middle ground are allowed to keep their full tangibility. So paradoxical an association between vision in depth and plastic values is, true enough, observable under specific atmospheric conditions in nature; but in the case of Degas it probably reflects his view of the world rather than a wish to imitate exceptional phenomena in nature. This is proved by the fact that the development in each of the three dimensions expresses the same idea, but with ever-increasing emphasis on the negative.

In the dimension of width the square format, a figure of repose, is distorted by centrifugal forces which displace the accents to the far sides, where they are nevertheless held together by a centripetal force. In the dimension of height the opposing forces are directed not outward but inward, i.e., they move not away from each other but toward each other; the woman's back not only receives them but endures them. In the dimension of depth the resistance of the middle ground is further weakened, and this middle ground is reduced to an ideal suggestion. Degas comes to only *one* conclusion: the metaphysical inadequacy and worthlessness of action and consciousness alike.

On the whole, the changes in the composition are less important than those of realization and means of representation; but, together with these, the composition is liberated from its schematic character and acquires relative autonomy.

A succinct formula for his working process, the method of Degas' artistic imagination, might read: the first version supplies a pictorial scaffold by means of strong contrasts both of line and of light effects; in it bodies, space, and motif are crystallized into a single compositional scheme, which by the subjectivism of its line expresses a temperament both voluntaristic and intellectual. The fifth version abandons this subjectivism and aims at pictorial form by adding volume to both objects and space through the internalization of, and mediation between, the contrasts. This makes possible stronger differentiations and more varied integrations of objects, space, and motif. This process of objectification aims more at the substantial autonomy of the picture as a whole than at the ultimate spontaneity of objects, space, and technique. This last distinction will become entirely clear to us only when we now proceed to analyze the fourteenth version. (There are seventeen versions in all.)

Here, too, differences will at first appear both very small and very great. Very small, because the square format has been retained and the principal objects have not changed position. Very great, because the total effect is new with respect both to the main content and to the technical treatment.

For the first time we can say that the space is filled with a specific atmosphere—the tepid, humid, almost slippery, steamy air of the bathroom. Now the water possesses a definite temperature and radiation; the woman's body is enveloped in a light mistiness that settles on the wall and differentiates its mass into lighter or darker, cooler or warmer, drier or damper areas. The air frees the objects from their rigid outlines, most of all the woman herself, who now has a form that is held together internally even though her contours have been weakened and in some places have entirely disappeared. The air links objects: bathtub with the water in it, water with the woman's leg—note the circular ripples—woman with the towel behind her, right armrest of the chair with the rug, etc. The various textures (the white of the porcelain, the linen towel, the flesh, the enamel of the bathtub) are no longer unrelated, though it cannot be said that their differentiations have all been made to emerge from the homogeneous atmosphere; they are held together by their co-ordination. Furthermore, the objects are detached in space by the action of the air: now there is distance between the head and the door, between the towel and the wall, and between the towel and the fringed chair. Thus, for the first time, there is interplay between atmosphere and things: either the objects assert themselves (the vase of flowers, the towel), or they endure the atmosphere (the rug on the floor, or the back wall), or else a mixture of passive and active attitudes occurs (the woman's body). In every case the rational, unequivocal definition of objects has yielded to a kind of play between thing and air, at once momentary and continuous inasmuch as it oscillates between physicality and nonphysicality, between being and nonbeing. The print has acquired a more sensual appearance, and within it, on account of it, a deeper, more universal, and more comprehensive significance: as it has become more sensual it makes more sense. The physical act of climbing out of the bathtub in the stifling, steamy air has become symbolic; something immaterial is now effective in matter, something irrational. It was only after thirteen attempts that Degas achieved the sensuality and irrationality that are generally regarded by the everyday philosopher as the most direct data of life: what came first in the artist's experience was last to be expressed in art.

Since this deepening of the content is artistic, not literary (i.e., figured, not merely intended; formed, not merely stated), it must be evident in the technique of etching which—being the ultimate expression of the creative method—can alone bring together the most sensual and the most sensible elements. It is almost as though line and light had been pulverized—an effect diametrically opposed to the massive effects of the fifth state. To be sure, there are still compact areas of shrill white and impenetrable dark, and we see in the towel some of those biting lines which reflect the artist's temperament. But the over-all impression is set in a cool intermediate tone, in quality powdery and porous, in which infinitely small points of fullness and emptiness, of darkness and light alternate, so that there is a continual hovering movement, a kind of vibration from point to point. This new technique is to be seen most clearly in the dots that now appear on the lower part of the cloth on the flower shelf. Similarly, extensive areas have been atomized into infinitely small, fixed points of light and dark—the woman's right leg, for example, where the use of such points in various degrees of concentration has served to provide a link with the highly varying lights and darks on towel and rug.

A similar but vaguer effect of shimmer is now obtained from the tension between individual lines and masses. The single line has lost its isolated beginning and freely vanishing end, such as it had in the first state. Having become impersonal, it is now integrated in the over-all structure. Line and emptiness now appear to be completely regular and very subtle. Dimming has been effected by means of small dark spots which are relatively independent and set in rhythmic intervals to each other; on the right, almost the only example is the dark foliage of the flowers.

To the analyzing intellect the technical means of expression seem greatly enriched and at the same time more uniform inasmuch as smudgings, as in the case of the water in the tub, have disappeared. For the sensitive eye, rigidity has given way to tingling vibration, thus heightening stimulation and lessening shock effects. As object and meaning have been transformed, the treatment as a whole aims increasingly at bringing out the differences between the warm vibrance of the air and the heavy coldness of the objects. Textures and compositional problems are now of secondary importance.

Accordingly, the over-all tonality—i.e., the position of the dominant tone in the scale of tones—is completely altered. In the first state light tones were accented; in the fifth state intermediate tones served only to muffle glare. For the fourteenth state Degas has chosen a single intermediate tone which he has made so important that it asserts itself against both the lightest areas (towel, vase, light area on the floor) and the darkest ones (lower left corner, and the cloth on the flower shelf). Through this intermediate tone a balance of tones has been achieved and then supplemented by a very refined balance of masses, which was not even hinted at in the two earlier states. This dominant intermediate tone is achieved by the comparative brightening of a dark area (e.g., the wall, the rug) on the one hand, and by the subduing of a light area (e.g., door, bathtub, water) on the other. The brightened dark areas lie as close (almost closer) to the darkest areas as the subdued light areas to the lightest areas. Thus large porous surfaces have been introduced for the first time; but the result is not active tension between the two—they remain co-ordinated. Also co-ordinated—with areas greatly reduced—are the most intense lights and shadows; even where an intermediate tone is situated between them, as between the flower shelf and the floor, they do not flow into each other or grow out of each other. Degas—in contrast to Rodin—disliked metamorphoses; even in his sensualism he remained antiromantic, however much he may have wished to turn his back on his idol, "Monsieur Ingres," and advance in the direction of impressionism.

The middle tone on the scale of light and dark is at the same time an intermediate tone on the warm-cold scale—a lukewarm tone, now warmer and now cooler in continually varying mixture, against which the most intense lights and shadows (towel, flower shelf, vase) appear cold. Just as Rubens made the sensuality of his female bodies more remote by the use of cold colors, Degas rendered a humid, tepid atmosphere by contrast rather than similarity.

Another essential change in the means of representation consists in the elimination of outlines and thus of the earlier dualism in the use of lines. Now that the atmosphere frees the objects from their prisonlike fixedness, rigid drawing is superfluous. This can be seen particularly clearly where the woman's back meets the towel. The collision of two differently directed shadows on different objects is eliminated; only a single series of vertical lines now connects the woman's back and the towel—a relatively independent connecting tone. This may not have been Degas' last word, but it shows how far he was ready to go in dissolving form, at least experimentally, in the course of his work. Where true outlines remain (bathtub, back of armchair, door), they are more closely blended with the adjoining values. Definition of forms and placement of light cease to be separate, let alone contradictory. The woman's body is more modeled, though the hatchings have disappeared. The arm is rounder, the flesh more pliable, the ridge in the modeling has lost its sharpness; the tension of the torso is produced internally, so to speak, by the duality of the movement.

This result of our analysis may help us clarify Degas' central confession as theoretician: "Le dessin n'est pas la forme, il est la manière de voir la forme" ("Drawing is not form, it is the way we see form"). Why did he repeat this enigmatic statement so often, and why was he so irritated when it was not understood? For Degas, line was a means—and, as we have seen, only a provisional means—for enclosing, for defining form, i.e., it was less a "manière de voir" than a method of representing. In the age of impressionism he could not be content with so classicistic a method. Thus, in opposing a "manière de voir"—or, more accurately, a "méthode de représenter"—to form as it is perceived, or actual form,[4] he expressed the side of him that was furthest from Ingres and closest to Monet; in short, his ambivalent desire to achieve the synthesis of two antithetical elements: the isolated autonomous form and the form in light.

4. [For "actual form" (*Daseinsform*), see p. 23, above, and the Appendix, pp. 210, 217.]

A second factor must be added, however, which is suggested by the variant of his dictum reported by Georges Jeanniot: "Le dessin n'est pas ce que l'on voit, c'est ce qu'il faut faire voir aux autres" ("Drawing is not what one sees, it is what we want to make others see"). With these words Degas reveals the difference between actual form and effective form, whereas the dogma of classicism held that relativity can be eliminated only in the one absolute form, which is the actual form. But to recognize the validity of effective form is to recognize the validity of relative as well as actual being—in this case, relative to the viewer, as, in the other case, to the atmosphere. By the same token the problem of form is expressed in new terms, which are no longer classicistic or dogmatic. The same contradiction between actual form and effective form (actual being and relative being) was also confronted by Cézanne. It made of both artists perpetually unsatisfied seekers after perfection. The great difference between their solutions to the problem is accounted for not only by their temperaments but above all by the different traditions in which they were rooted. Cézanne's "Poussin refait sur la nature" might have been matched by Degas with "Ingres refait sur la nature"—and there is an essential, infinitely profound difference between Poussin and Ingres.

The tendency to uniformity, which we have just shown with respect to line and light, is also observable in the treatment of space. Gone is the rigidity with which the foreground was separated from the background in the earlier states (by the back of the fringed chair) and the middle ground reduced to zero under the impact of their collision. By means of a number of changes (more oblique hatching on the towel, altered position of the chair in relation to the picture on the wall, the new funnel-shaped fold of the towel, larger and taller flowers) a greater dovetailing, a more intimate interpenetration of the parts of space is effected, although the gap between foreground and background has, if anything, been emphasized. Even now, when Degas has eliminated the opposition between the atmospheric and the concretely picturing halves of the print—or has at least weakened it to a differentiation within the atmosphere—he does not relinquish the contrast between continuity and discontinuity, perhaps because, with his fondness for viewing floors from above, he found the contrast between the dimensions of depth and height too great, or perhaps because of his need for rendering depth in terms of rising movements and height in terms of downward pressures. Degas regarded this conflict as constant, so much so that the height of the horizon in all three states studied here remains unchanged. The etching in this dimension is divided in the approximate ratio of 3 : 2 (the golden section), which is not stressed otherwise. But although the duality has been preserved, the effect is one of homogeneous space.

Another change concerns the walls: the left wall has been reduced by half and the back wall extended closer to the edge. This serves the purpose of accentuating the centrifugal extension in width of the middle ground at the expense of the centripetal movement of the foreground. The same purpose has been served by making the door narrower and by moving the picture frame closer to the door. But the now greater interval between the picture and the right edge of the print has been filled with flowers, so that the movement into depth is here being checked for the first time. Two things are achieved by this continuous flow of movement in depth and width: the spatial motif of the fifth state is perfected, and it is better balanced in relation to the figurative motif of intersecting diagonal planes, which predominated in the first state. The spatial and the figurative motives are integrated, where before they had diverged; but this integration does not go beyond mere co-ordination. The objects do not create the space nor does space create the objects. To achieve unity despite this primary duality between space and forms, Degas applied various principles to both: the opposition between impulse and resistance (floor and wall, woman and towel), the curve (fringed chair, woman's back, movement along the spatial boundaries), etc. But neither this application nor the impressionist atmosphere nor the co-ordination of the various elements has prevented the space from being a box, an emptiness into which objects have been placed—for all that Degas did his best to avoid a boxlike space by conspicuously omitting the ceiling.[5] In this respect he differs fundamentally from Cézanne, who did not recognize an a priori empty (absolute) space but built up objects and space simultaneously from the same spots of color.

The significance of this fact will become apparent when we examine the changes in motif and composition.

We have seen that in the dimension of width Degas placed his accents at the sides, thus putting the centripetal movement of the foreground in contrast with a centrifugal movement in the background. From the outset he had also felt the need to relate these opposed movements to a checkpoint of repose. This point was the fold falling from the right corner of the towel. But this important spot was curiously undefined—not with respect to location, but with respect to form and size. Earlier corrections did not satisfy him; moreover, in order to clarify the spatial motif he was compelled to move the picture frame. But one thing he was certain about—the location of the checkpoint: it had to be at a ratio of 5 : 2 within the dimension of width. In the fourteenth version Degas brings in a new motif to express this function—a white funnel-shaped fold of the towel, suspended from the right corner, crossing the horizon, and falling over the dark fringed chair. This addition has many important consequences: the white of the vase is now connected with the group of whites at the left, and thus the composition is prevented from falling apart at this important junction point; furthermore, the bottom of the funnel-shaped fold forms a horizontal, which serves to measure the unequal distances from the accents at left and right and also effectively defines for the eye the differing

---

5. [A bit of ceiling is clearly shown in each of the three versions, but its restricted size seems only to confirm the author's analysis of space.]

heights of the obliquely rising flower shelf and the obliquely falling woman's arm (all the more effectively because the eye has been prepared below by the fact that the lower edge of the fringed chair, the bottom of the towel, and the top of the armchair are now practically at the same height). But, most important, the point of balance is now occupied by an object and no longer has to cope with the destructive competition of a void next to it. This gives rise to an entirely new expressive value. The axis has lost its terrifying, empty, inadequate quality, and it is doubtless no accident that the fold emerges unseen from the back of the towel, almost suddenly revealing its effect. Were we to be shown the fold in its entirety, it would not have this effect of surprise and mystery. In any case, a crucial step has been taken toward bringing the diagonal composition (formerly exclusive) closer to the requirements of the picture surface—i.e., to relate the dynamics of unfolding space more closely to the statics of mass and the movement in space to the fact of space. (This is a prerequisite for establishing a link, however secondary, between space and atmosphere.)

A number of smaller changes have the same purpose—to enhance the static aspect of the composition in relation to the dynamism of space. The far edge of the bathtub and the right edge of the rug are now so arranged that their prolongations would meet at the servant's head and the right side of the picture frame. In order not to make this too obvious, Degas has eliminated the part in her hair. Even more striking is the fact that the two outermost oblique lines of bathtub and flower shelf now meet inside instead of outside the picture space; as a result the print is closed at the top. Now the curves on the the servant's head—all clearly rounded—help to close the obtuse angle between the two upper corners of the towel (the curved form of these bands echoes the bottom of the funnel-shaped fold). A further important change concerns the accents at the edges of the etching: Degas has introduced several factors to weaken the centrifugal force. Prolonged, the right edge of the back of the armchair in the foreground now meets the woman's leg where it is emerging from the water and (farther up) her elbow, with the result that the displacement of the accent toward the left edge is checked by this imaginary line. Only now is the vertical edge of the door fully effective as a concrete boundary. On the right side of the print the edge of the flower shelf, prolonged, would meet the right upper corner of the towel, as in the earlier states, but now it creates, with the line of the left thigh and buttock (bending into the edge of the tub), an imaginary triangle which both points to and checks the forces directed toward the right edge of the etching. The funnel-shaped fold stands for the altitude of this triangle, i.e., in it the sides of the triangle are balanced and come to a point of rest. All these changes disclose the same intention: to keep the opposed directions *within* the etching, to balance and fix them within it, thus tying them more firmly to the compositional scheme.

As a result of the more numerous relationships established between points situated at different heights, upward and downward movements seem to press harder in the area of the woman's back. In response to this pressure her position is a little more erect. The lines come into the print from outside the picture space but, once in, are as though in a prison whose invisible guard takes painful pleasure in setting them against each other until they find their point of balance in a mathematical equation of icily burning emotions that would be a mathematician's despair. In any case, escape from the prison is impossible. The semblance of pictorial openness that remains has, in Degas, nothing to do with pantheism, as in Monet or, at a higher level, in Giorgione. It is an ironic counterpart to the imprisonment of all objects, light areas, and shadows in a web which the artist, with the unconcern and malice of a spider, has woven as close and as inviolable as a law of nature.

In the dimension of width, too, there have been changes. As in the first state, the picture depth is intended to be seen simultaneously from both sides; but the respective starting points are now a relatively warm intermediate tone at the left (in the water) and a cold white area at the right, which is reinforced by a compact mass of cold black. This contrast in the dimension of width makes it seem as though something were going on between the extremes. But the activity escapes between them into depth and to the top, and all that remains is the chilling irony of an open void.

Probably the most important of all the changes within the internal composition are those in the depth dimension. The increasing three-dimensionality of the area approaching the middle ground is now for the first time answered by a dematerialization of the background, which is all the more surprising because the back wall remains as close to the middle ground as before. In addition, the light areas, the door and the picture frame (and, even more, the towel), press forward. The former hardness and solidity of the wall have given way to an oscillation alternating between a condensation of the atmosphere and decomposition of the wall. But even this hovering between the material and the immaterial, between being and nonbeing, offers us no escape. Our physical vision is more gently treated but our intellectual vision is now trapped in a web of being all the more irrevocable. Degas' final message is not one of comfort. There is a greater illusion of freedom within the realm of necessity, but ultimately we discover it is only a cruel, ironical joke.

The changes in the three dimensions add up to this, that the etching now has a boundary controlled from within, but its openness at the sides, though lessened (particularly on the left by the shading in the bathtub), survives thanks to the fact that several objects are cut off by the edges of the print. Although the tonality has been cleared up, the colliding forces are heavier and more confined: the intersection of the diagonal centrifugal and centripetal forces, which originally dominated the sketch, is now supplemented and brought into balance with forces pulling left and right, forces exerting downward pressure, and forces driving into depth. To Degas, such a system of mechanical forces had universal validity. He therefore was obliged either to introduce elements of nature, such as atmosphere, into the work or else open the closed system to surrounding nature. Such an opening imperils the complex balance of opposing forces, while atmosphere is not only of a quality different from that of objects, but also obeys laws of movement different from those of the other forces—its laws are those of oscillation and vibration.

Degas was not the first painter to represent the world as a play of mechanical forces. Before him, Courbet had conceived only nature, especially the sea, as a machine. Degas went further: he conceived man, society, and art as a machine. Courbet was still able to dramatize man's self-alienation or to veil it with "beauty"; to the somewhat younger Degas, the alienation had become so extreme that no such escape was possible, or, if attempted, would only lead to greater failure. Both conceived of the world in terms of mechanism because they did not understand their period. Courbet sought this understanding in Proudhon, hoping thus to create a bridge between his art and his time; Degas, on the contrary, fled understanding—was compelled to flee it—like Cézanne. His fanatical hatred of Dreyfus, of both Jews and Protestants, means that he could only envisage his epoch in negative terms; he could not understand it from a positive point of view. The only bridge he could build between his society and art was not affirmation but criticism of reality. He found the sole source of his inspiration in social criticism, and it was essentially confined to criticism of the bourgeoisie.

This accounts for the fact that many studies were required, a long detour, before *sensual* pleasure came into the work. In the first version the appeal is merely to our sense of construction; in the fifth, to our tactile sense; but neither the one nor the other is fully satisfied, and the eye is scarcely attracted. It seems as though Degas had worked only for himself, with no thought for the viewer. But the true reason must lie in this, that the complex system of mechanical forces by which he understood the world knows only one pleasure—the pleasure in the artistic means of representation. And this pleasure could be realized only when the mechanical forces functioned of themselves in a definite relationship and a definite arrangement. Then the artist could forget the end and lose himself in the enjoyment of the means. Degas renders a world without joy, a world incapable of pleasure; but at the same time he renders the pleasure he derived from it: the pleasure in his work, in the means of work. *L'art pour l'art* was his only solace, the only principle of morality that he and those like him could still find in the society of industrial capitalism.

The compositional scheme of the first version, with its strong contrasts in the means of representation and its subjective technique, has given way in the fourteenth (but not last—and even the last was provisional to Degas!) to concrete sensuality, the free play

of atmosphere, and the self-sufficiency of the work itself. The artist had met the requirements of three-dimensionality, of the laws of the object, of space, and of lighting, and of
the balance of opposing forces. In the first version, where his personal temperament
could be felt most directly, his personality showed least depth and scope. Later, when
his personality seems to have been entirely submerged in the atmosphere of the bathroom, it expresses—indirectly and metaphorically—its ultimate insights. We see clearly
how Degas complicated his problem at each stage of the working process, attempting to
transform a fragmentary perception into one as definitive, as total as possible. This
multiplication of difficulties obviously stimulated him.

Why the difficulties of creation were so great for Degas should be clear from our
analysis, although we did not emphasize them, being interested only in his working
method, and this only to the extent to which it may serve as a concrete illustration of the
workings of the artistic imagination. But we may, in conclusion, briefly note why the
fate of such a worker was bound to be tragic in his day—it was the fate of Cézanne and
many others. Degas was a specialist who wanted to be a universal man, who wanted to
build in a disintegrating world, a sensual man in a world that made pleasure impossible,
an artist in an age of the machine—he was a creator at a time when man's life was
wholly governed by abstract relationships and dependencies, the performance of services,
and the exchange of commodities. Industrial capitalism had put mankind, not only art
and artist, in question. The artist may accept this challenge and give form to his feelings
in reaction to the historical conditions of his life, but he cannot explain them either to
himself or to others. That is why he must search for an explanation outside himself.
Degas' own social stratum lived behind a veil of self-deception which the artist might
tear apart but could not see through. The social class that was the enemy of his class provided an explanation but, while radically negating the bourgeois basis of art, was as yet
unable to provide a new basis.

What this means will be clearer from a general observation. In previous epochs the
most favorable conditions for artistic creation had been the existence of a class of crafts-
men (since art is craft), of a ruling class capable of enjoyment and display, and of a class
of intellectuals capable of explaining the world (priests, philosophers, etc.). But in the
last third of the nineteenth century crafts were disintegrating; the ruling class could no
longer take pleasure in the display of its wealth because it had too much to conceal from
its class adversaries; and the intellectuals had become too specialized even to pretend
to be capable any longer of understanding the world as a whole. Under such circumstances Degas saw only one solution for the artist: to withdraw into solitude, to spit his
disgust with the world in the face of God "our Father," and to live for the occasional joy
of forcing intractable matter, from which he created art, to sing for a moment.

III. THE ARTIST'S DEVELOPMENT

Giotto: *Lamentation over the Body of Christ* and *Death of Saint Francis*

(PLATES XI, XII)

> FAUST: What am I then, if all too far
> Above me lies the crown of man's desire,
> To which our senses all aspire?
> MEPHISTOPHELES: You are precisely—what you are!
> Place on your head a wig that reaches to the sky,
> Stand upon buskins meters high:
> You still remain—just what you are!
>
> GOETHE, *Faust*, Part I

XIII*a*   GIOTTO. *The Death of Saint Francis* (after cleaning of 1957)

XIII*b*   GIOTTO. Friar's head. Sinopia drawing for
The Death of Saint Francis

XII   GIOTTO. *The Death of Saint Francis* (after restoration of 1853). After 1317. Fresco. Bardi Chapel,
Santa Croce, Florence

XI GIOTTO. *Lamentation over the Body of Christ.* 1304. Fresco. Arena Chapel, Padua

Just as every man is no more than an individual part of the whole, and his task consists in making the most of what *he* has—i.e., in bringing to life, within his own limits, the whole and the universal—so every artist is confined in his own, alas all too narrow prison. He has only a limited range of potential subjects to express, forms to represent them with, and artistic values to realize. That is why the same subjects, motifs, and compositional forms recur at the various stages of his life and, however great his vitality, he can only "fulfill the law under which he began." Consider Goethe, for example: *The Sorrows of Werther*, *Tasso*, the *Elective Affinities*, the "Marienbad Elegy," the works of youth, maturity, and old age, all are variations on the same theme. The music at the close of *Egmont* says the same thing as the conclusion of the "Trilogy of Passion" or Part II of *Faust* and marks Goethe's limits in relation to the tragic, to Shakespeare—limits of which he himself was aware. Man does not create from nothing. Because his highest gift is finite, he strives the more for supreme perfection at every moment during his life, strives to give wholeness and unity to the mere succession of moments. Whenever creative energy—the axis around which the greatest conflicts revolve—lacks the strength to achieve artistic unity, it disintegrates into madness or religion.

These intimations of the artist's individual limits point to the dual character of his development: the natural aspect, extending from youth to maturity and old age, and the artistic hierarchy of values, a rise or decline in the realm of perfection. When we compare Giotto's *Lamentation over the Body of Christ* in the Arena Chapel at Padua (1304, Plate XI) with his *Death of Saint Francis* in the Bardi Chapel at Florence (after 1317, Plates XII, XIII*a*), we need not distinguish between the two aspects, because here we have an artist who, with age, produced the maturer works—although the uncertain dating of his birth (1266 or 1276) bars us from making a systematic interpretation of his psychological development. We shall confine ourselves to the question: What artistically significant changes have been brought about by the passage of fifteen active years?

Abstractly considered, the two themes appear closely related, easily subsumed under a single concept: grief over the death of a great and well-loved man. Such an abstract view will accordingly stress the common features of the subject: the laid-out body; the mourners surrounding him with love, grief, and veneration; the reference to a future life. If we take a historical view, however, we shall primarily notice differences. Christ dies as the (crucified) Son of God; at his death, in addition to the apostles and followers, heavenly angels are present, while of course no reference is made to Church or religious ritual. Saint Francis, on the other hand, was a monk; in life he vowed himself to the imitation of Christ; in death the miracle of the stigmata is revealed, and the soul of the saint, borne by angels, mounts to heaven; the funeral ritual of the Church is being performed. Each of the two works shows a single scene from a cycle depicting a life dedicated to mankind. The important thing in both is not the dead man's acts or his suffering on behalf of mankind, but mankind's attempt to pay an infinite debt by expressing its gratitude. The emphasis on the human element seems to correspond to the fact that mourning figures cut across the body of the dead at several points; once in the *Lamentation*, three times in the *Death of Saint Francis*. Intervening figures of this kind were not customary either earlier (*Death of the Virgin* in the Strasbourg Cathedral) or later (*Lamentation for Christ* by Hugo van der Goes[1]). Here the artist wanted the laid-out body of the dead Son of God or the saint closely associated with the human emotions it aroused.

We discover a like combination of similarity and difference when we approach the two works from a formal point of view. A schematic view would reduce the two compositions to the form of a horizontal closed at each end by a right angle |_____| and point out the ovals of the groups of figures surrounding the dead body. A more concretely disposed eye, on the other hand, would be attracted by the differences, especially by the way the marked diagonal slope of the hill in one work, cut across by the figure of the Apostle John, has been replaced in the other with a wall divided into rectangular panels. Also, the harsh, elementary opposition between the human figures and the angels, between the earthly and the heavenly, in the first picture, has been replaced by a threefold division between man, space, and heaven. We shall first analyze the changes in the common aspects and then go on to examine the new differences which, as we shall see, serve the same end.

The |_____| scheme is, in the work at Padua, fitted into a nearly square format: $a : (a - 1)$, and the perpendicular is formed by two standing figures on each side, which reach only to mid height. This results in a division with sharp contrasts: at the bottom, the figures solidly grouped around the body of Christ, with a good deal of overlapping, and almost entirely hiding the ground; at the top, free from constrictions at the sides, the completely different world of the angels, who are flying out of the sky in marked foreshortening or across it, their undulatory courses loosely patterned like brick bonding.

1. [In the Kunsthistorisches Museum, Vienna.]

These two worlds, so different from each other, do not come into contact, or do so only at the right edge where a leafless tree links them. A low stretch of empty sky intervenes and creates a sharp break between them. The heavy, massive human figures are not lamenting any differently from the lightly soaring angels, but the human beings do not hear the angels' voices; they seem unaware of them, immersed as they are in their own grief.

Unlike the *Lamentation*, the scheme of the *Death of Saint Francis* is fitted into a rectangular format in the ratio 3 : 2, i.e., the golden section, the proportion that most closely links the whole with its parts. Furthermore, there is no tension between format and compositional scheme, for the verticals at left and right extend nearly to the top of the picture. These verticals are architectural elements (doorways with gabled canopies), and they are strengthened by standing figures which, though just reaching above mid-height, are arranged in groups so that they are seen next to or behind each other in perspective. External unity has been matched by internal unity: the development goes from the representational-human element (which is geometrically ordered) to the abstract-mathematical element (which employs representation—the wall, for instance—only as a pretext), and ends in the sky, conceived as the absolute. At the same time, however, the sky extends farther down, on the right side as far as the horizon, and portions of it are visible through each doorway. The sky thus encompasses, with its immateriality and infinitude, the entire formed world of bodies and space. As a result the external juxtaposition of heterogeneous worlds, cut off from each other in the Padua work, has given way to a more continuous development from the earthly to the heavenly, from the conditioned to the unconditional. Emblematic of the latter is the cross and banner, carried by the monks, which extends into the sky. The three worlds—earth, heaven, and the absolute—have become a triune world of bodies, geometry, and being; and as unity has triumphed over the contrasts, the qualities of these contrasts have themselves become different.

This development is essential to the understanding of Giotto's art; we must, however, keep in mind that the compositional scheme itself remains constant, particularly with regard to two features. First, the dead body is parallel to the horizontals of earth and horizon; in the later painting, parallelism is further emphasized by the addition of the deathbed, which raises the corpse and keeps it from sagging, and by the direct statement of the horizon. Second, the pictorial structure as a whole is related to the basic structural lines of the surface, the mathematical order of which reduces the occasion for subjective emotion and at the same time invests perception and vision with the character of necessity. This second feature, too, is more clearly marked in the later painting because there is less use of diagonals, while the number of verticals and horizontals has been increased (particularly the horizontals—the shroud, the deathbed, the bands across the top of the wall). Now the congruence of human form and picture form has acquired much greater weight and pre-eminence, whether the diminished incongruence results from the priority of a transcendent world or from that of the human emotions whose expressiveness resists objectification.

Another feature common to both works is that the corpse lies within an imaginary horizontal oval. But the ovals differ in important respects. In the Padua painting the nearer part of the oval is provided by the bottoms of the women seated in the foreground and its farther portion by the backs and heads of the women just behind the body. These human figures are squeezed into the oval, which in turn is bound to them; the geometric form seems to be a priori in relation to the masses along its periphery; the slightest displacement of any of the masses would break up the form. In the painting at Florence, the relation between human figure and oval form is a good deal freer. The curve of the oval begins in the middle plane at the shroud: it swings to the pillow and halo at the left into a farther plane, where it continues, tangent to the heads of the kneeling monks, and comes to the nearest plane via the backs and arms of the two monks kneeling at the right end of the bier; the girdles of the friars kneeling in the foreground complete the oval. The lower parts of the bodies of the three figures kneeling before the bier thus remain entirely outside; they perform new functions—they effect the shift from the vertical to the horizontal and at the same time develop parts of the curve relatively independently of the whole. The oval is no longer defined by the coincidence of two functions—the active one of enclosing the human figures and the passive one of being filled up with masses from the periphery toward the center; it is constituted both as a whole and as a sum of parts, and the movement of the whole is in a direction opposite to the movements of the parts.

The continuous to-and-fro movement within space produces not only greater freedom between the human figures and the oval form, but also a closer relationship of these elements with the picture as a whole. In the Padua painting Giotto emphasized the ends of the oval by placing a woman on each side of the body; this gives finitude to the oval form, detaching it from the rest of the picture. But in the painting at Florence the handles of the bier fall outside the oval at both the left and the right and open it up horizontally, while enclosing the corpse more tightly within it. Thereby the geometric form loses its monadlike isolation and is incorporated into the horizontal.

The same integration takes place in height and depth, the two being closely related in both works. With respect to height, we see this most clearly in the three similar curved lines which begin at ground level in the kneeling figures in the foreground, traverse the oval and, with slight changes, terminate in the vertical divisions of the wall. The curve farthest left begins with the right edge of the ermine-collared mantle, swings left over the shoulder and head of the Franciscan friar and along the outstretched hand and face of the friar behind him; it then swerves down along the latter's right arm and the shroud and ends along the shadow under the bier. The outline of this slanted oval is at first attached to an accentuated object, then to an unaccentuated object, and finally not even to an object but to a shadow. This suggests rhythmic sinking from being to non-being. But even before the accentuated part passes into the less accentuated one, a narrow strip of the wall (between two panels) rises upward. Significantly, it is situated *between* the raised arm with hand bent back and the tilted head with eyes looking up, so that it leads the eye heavenward to the ascending soul of the saint more strongly than the figure does, even though its upward path is checked by the horizontals. Thus, the first curve takes on contradictory references—to eternal life at its highest point and to death and disintegration at its lowest point.

The second curve begins very near the first, as though to repeat it, but soon turns away from it to the right and rises toward the central axis of the painting. This irregular S curve does not encircle the horizontal of the corpse but cuts across it; if we are to see here another symbol of the cross, this one approximates the Greek cross, while the corresponding cross in the *Lamentation* is distinctly Latin. The first two curves, so unlike each other, form an acute angle that opens obliquely upward so that even its right side remains to the left of the heavenly vision. Where the sides of the angle actually end, we can see with what contrasting tensions Giotto now worked: at the highest point of the first curve, where it turns down to the corpse and away from the vision in the sky, a gesture points upward to the vision; where the second curve stops after its upper portion turns away from the saint, a gesture refers back to the saint. This reference checks and breaks the ascent of the curve even before it meets the horizontal, and serves as a connection with the third curve. The latter begins at some distance from the second curve and also on the ground, where at first it parallels the other two; at the height where the others turn, this one forks in the Y shape. The right branch of the Y is almost vertical and separates the group around the saint from the group at the right; the left branch continues in the initial direction until it approaches the second curve, to which it is linked by the expressive face between them. The two dissimilar curves form an oval that is open at the bottom but firmly, almost oppressively closed at the top; it rises, slightly slanted, but does not reach the horizontals of the wall.

The three different curves thus form two variants of the oval around the body of the saint and serve a double function: they provide a transition from the horizontal to the vertical, and they link the horizontal with the dimension of depth in two ways—from front to back and from back to front—the first time by a mere succession of the opposed directions, the second time by a succession involving also a mutual penetration of the opposites, that is, of the movements into and out of the picture; this represents a formal heightening of the first.

In the earlier painting Giotto tore the oval into two parts: a smaller part at the left around the head and shoulders of Christ, and a larger one at the right around the legs. In the open space between these two concrete portions lies an imaginary slanting plane (inclined plane) which extends over Christ's body from the left (foreground) to the right (middle ground) and terminates at the hill and the saint's halo. At either end it is crossed by two other planes: one formed by the back of the seated woman, which also recedes into depth but this time from right to left; and the other formed by the woman bending forward, holding the upper part of Christ's body in her lap. These tipped planes are cut off, the first in the back, the second in front, so that the opposite directions of the two planes by-pass each other (⟋ ⟍). Such a configuration of two noncomplementary movements must have been a fundamental experience of spatial dynamics for Giotto, for it occurs also in the later painting between the kneeling figures in front of the dead saint and the three kneeling figures behind him—although here it differs in two crucial respects. The opposing movements are used three times instead of once, and instead of completely by-passing each other, they meet at one point and are thus related. This is one of the reasons why the distance in depth between the lower and upper part of the oval comes out so much more clearly. In the earlier painting the vehement and direct movement into depth (along the vertical) was stopped behind the overlapping figures; but in the later painting the slower movement into depth is answered by a stronger forward movement from behind. Thereby the forward and backward movements in pictorial space are formally related as parts of the plane and the path traced by the oval motif becomes dependent upon them, whereas in the earlier painting the path of the oval was primary and the movement into depth was added to it in order to open up the originally closed oval space. This implies that the second work involves a fundamentally different conception of space and modeling, to which we shall return.

These differences in methods of achieving the oval and integrating it with the various dimensions of pictorial space—i.e., in the means of representing the world—must not lead us to overlook the feature common to the two works: in both, the oval encloses a corpse which lies along its major axis and is perceived through it. To be sure, the body is differently laid out in the later painting: it is perfectly horizontal, whereas in the earlier painting it sags in the middle. The visible parts of the two bodies are also different. The two paintings nevertheless have a conception of the world in common, more clearly stated in the earlier, but rendered with greater art in the later one.

Assuming that the body of Christ, in a perfectly horizontal position, would be halved by the major (transverse) axis of the oval which now touches his left hip, we see that the part which sags to find support is lower by half the width of the body, head and left hand are raised by the whole width of the body, and the legs return to the height of the transverse axis. The regularity with which the body rises and falls gives it a quality of rigidity; it is self-contained, remote, and ultimately removed from the mourners around it. The different attitudes of the mourners all recognize this aloofness. However tenderly the woman at the lower left may hold the head of Christ in her hands, its weight is incommensurable with her gesture: it is almost too heavy to be borne; that she holds it at all is a kind of miracle. However lovingly Mary may embrace the head with both arms, it remains entirely apart from her gesture; not even her tears can reach it. And Mary Magdalene, whose grief is more contemplative, is at a distance for all her closeness; she does touch Christ, but only by one foot. Each of these women is alone with her personal sorrow; those closest to the body appear inwardly the most remote from each other. All they have in common in the loneliness of their respective grief is the desire to attend on Christ and caress him, and the individual nuances in their sorrow are gradations and variations of *one* contemplative grief, in contrast to Saint John's outburst; his agitation is echoed in the woman standing at the far left, in sharp contrast to her neighbor. But whether their grief moved them inwardly or makes them outwardly agitated, all are seeking Christ without finding him.

The formal equivalent of this type of human relationship—which rests entirely on Christ's mediation despite his great remoteness from each mourner—consists, to begin with, in this, that each of the women is inscribed into a geometric figure. The three in the foreground constitute triangles or pyramids (with a good deal of variety in detail); the two women on the other side of the body constitute ovals. But Mary and the other figure, sitting cross-legged at the lower left, together form an imaginary inclined oval which encloses the head and chest of Christ, whereas the three women at the right more nearly form a trapezoidal broken oval within which Christ's lower legs serve as the focal point of various movements. The latter two geometric shapes express the common aspiration of the figures—their common relationship to Christ; but the two are separated by an interval, and this interval is occupied by the upper body of Christ. What holds them together inwardly is thus revealed, while the external connection between them is supplied by the larger though almost broken ellipse. Consequently, it is not the elliptical curve alone, nor even the fact that it is divided into or composed of individual forms of different kinds, that expresses so adequately the contemplative grief of the isolated mourners and their equidistance from Christ, but rather the way in which he himself—head, arms, feet showing the wounds—appears among the groups and between them, while his strong upper body, unattended, is offered to the beholder. The mathematical and figurative are only the external shell of the religious; only in so far as the Son of God broke through the highest forms of reality—i.e., of artistic consciousness—in order to offer himself as the kernel within the shell, only to this extent has the form been given content and meaning. This does not imply that in the painting itself there is an artistic dualism between geometric forms and spiritual expression, but it does imply that unity is achieved on the basis of an extra- or supra-artistic principle: the oppositions are not directly synthesized, but related to a third term, which lies outside them on a level of being that transcends them.

So far we have discussed the most striking similarities between the two works, and have found that all the changes from the earlier to the later painting pursue the same goal: the Christian conception is deepened and clarified and its pictorial figuration is perfected through the treatment of the group motif and its integration within the dimensions and directions of plane and space. We shall now pass to the most striking difference. The diagonal that plays such a central part in the Padua painting is absent from the other. In representational terms this diagonal is shown by the ridge of a hill which, descending along the width of the picture, rips the plane into a projecting background at the left, in *contrapposto* to a receding foreground at the right; the ridge itself, with its strong light, forms the entire middle ground. It might be thought that the expressive force of this diagonal lies in its uniqueness and autonomy. But such an assumption proves false when we note that it is approximately the diagonal of the two lower of the three rectangles of the compositional scheme; or, in arithmetical terms, its gradient, which is objectively represented as the hill, measures the middle third of the height of the picture: the remaining part, which is invisible, has a distance from the border that is precisely defined by the geometric diagonal. The emphatic vehemence of the gradient actually rests upon the fact that it is *not* rendered as a straight line on the surface, but by means of two space-opening planes, i.e., planes not parallel to the surface. One of these planes, the lighter one, descends and comes forward; the other, which is shaded and which arrests and supports the first, also descends, but at the same time recedes, so that the edge where the two meet defines the foreground. This figuration of space through modeling along a sloping parallelepiped produces a spatial dynamism that enhances the expressive force of the diagonal, partly by the emphatic contrast between light and shadow, partly by its relation to the metrical scheme of the picture.

Another diagonal intersects this one, embodied in a figure reduced to two gestures, upper torso thrown forward while the arms are thrown back. This intersecting diagonal, too, acquires its expressive force largely from the fact that the linear motif of the surface is transformed into a spatial motif in the following manner: most of the lower part of John's body is covered by a kneeling woman, while his right arm is masked by his body, so that we see only the right hand, raised between head and shoulder. The planes of his mantle—now concave, now convex—are bent back toward the planes of the ridge, with whose edge they clash shrilly. This results in a single and relatively narrow area of intersection, dividing the ridge into two very different lengths (1 : 2).

Moreover, we must note the manner in which Saint John's expansive gesture is fitted into the picture as a whole. The vertical axis of the painting runs through John's face just left of his neck, so that the head is much more closely related to Christ than the rest of his body, which in turn is closer to Christ than his arms. We get the impression that this single agitated man among the many women is trying to get closer to his dead Master from an endless distance but reaches Him only with his tear-pinched eyes. Furthermore, by a precisely calculated proportion, John's left hand is detached from his body and held at a fixed point: the distance from the right edge of his garment to the right edge of the painting is equal to that from the left edge of the painting to the right edge of the second standing woman's garment. This proportion is unusual, for it does not coincide in location or extension with any of the metrical distances, which we will later note in greater detail (see p. 100). This twofold contrast—the fact that the backward movement of John's arms cannot fall in with the forward surge of his body and that this surge remains isolated from Christ because it is arrested by the vertical axis—holds John fast to the wall-like hill despite his vigorous gesture. But even this contrast between the dynamism of his gesture and the immobility of his body against the hill is shown at a carefully calculated point within the painting: the point of bisection divides the hill in the approximate proportion of 2 : 5 (respectively, at left and at right).

Nor is the intersection of slanting planes in depth suddenly presented as a *fait accompli*; it is carefully prepared and resolved. It is prepared, above all, by the figure of the woman who is shown in the foreground in three-quarter view from the back; it is her body that divides the body of Christ by a new opposing slant into depth, so that its visible parts are in a proportion of 5 : 2; if we could see the portion of the ridge at the left now covered, we would see that the larger part of the body of Christ forms an acute angle with the shorter part of the ridge. It is resolved not in the dimension of width, but in that of height: the angels, despite Giotto's fondness for foreshortening and a seemingly random arrangement, do not once overlap. As a result, the motif of intersection occurs only in the earthly sphere; it would introduce too harsh, too painful a note in the heavenly one.

This is the heart of the matter. Where we today see little but the formal play of two intersecting planes, medieval man must have seen the symbol of his faith: the Latin cross. Here it seems miraculously to be resting on its smaller beam after tumbling down from a height. The observable formal motif of intersecting lines evoked to the faithful of former times the spiritual meaning of the Cross, and in the portrayal of the Lamentation for Christ made the past events of the Crucifixion and the Deposition just as immediate to him as the portrayal of the angels made the future events of the Ascension and the Enthronement. What may today seem merely dogmatic mythology, as dead as the myths of Artemis and Apollo or Isis and Osiris, was once seen as a most real moment in world history. The death of Christ on the Cross was to have redeemed mankind for all eternity if only men would mourn him and follow his teaching. This conception of world history has changed and belief in its mythological base has died; Giotto, however, recorded both conception and belief in visible forms which, for all the passing of their mythological content, bestow the only timelessness of which man is capable: that of artistic creation.

The differences we note in Giotto's *Death of Saint Francis* will become clear only when we understand how the compositional scheme, the oval of mourners, and the cross motif are interrelated in the earlier painting. These three factors are obviously unequal in emphasis both in spiritual and sensory terms. The cross is the central pictorial motif which relates the picture to sacred history. The ellipse supplies the motif for the group which expresses the direct meaning of the scene. The compositional scheme seems to play a purely regulative role; in actuality, however, it expresses the most general metaphysical hypotheses of the Christian religion and their relations to the basic elements of artistic creation. From the point of view of the theory of knowledge, the three factors in question are located at three different levels of reality. But Giotto presents them not only as belonging to a *single type* of reality, but also as having the same degree of reality—as though of equal importance, in competition with one another. Only in the narrow strip of empty sky do we find another type of reality, as we find another degree of reality in the angels. This lack of differentiation, at this stage, is no doubt accounted for by Giotto's inability to tie together the different motifs by purely artistic means. We see this most clearly in the relation between the oval of the mourning group and the vertical figures at both corners of the picture. The figures are shown standing and recede into depth; with the figure of Saint John and the ridge they form a curve in depth which might be thought of as a variant upon the oval and at the same time as a transition from the oval motif to the cross motif. Moreover, contact between the seated figures at the bottom and the standing figures is created by the fact that the former overlap the latter in two cases on the left and once on the right. But this does not alter our pervading impression that the group of two figures at the sides are purely static repetitions of the vertical edges of the painting; whereas the two motifs are rendered with strong and varied dynamism: the oval is shifted from the center to the left, so that the larger part of Christ's body lies in the left half of the painting, while the analogous leftward movement of the ridge is arrested by Saint John a little to the right of center. Between the calm displacement in the foreground and the violent interruption behind it—i.e., between the horizontal and diagonal branches of one and the same movement in different tempi—connection has been established by a slant which, running from back to front, leads from Saint John's head to the head of the seated woman (seen from the back) in the foreground. The inclination of this slant gives us the extent of the displacement from the static vertical, but the connection thus established between the static and the dynamic remains purely external.

What an internal connection would be can be seen in the later painting, which differs from the earlier one above all in its treatment of the groups at the sides and their relationships to the oval. The formal positional symmetry of the side groups has, in the *Death of*

Saint Francis, given way to a concrete asymmetry. The right group is shown in three-quarter view, but the left in almost orthogonal foreshortening—i.e., the former is broader than the latter (approximately 5 : 3). This means not only that the four elements of which each side group consists—dark empty area, architecture, and two rows of men—are more crowded at the left than at the right, where Giotto permitted the sky to extend down to the horizon to encompass the whole pictorial space and the architectural scaffolding and to relativize them (of which more later); it means also that the profile view of the group on the left and the three-quarter view of the group on the right are connected with another sort of movement. At the inner groups, respectively, we find on the left a curve rising at a slight inclination in front and coming to a halt in the almost vertical descent in back, whereas at the right we have a curve rising vertically and then sloping toward the inside. Therefore the group on the right seems still to be marching in procession, while the group on the left seems to have come to a stop. In other words, the group on the right, which takes up more room, seems to press against the central oval, whereas the group on the left arrests this movement; at the same time this movement is related—though only provisionally—to the vertical axis, which, indicated only ideally, disappears at the bottom in empty space between the monks but becomes visually more concrete as we move upward. The static symmetry is linked with—indeed, made dependent upon—energies of different intensity at each side: at the right they push strongly against a weaker resistance, while at the left they push weakly against a stronger resistance. The impression produced is that the location of the groups has been determined by dynamic forces: the static structure results from a play of energies that seems to unfold before our eyes. Not a trace of all this is to be felt in the painting of 1304. Although the oval is moved leftward from the axis, the numerous deviations from symmetry do not produce unmistakable dynamic forces in the groups at each side. Rather, these merely fill the space the motifs did not take up. The static elements were determined in advance, and only their distribution has been varied. No unified principle, however, seems to govern the secondary asymmetrical elements and tie them to the painting as a whole.

The corner groups of the later painting express one direction of dynamic movement, which relates the static and dynamic elements only externally; another, opposite movement, and a closer relation between static and dynamic energies, are to be found in the rectangular panels of the wall. Because there are five of them (if we disregard the incomplete sections at the sides), the vertical axis is the more emphasized. This axis divides the center rectangle into two unequal parts in the proportion of the golden section, like the proportion of the picture's height and width and like the comparative widths of the groups at each side. This unequal division of the central panel is related to the fact that the panels are not of equal width. They follow a definite rhythm, however: the narrowest is at the right, the one next to it is wider, and the center one again less wide than the second (but not as narrow as the first) in order to support the crowding of the figures beyond it; the fourth panel is wider (approximately equal to the second) and the one at the extreme left is the widest of them all. If we use ∪ for narrow and — for wide, we get (from left to right) the series: — — ∪ — ∪. Thus the measurements decrease in alternation from left to right, counteracting the dynamic movement represented by the displacement of the bier. In the human groups, on the other hand, the width of the masses becomes less as we go in the opposite direction, from right to left. This brings about the following contrast: large group / small panel at the right, and small group / large panel at the left. This rhythmic alternation is further bolstered by the fact that the upper parts of the two left panels are more exposed than are those on the right. Thus we do not get what we found in the earlier painting, a single direction of movement in two tempi, but two opposed directions of movement. These latter begin at the right edge, not with a static figure but with a static group; then they come to a stop at the left, only to become movement again as the eye is led back to the starting point.

But this does not exhaust the differences of the later painting with respect to movement. This movement is articulated by two V-shaped gaps between the oval central group and the standing groups at each side. This prehistoric symbol of life[2] is the main motif of the later painting. When the eye addresses itself to this broad-surfaced painting, starting at the left, it is led downward along the steep folds of the clerical robes until it hits the ground; from there it feels its way up along the mildly slanted legs of the bier and, briefly checked, along the even more slanted lappet of the shroud; when it reaches the figure of the monk who is looking up, it receives its first intimation of the celestial vision, still very far away. Then the eye wanders along the full extent of the central oval and moves downward again along the back of the monk farthest to the right behind the bier. There, *behind* the overlapping robes, the eye is led into an unbounded depth, so to speak, and yet at the same time is arrested in front. Ascending the robe of the hindmost choirboy, it is led along the banner with the cross up to the heavenly apparition and this time brought very close to it. The two V-shaped gaps and their varied resolutions constitute the lifeblood of the painting. If we pretended they were not there, it would appear meaningless and dead.

Now, it is interesting to note that the two V shapes are hinted at in the earlier painting: over (behind) the left forearm of Christ and below the left hand of John. Although both are emphasized by the metrical divisions (as determined by the frame; see p. 100) and by other compositional factors, they are comparatively ineffective: the left of the two is too wide, and that on the right does not reach down far enough; nor are they sufficiently related in terms of either size or movement. They are merely empty areas, points of repose for the general agitation of gestures and emotions. In the later

2. [Cf. the author's *Prehistoric Pottery and Civilization in Egypt*, pp. 76*ff.*]

painting, however, it is exactly this double hiatus which is alive and stirring. For as the eye drops into the void and rises from it again—the first time arrested by a horizontal, the second time led beyond it by the banner with the cross to the ascending soul—the viewer becomes the actor, and since his action takes place in the void, he becomes the vehicle of the strongest action, before which all other actions pale and appear relative.

The important thing here is not merely that one pictorial motif (the cross) has been replaced by another (the sign of life triumphant), because the painting does not represent the Saviour, but a saint. The new motif has a different quality. This is most apparent in the sky. The empty area in the earlier painting between the heads of human figures and the angels, although strongly emphasized, lay in another plane behind the human figures; the latter acted in front of it; they did not participate in its emptiness— just as life with its gestures strongly projected outward stands in opposition to death, as long as death remains an outward event. From such a point of view motifs can only be figurative—i.e., be formed by objects—whether symbolic signs like the cross or geometric shapes like the interrupted oval. In the later painting the sky has been given a mode of being different from that of the objects and human figures; its emptiness relativizes them, providing them with an absolute; it permeates them to form an interfigurative motif that is bounded by objects but otherwise immaterial. The change of subject by the artist is connected with a deepening of religious feeling despite the fact that the central character represented occupies a lower rank in the religious hierarchy. It is no longer faith which imposes its scale of values on art, but art which imposes its scale of values on faith.

Now it becomes clear why the different quality of the new motif could not have been developed in the earlier painting. The diagonals which supplied the dominant linear motif in the earlier composition—for all the symbolic significance of their intersection (the cross)—are too subjective, too emotional, too immediate in their force as lines to be expressive of serenity. The diagonals had to be abandoned for a system of verticals and horizontals rooted objectively, impersonally, in the surface. Only thus can life and death unfold their exalted language of silence and emptiness.

We have already discussed the verticals in detail, as they occur in the groups of figures at the sides and in the rectangles of the wall. The horizontals are found in the deathbed, and then above and behind it in a threefold series on the wall: first as an interrupted sequence of molded short sides of tall rectangles; above them as a continuous plain horizontal (masked at left and right by the consoles of the gabled doorways); and finally as a sharply profiled continuous horizontal, which runs into the architraves of the gables at both sides. These horizontals have in common the function of separating the representational and the abstract elements of the earthly region from the celestial absolute. At the same time the differences in molding among the three horizontals create differences in the degree of reality. The lowest degree is found in the middle horizontal, so that the initial emphasis reaches a maximum by passing through a stage of nonbeing. The differentiation according to degree of reality is handled with the greatest assurance and subtlety in the later work. The lesser degree of physical reality is often the greater degree of emotional reality; when both disappear, a spiritual reality still remains. The quantitative differences have become qualitative ones, and the latter in turn a system of modes of existence, a graduated whole which, with all its differences and tensions, encompasses the high-medieval concept of being. In this sense the younger Giotto also knew a system of degrees of being, but these lie separately one above the other (people, sky, angels), whereas now they interact without thereby excluding transcendence.

This qualitative difference gives rise to the difference in effect. In treating the figurative motif of the earlier painting the artist sought to enhance all its components to the extent of overwhelming the viewer's capacity for understanding and empathy. And this actually happens. Even though we may be able to comprehend wholly either the force of Saint John's emotional outburst *or* the more inward and contemplative grief of the women, scarcely anyone could dare to feel both of these simultaneously, with equal intensity, in the full tension of their contrast. The motif of the interfigurative void in the later work is not exposed to the competition of the human figures or their gestures; the viewer is directly confronted with a task which by its very nature is infinitely beyond human strength. This time the viewer does not measure himself and what he sees against the artist, but measures the artist and himself against the absolute. In the interfigurative motif of the void the absolute becomes visible; in the figurative motif what becomes visible is only a superior finiteness (to which religion alone, and not art, ascribes the reality of an infinite substance). Thus we arrive at the seemingly paradoxical result that the lamentation for Christ, though it sets the angels in heaven in motion, is an occurrence confined to his disciples, whereas the death of Saint Francis is an event of universal human significance. Giotto had learned in the interval how to express in artistic terms the dimension of the absolute which is implied in the Christian religion.

To these differences of motif corresponds a new configuration of the work. The painting in Padua seems the result of the artist's suprapersonal will in pursuit of necessity, whereas the later painting seems to have grown out of itself, so that it not merely opposes man's immanent will to his transcendent being but unites them. So close and internal a synthesis of opposites, however, is possible only thanks to their underlying unity. Between the earlier and the later work the artist's world view has changed, and his method of portraying it as well. Whereas in the former the spheres of reality as defined by religion are shown separate, in extreme opposition to each other and hence merely juxtaposed in an external way, in the later work they are developed step by step out of their all-encompassing unity, so that even the greatest contrasts are internally related at the same time that they are set off more clearly. In the painting of 1304 Giotto proceeded analytically and compositionally, merely assembling static and dynamic elements; after 1317 he proceeded constitutively and synthetically, bringing pictorial statics and balance into methodological integration. In the former case the artist envisaged method as something imposed upon objects in order to construct a painting; in the latter as something that helps the objects to realize their own meaning, to become a whole. This wholeness was intended in the earlier painting; when it was realized in the later one, however, richness was not sacrificed nor was the tension of opposites weakened. Rather, both had grown greater in their new relation to underlying unity. These differences in method will be clarified by analysis of the means of representation and of the formal aspects of the motif as realized in terms of surface, volume, and space.[3]

In the earlier painting we can very well distinguish the material characteristics of the objects represented—hair, flesh, cloth, linen. But the painting is characterized by an over-all, even abstract materiality, in relation to which the specific sensory properties play only a subordinate role; but this over-all material character is of the utmost physical reality, as is that of the bodies whose surfaces it represents. This is no longer the materiality of medieval realism, according to which the universal possessed a more primordial being than the particular. Nor is it the materiality of medieval nominalism, for which the universal was only a name and the particular had more concrete, immediate reality. Rather, materiality is based upon reasoned comparisons between phenomena. By successive acts of abstraction the quiddity has become the "concept"—and the concept is identified with the thing itself. That is why there is little difference between a garment drawn tightly over a body and a garment hanging loosely on it; that is why Giotto's materials are so often treated with the same tautness and the same nonporous denseness. The fact that none of the bodies has a transcending radiance and that there is no concrete atmosphere to the picture as a whole which could show an emotional unity in terms of space corresponds to this creative act, isolating each separate thing in order to deprive its appearance of contingency and sensuality.

Any artistic treatment of the surface implies not only a specific attitude toward the material aspects of objects but also, and at the same time, the material realization of the emotional and spiritual meanings they suggest. We may refer here to the earlier painting's distinction between active and contemplative displays of emotion and to the ways

3. [The author died before the cleaning of the Florence frescoes was begun in 1957. The recovery of original color and elimination of spurious color (result of the repainting of 1853) has little effect on his analysis, but his account of line, ornament, frame, and style may require revision (see Pls. XIII*a* and XVI*a*). See the general accounts by Eve Borsook and Alfred Frankfurter in *Portfolio and Art News Annual* (New York, 1961) and two works by Ugo Procacci: *La Tecnica degli antichi affreschi e il loro distacco e restauro* (Florence, 1958), and *Sinopie e affreschi* (Milan, 1961); also Millard Meiss and L. Tintori, *The Painting of the Life of St. Francis in Assisi, with Notes on the Arena Chapel* (New York, 1962).]

these are varied. Facial expression and gesture serve to render both, but though representing no doubt permanent characteristics of the whole body and not simply passing moods, they do not derive from a common atmosphere of which they would be the concrete expressions. There is a good deal of emotion expressed in the earlier painting, but this is not reflected in animation of the surface, which would at best reflect a conscious tension in the artist.

Much the same observations might tentatively be made about the paint. It does not possess its own material character, but is raised to the level of a universal which serves at the same time to dematerialize it and yet to enhance its expressiveness. Material properties, spiritual expression, and paint combine to render and concretize the universal.

The later work shows—very differently from the earlier—a common mood prevailing over the entire painting. It is appropriate to the subject matter represented, for the use of space is uniformly coherent, although varied in terms of objects, emotions, and materials. The over-all materiality has brought out an immanent-mathematical character around which—as center—revolve a more immaterial (more spiritual) and a more concrete (more material) sphere. In this atmosphere everything vibrates, the loftiness of solemn devotion, the intimacy of silent grief; the almost matter-of-course event of the miracle, just as much as the subtle differences in the material properties of the robes and the fur: the substance and expressiveness of the material have been dematerialized as well as made objective. Note how the monks' habits, their bodies, and their expressions have become one—how, for instance, the quivering line of the garment worn by the brother kneeling at the center suggests the aged body beneath it, palsied with childlike devotion. Here material texture and emotional expression are both blended and contrasted to form a whole. The same degree of unity is achieved, in the group bearing the banner, to express an entirely different mood: stiff, light-colored, cold-textured materials; erect youthful stance; and impersonal liturgical devotion.

In summing up we might say that the various material characters have become more individual and concrete but at the same time more immaterial and spiritual. The range of contrasts is broader but at the same time they are brought together more intimately, on the basis of a definite order. The spiritual aspect predominates, now no longer reflecting the artist's conscious tension only but the controlled emotion of the persons represented; it is embodied first in objects, then in paint. As a result we have a continual transformation of the spiritual into the material at every point, whereas in the picture as a whole the method takes us from the physical to the immaterial-absolute via the mathematical-abstract. Because of this contrast between the whole and its parts, the material characters vary from one compositional segment to another. This is what produces so richly unified a surface in contrast to the comparative monotony of the painting in Padua.

Corresponding to this is the development in the means of representation, in particular of line (see Plate XIII*b*). The unbroken lines in the earlier painting (e.g., in the border of the cloak worn by the figure at the extreme right or in the folds of the white stole worn by the next figure) flow in one direction only and, for all their precision, are somewhat soft. In the later painting the curving line which defines the nearest bearer of the banner is taut as a straight line, nearly vertical where it slopes and slightly wavy in the folds of the sleeve. The lines contain their opposites in themselves, and as a result of this inner conflict they come to life. We may look in vain for anything like this inner tension in the earlier painting. There, line serves only to define and articulate; it seems arbitrary, extraneous, whereas in the later painting it has acquired an independent existence, an inner dynamism. That is why lines in the later picture appear in varying thickness to indicate different degrees of tension between the oppositions that constitute them. At the highest pitch of their geometrical energy they display a musical character utterly alien to the former use of line, which had no oscillation between nuances and could not express intermediate degrees between being and nonbeing.

Furthermore, while line in the earlier work had moved but one way, in the later work it moves in both directions of a dimension. Take the simplest example, the one offered by an inanimate object: the doorpost at the right. It moves upward in accordance with our architectural expectation, but at the same time we feel a gradual diminution in the force of the ascent, which reaches a weak point and almost stops before the architrave intervenes. From this point on, where the console and the projecting roof are located, there are two things to be noted: the wall continues to rise while optically becoming narrower, but at the same time the ascending line of the doorway makes a curve, forcing the eye to descend. The human figures display this same sequential up-and-down movement, which is also an interplay. This is clear in the foremost figure of each group of three standing figures at far left and right: the viewer whose eye follows one edge of the robe upward will be obliged to see the other edge as a descent. The actual direction his eye follows will depend largely on whether it has proceeded from a side inward, from the middle outward, or from side to side: all these directions of movement are possible and almost equivalent. Furthermore, the up movement is not only related to the down movement, but both are related to the drooping curve of the sleeve, in contrast to which both seem to be upward.

A third difference, which is connected with the first two (absence of conflict vs. presence of conflict; one-way movement vs. two-way movement), concerns gradations in intensity. In the painting of 1304 each and every one of the lines has either the same intensity throughout or passes without transition from being into nonbeing. It is true that we feel the woman seated at the far left and the man standing at the far right as less intense than the other figures, but the total impression is nonetheless one of uniform strong emphasis. In the later painting we find oppositions such as between the completely relaxed, loose, quivering line in the cloak of the figure kneeling in the middle and the stiff, sharp, almost geometric outline of the banner bearer—a polarity which allows for countless intermediate degrees of intensity. The latter, however, are nothing but degrees of intensity in individual lines distributed among various figures. Such distribution makes possible a diversity of expressive values: the quivering line just mentioned represents the old monk's mental state just as clearly and unambiguously as the sharper line represents the young man's power of concentration and less intense emotional involvement. In the earlier painting, however, the consistently uniform line confines expressive possibilities to typical differences (those between contemplation and action, for example).

Space and line do not become form until modeling has been added to these means of representation. The modeling differs in the two paintings. In the *Lamentation* the back view of the woman seated on the ground is composed of two parts, which together give the impression of a three-dimensional body—a recessive rectangle and a lateral triangle. But because the base of the two geometric forms is the same straight line at the lower edge of the painting and because the apex of the triangle runs into the rectangle, the two are not clearly separated, the less so for the fact that both are parts of a single garment concealing the articulations of the body. The extent to which a uniform three-dimensional volume is intended, rather than a structure of comparatively independent planes, is shown by the ridgelike fold in the rectangle of the back, which divides a lighter from a darker area; these slant in different directions, like gables, yet merge at the shoulder. Volume and depth, i.e., modeling, are achieved by recourse to two opposed methodological principles. One consists in composing several planes around a ridge as a single stereometric figure; the other consists in bisecting a single plane, the parts of which tend in different directions. The two principles are limited by and subjected to the a priori concept of one volume, as well as that of a plane arresting all movement into depth, thus excluding the illusion of a rounded body.

The corresponding figure in the painting of 1317 shows two essential differences. First, the modeling of this smaller volume produces the effect of a rounded body. This is due partly to the fact that the lateral and back planes of the lower part of the body have no common horizontal at the bottom, but are clearly separated in light and dark areas from top to bottom by a dividing ridge. The dividing line now serves as a meeting line[4] for the eye, which simultaneously perceives the two planes as extending in different directions with different widths and depths. In the earlier painting the plane of the back was seen wholly from the right side and the lateral plane from the front, and as a result the ridge provided no meeting line for the eye between them. The baggy volumes of the indi-

4. [For "meeting line" (*Trefflinie*), see Pl. XXV and the Appendix, p. 222.]

vidual figures were differentiated according to their parts in the total composition, without taking the other figures into account. In the later painting, however, a single meeting line serves as modeling principle for several figures. This is why the back of the monk who kneels in the right foreground is shown more nearly in full, i.e., the plane of the back is less recessive than the lateral plane (in contrast to the position of the kneeling monk at his left), and why no one side of the ermine-collared figure is shown independently; in this instance the principle of the dividing line has given way to that of the cylinder. The second main difference is that in the *Lamentation* the volumes of bodies were rendered by a single type of curvature, most often being convex; concavity was used largely to delimit surfaces and to effect transition to the picture plane. In the *Death of Saint Francis* the concave passes into the convex in the two monks kneeling in the right foreground and this undulatory movement is complicated by a twist of the upper part of the body, by certain overlappings (masking of left forearms), and by linear elements (the fold made by the cords at the waist turn up and in). Thus, the viewer's eye is made to move around the figures instead of stopping at the outline. Compare, for instance, the upper edges of the monks' cowls with the woman's headcloth in the earlier painting.[5]

To take another example, let us compare, with reference to differences in modeling, the figures standing second from the right in each painting. In the painting in Padua the figure is a slightly turned plane; the eye does not perceive it as a body in the round. In the painting in Florence the garment is a cylinder which gives an unmistakable impression of volume. This is not to say that the plane in the earlier painting is flat—far from it; it is animated by the white stole with its varied folds of different depths. The stole, however, like the pattern on the chest and the inclination of the head, achieves no more than a modicum of surface animation because the spatial differentiations are not related to a *single* axial plane. In the later painting, such an axial plane traverses the body and performs several functions: it holds together the two differently moving lines of the contour (the left comes closer to the viewer at the bottom, the right closer to him at the top); it accentuates the difference in depth between the two planes on either side of the ridge on the cylinder whose shape is delicately nuanced by the fluted folds of alternating light and dark, which make it both come forward and recede; it pulls the shoulders forward and together, so that despite the three-quarter foreshortening we see a portion of the figure's back as well as a portion of the chest; and it connects the opposing movements of the left forearm and the foreshortened right arm (partly masked by the former). (Compare the corresponding points in the earlier painting.) All this results in a number of lines which lead into a depth no longer visible or stimulate the eye to move around the figure. Whereas in the earlier painting the arms shade off into the background, in the later one the strong contrast between light and shadow suggests relief. The effect is that of a

5. [The author refers to the woman who holds the left wrist of Christ.]

stereometric mass which is concentrated around an axial plane parallel to the picture surface and which suggests space behind it. In this way the human figure, beyond its function of indicating depth, has acquired a certain degree of three-dimensional independence, the reality of a body in the round, which it did not possess in the earlier painting. In the later painting the modeling seems to be a natural, intrinsic attribute of the figure, whereas in the earlier painting we feel that it has been superimposed.

These different methods of figuring three-dimensional form are matched by differences in the figuration of the human body. In the earlier painting volume is all. The articulations of the bodies are not shown; the clothes envelope the figures like tightly filled sacks, the forms and dimensions of which are determined by gravity and the specific spatial and compositional functions of the figure. The over-all tendency is to bring out volume as much as possible and let body and garment volumes coincide. Only in a few cases does the body mass stick out completely or sink in.

In keeping with this tendency to stress volume, the forms of the dead Christ suggest the body of a vigorous man. The position and function of shoulders, thighs, ribs, abdomen, reveal the artist's knowledge of anatomy; some of the clothed figures, too, leave us in no doubt on this score. The apparent failure to show wrists and ankles in the dead body reflects a stylistic intention rather than ignorance of anatomy: for how knowingly does the hand of the woman support the head of Christ! Giotto does not use the joints of the body as a chief means for articulating his masses; thus he covers them whenever they would conflict with the means of differentiation he actually employs—emphasis upon spatial and compositional functions (for instance, where the neck of the dead Christ joins the torso). A specific and richly varied need for expression determines the *amount* of articulation given each volume. This results in frequent contrasts between non-articulated and overarticulated areas, both in individual figures and between several figures; but nowhere does the artist indulge in the ornamental play of drapery for its own sake.

In the earlier painting there are two or three types of volume. The human figures expand in every dimension and volume is set beside volume, either in the same plane or alternating in depth somewhat in the manner of brick bonding, i.e., the figures shown behind other figures are located in spaces between the latter. Even where they are drawn with different degrees of articulation the volumes are approximately equal. But in the upper part of the picture the volumes are relatively small and foreshortened, and for all their "bond" arrangement, each figure stands alone against the background. The angels do not constitute masses extended evenly to all sides and obscuring the background; rather, they are mass-points or lines of flight which break out of the background, thereby underscoring its importance. Giotto obviously had it in mind to represent the angelic mode of existence, so different from the human one, and thus to create two realms—an earthly one below and a heavenly one above. There is a gulf between them in which no volumes appear.

In general the clothed bodies seem to be similar in character to the naked body of Christ. The lower limbs are comparatively thin (the lower arms are also quite slender), while the torsos are more sturdy, the shoulders sloping. The figures average between eight and nine heads in height and possess both flexibility and physical control. Their gestures are uninhibited, without excessive self-restraint, "natural" rather than "graceful." The foreheads are for the most part low and the chins strong; the eyes are elongated and slitted, almost suggesting blindness or narrow, piercing vision. The noses are prominent, with a slight indentation below the forehead. The circle of Jesus' intimates would seem to have been made up of strong and healthy people of urban culture but peasant origins.

These healthy bodies are inhabited by healthy souls; there is nothing here to suggest overindividualized, one-sided, hysterical brilliance or sentimentality. Rather, the souls are generalized into an abstract concept, a typified psyche. The tension between receiving and giving, vegetative and intellectual, are concentrated in the emotional expressions to produce a kind of least common denominator of which the various factors have lost their specificity. Such a soul is not a force shaping the body; rather, it is an obligatory expression of the body. The mass, position, and outline of the latter are its psychic expression, out of which gestures arise naturally as its most concrete manifestations—often quite literally, when hands, arms, profiles are completely isolated, or else gestures are wholly lost in the mass.

In all these respects the later painting presents very great differences. Wherever Giotto still stressed volume he constituted it (instead of merely outlining it), realizing it as a stereometric illusion. Volume is no longer rendered in terms of mere bulk, but as an animated play of energies—pressing down or ascending, centrifugal or centripetal. The volumes now are not just there: they grow and complete themselves before our eyes (in analogy with the previously discussed type of shifting balance). Accordingly, the articulations of volume are not determined on the basis of spatial or compositional functions but are subordinated to the stereometric form, derived from and integrated with it. For this reason, stress on anatomy is less marked: only twice is a neck shown, and wrists are exposed at only five places among the twenty-two figures represented—a fact that cannot of course be accounted for by the monks' robes alone, and certainly not by any lack of knowledge of anatomy in Giotto.

Most striking is the new distinction between degrees or types of reality in the figures: they correspond to relative distance from the body of Saint Francis. The latter is smaller than Christ's, its volume diminishing rather than increasing; from the tight-fitting garment, however, emanates a strong soulful transparence. When we compare the kneeling monks with the women of the earlier painting, we find that the monks' habits fall loosely over their bodies, yet do not conceal their agitation. Even without knowing anything about the rules of the Franciscan order we feel that these men have been formed by their vows of poverty and mystical love—and Saint Francis most of all. Never has genuine Franciscanism been portrayed more simply or more exhaustively than here. We cannot doubt the devotion of these authentic "poor" who have renounced all possessions in order to achieve an *imitatio Francisci*, as he himself had undertaken an *imitatio Christi*. In contrast with the kneeling monks, the groups at the two sides are treated in full volumes; they thus set off the more personal and mystical devotion of the former with the impersonality of cultic devotion, cult being the possession of the holy made visible. Only thus can we interpret the exalted solemnity of the groups at each side and not as a contradiction between mystical inwardness and ritual outwardness. Liturgical observances are as indispensable as asceticism and mysticism to Catholic Christianity, and Giotto has brought them together here as in a kind of Thomist *Summa*. What is figured here is not a single scene in the Passion of Christ (as in the *Lamentation*), but the spirit of the Christian religion itself.

Accordingly, the type of human relationships portrayed in the later painting is also different. The members of the group around the body are as isolated from one another as they were in the *Lamentation*. The monk who kisses the saint's hand in front of the bier is as unrelated to the monk who kisses his foot as he is to the monk kissing the other hand, from whom he is separated by the body of the saint. The one who examines the stigmata is completely apart from his neighbor (who kisses the saint's hand), etc. Saint Francis is no more affected by the brothers than is Christ by the love of the women. This isolation of the figures from each other is formally brought out by the comparative looseness with which the oval composition relates them. It serves as no more than a principle of grouping, to set off the curve formed by the shroud and the upper edge of the saint's body. The figures make a loose ellipse around the inner oval which—like Christ's body in the earlier painting—serves as mediator, the sole connecting link among the figures around it.

No such isolation, however, characterizes the figures in the groups at the sides. The two rows of three figures closest to the bier are each a *single* mass, and by reason of the composition both groups are more closely related to each other than to the monks right behind them, from whom they are separated optically by very slight means (variations on the hiatus). Thus the liturgical element is contrasted as a communal body with the more individualistic, mystical devotion embodied in the Franciscan order, and again it would be wrong to see only one kind of social relationship. The two kinds of human community, as we have said, are indispensable to the Catholic Church, and their connection is not external but internal. It is rendered artistically by the prevailing unity of

XIV   GIOTTO. *Lamentation over the Body of Christ* (with superimposed grid)

XV   GIOTTO. *Lamentation over the Body of Christ.* View with decorative enframement

XVI GIOTTO. *The Death of Saint Francis* (after cleaning of 1957). View with decorative enframement
(destroyed portion supplied)

XVII   GIOTTO. Wall in Arena Chapel, Padua

mood in the painting, which transcends all such contrasts and is itself rooted in the empty sky encompassing all.

This unity of mood, so different from the emotional uniformity of the earlier painting, is broken down into a torpid, even heavy, and a more conscious part. Examine one of these figures from toe to top. Each bit of the garment, lower and upper, knows its place in the ascending scale of conscious spirituality. In the standing figures at each side the arms mark a boundary between unreflective, unfree existence and spiritual freedom; in the kneeling monks the cords about their waists serve the same function. Usually the transition from one to the other is abrupt; that it is expressed here by curved lines bespeaks a Catholic emphasis upon mediation: the conflict is resolved not in terms of the forces opposed but by the intervention of divine grace. Aesthetically this gives the painting its epic character (as distinct from its dramatic action), even where, as in the earlier painting, external motion expresses internal emotion.

A still greater difference between the two paintings derives from a change in Giotto's conception of the relationship between body and soul. In the later work each human figure is as though possessed of his own core of immobility, around which his soul revolves, permeating his body and giving life to his robes. What we have here are not animated bodies, but embodied souls: the immortal soul has given form to the body—not in terms of abstract corporeality but individualized by its age and its other concrete features. While the immaterial has been given priority, the human figures have acquired a new freedom or at least a higher degree of freedom. There is nothing arbitrary about their actions in either work: no blind fate has assigned them their places; they are where they are in conscious consent to their fates. But in the later painting this surrender to fate is inward, profound, and impersonal, whereas in the earlier painting the figures are more personally affected and their actions appear more strident, without being more intense thereby. It is this greater detachment from the self that assures the more rigorous, more conscious *imitatio* of their present mediator. Moreover, there is another order in the complexity of the human being: immortality, freedom, fate take precedence as religious functions of the Church and Order; to them are subordinated the psychic expressions, now both more generalized and more individualized than in the earlier painting, where they had artistic priority. The human body *in abstracto*, endowed with psychic expression, has given way to a spiritualized being which is endowed by the painter with an individual body and an individual soul.

Since the treatment of bodies is closely related to the treatment of space, the new method of modeling necessarily involves a new figuration of the pictorial space and, of course, a different relationship between bodies and space. There is a stronger differentiation between, as well as closer integration among, the three dimensions and the two directions of movement each can express. The later painting shows clearly a succession of planes parallel to the picture surface, varying in their degrees of concreteness. They are connected by oblique planes as well as by complementary curves, but the primary connection is provided by a uniform (physical and spiritual) atmosphere which prevents the bodies from impinging upon each other. They are each separately and all together embedded in a superior unity. Thus the eye finds its first resting point in an imaginary plane connected with the quoining motif of the frame; next it moves onto a second plane, tangential to the ridge of the robe of the nearest banner bearer and to the feet and hems of the kneeling monks; next the nearest monk at the left establishes a plane, then the shroud, then the monk who stands in front of the fourth wall panel, then the wall itself and, finally, the sky. These planes, variously distant from each other, are concentrated around an imaginary axis of depth (which exerts a compelling force along both directions of depth and dominates the entire painting). It passes vertically through the body of the saint and through the middle monk in each row of three at the sides. In this way a diversity of spatial tensions becomes possible in a comparatively shallow pictorial space: everything in front pushes backward and, conversely, the back wall presses strongly forward. Though the space is shallow, the effect is not one of crowding because the varying distances between the planes and the variety of the ways they are related let in air over the entire pictorial space.

In the earlier painting there is practically no articulation of planes. To be sure, at the bottom an ideal plane parallel to the picture surface is implied by the foreground figures; but it is not clear, in the available state of the work, whether there was a plane that delimited space in the back. Whatever other planes parallel to the picture surface might be assumed (for instance, the one supplied by the bowed woman who holds Christ's hand) do not assert themselves against the space-opening force of the slanted ridge, which we have already described in detail, and the approximately half-circular curve that opens out between the groups at left and right via the figure of Saint John. Instead of a succession of planes parallel to the picture surface we have distinct layers of space consisting of stereometric bodies; and each of these bodies is modeled not around an axial plane but against a plane behind it, whose parts are turned into depth at constantly varying angles. These various movements into depth are both stressed and checked by interruptions and countermovements. Thus the principle of parallel planes is applied, as well as the opposite principle of counterstructural movements. In the course of his life Giotto came to give precedence to the former principle, no doubt under the influence of classical Greek sculpture, thanks to which Italy more than once served as teacher to the rest of Europe (cf. Rembrandt)—the latter principle being co-ordinated with and subordinated to the first. Not only this hierarchical order characterizes Giotto's development, but, even more, mounting stress on immanent laws and (connected with it) on objectivity. Everywhere—not only in the figuring of pictorial space—we feel the victory of the suprapersonal.

Space is similarly represented in the two paintings in that each contains a foreground extending into depth and a flat, extensionless background going into infinity, while the middle ground performs the function of a boundary of little or no depth. Within this purely formal similarity the treatment of space differs concretely in the two works: on the one hand we find an elementary, natural space, essentially alien and hostile to man; on the other, a man-created communal space. In the earlier painting the natural space lacks whatever might make it structural in visual terms—air to breathe and definite boundaries. The artist was primarily interested in opposing the weight and roughness of the earthly sphere to the winged animation of the heavenly sphere. In the later painting space is concretely supplied by air and mood alike; it has been given architectonic existence; the ground and the horizon line are both clearly visible; the symmetry of the sides is further reinforced by the paneling of the wall. The reality of the space is relativized by being set off against a nonspatial reality (analogous to eternity), just as time is made relative in relation to timelessness. All three of these factors are needed to complete the pictorial space, which is anything but a mere imitation of an existing space; together they constitute a new synthesis of Greek and Christian elements. Thus, out of the contemporary tradition which contained so many contradictions, a really new work was created, one that Masaccio and other Renaissance artists were quick to recognize as their most immediate antecedent.

The modern observer, accustomed as he is to small easel paintings, might well suppose our analysis of the painting to be ended, since the frame of the picture must appear to him an irrelevant decorative addition which merely serves to set off the work of art from its surroundings. This customary view is untenable both historically and aesthetically. The great painters and draftsmen of the Paleolithic Age never supplied frames for their works, yet this was not because they were incapable of creating works of art but because their daily life was completely dominated by the opposition between the infinity of space and the finitude of bodies. Their works of art had so immediate and communal a function, moreover, that it would have been inconceivable to have put frames around them and to endow them with a separate aesthetic reality. The artists of the twelfth and thirteenth centuries who produced the great stained-glass windows, and the baroque painters who decorated the altars and ceilings of churches, treated the frame as very nearly a work of art in its own right, made up of many different materials. This was not an expression of playfulness without any deeper meaning, but of a profound metaphysical principle of the Christian religion: God, the Creator of man, infinitely transcends the works and creations of man.

The frames that Giotto painted around his pictures did not serve merely to set off a given painting from others on the same wall. The very fact that the frames painted around the two works under discussion are so different in their forms and in relation to the works so framed obliges us to look for some deeper explanation, although—or precisely because—the two frames have one feature in common, namely, that neither involves representational elements: both are purely ornamental.

The frame around the *Lamentation* of 1304 consists of three painted bands (Plate XV). While there is no attempt to give relief, the spatial function of the frame is expressed by different degrees of light. The innermost band delimits the painting; the outermost separates it from the other paintings on the wall; the middle one, which contains no ornament, seems to serve only to set off the two others and measure their distance. The innermost border is articulated by repeated ornaments. Each consists of nine dots enclosed in a pointed form with slanted corners and is separated from its neighbors by up-ended squares. There are nine squares and eight pointed forms on every side of the frame—a numerical equality the more striking because the painting is not square: the width somewhat exceeds the height.

When we draw horizontal and vertical lines to connect the squares, the resulting grid (Plate XIV) throws light on the arrangement of the figures. The lowest of the horizontal lines comes just above the knee of the woman seated at the left and slightly below the knee of the woman seated at the right, and passes through the shaded area on Christ's body above the loincloth. It connects the left side of the picture with the right in *contrapposto* and supplies essential accents.

The next higher horizontal line of the grid cuts between the heads and the bodies of the seated figures and of the dead Christ. The third horizontal falls between the bowed women and the standing figures; it passes through the waist of the woman standing at the left and the forearm of the man standing second from the right; the halo of one of the bowed women extends above it, while the other falls below it. The eyes of the standing figures are on a line with the fourth horizontal except where heads are strongly bent forward; the head at the left falls a little below it, while that of Saint John extends a little above it. These horizontals clearly serve the function of indicating levels of height and of relating them in *contrapposto* across the width; the process can be followed throughout the painting. But for all the interplay of rigidity and free deviation, the function remains purely ideal.

The vertical lines of the grid fulfill a similar function. The first from the right passes along one leg of the figure standing at the right and causes this figure, together with the tree above it, strongly to close the picture. The second from the right is approximately tangential to one of the wings of the first angel at the right, then passes through one hand of the second man standing and finally through the neck and forearm of the seated woman. The third vertical passes through Saint John's back and, farther down, the ankles of Christ, so that His feet, with Mary Magdalene's hands and head, fall within the same square of the grid. The fourth vertical separates heads from torsos. The fifth severs Christ's hands from His forearms, so that the expressive parts of the bodies, separated from the unexpressive, are brought together in a single square of the grid—a relation further stressed by the angel in the skies which is seen almost frontally. Thus the grid serves as more than a rigid regulative scheme; it performs specific compositional functions, now assisting in articulation, now in relating expressions and bodies at crucial points. In other words, it serves as a strict metrical system within which it is possible to combine the greatest clarity with the greatest freedom, because it is subordinated to an individual conception even though it seems to originate in an a priori mathematical division of the picture plane.

This division into eight parts is combined with the division into three parts of the ornament in the outermost border. Here, too, the same number of identical motifs occurs in the top and bottom bands as in the sides (though the dimensions are not equal): three narrow rectangles indented at the small sides (except at the corners of the frame), so that up-ended squares fit between them. Both rectangles and squares are subdivided in so intricate a manner that we can only clarify its main principles. A horizontal square is set within each up-ended square and contains in turn several up-ended squares, constructed from the centers of its sides and broken into triangles by an alternation of light and dark. Each rectangle is divided into eight overlapping and complicated groups of figures. Each figure consists of two concentric hexagons; they are separated from each other by a differently-colored dodecagon with re-entrant angles. The intersections of each two hexagons form a rhombus whose corners touch the points of the inner, smaller hexagons. To what extent this geometrical use of ornament may reflect the secrets of the masons' lodges (*Bauhütten*) cannot be gone into here; what is important for the painting is the alternation of light and dark in the frame, which produces a triple system of vibrations and thus endows the frame, for all its rigidity, with great spatial movement.

This is the Gothic form of the function, later fulfilled by the baroque picture frame or ceiling ornamentation. *The frame encloses the painting according to a transcendent principle which at the same time enters into the structure of the painting.* This principle remains valid when, to the two bands divided into eight and three parts respectively, we add the vertical panels on either side of the picture, which, starting at the top of the pedestal, run the full height of the wall (Plate XVII). Their strongest accents serve to articulate the painting into an upper and lower part, thus separating the earth with its people from heaven with its angels.

The number of articulations in each border may be interpreted symbolically as well as aesthetically. For medieval man the number 2 could symbolize either the union of related things or the division of one thing; the number 3 symbolized the Holy Trinity;

and 8 symbolized the New Covenant (since the Resurrection occurred on the eighth day). The number 8 is the third power of 2; 2^3 then stands for the fundamental earthly dualism combined with the Trinity, a Christian equivalent to the Egyptian formula $3^2 + 4^2 = 5^2$. (Another combination of the numbers 2 and 3 $[3^2]$ results in the number 9, also frequently used.) It is quite possible that purely arithmetical considerations obtained: the numbers 2 and 3 are the smaller and larger parts of the golden section in the classic approximation $2:3 = 3:5$, while the numbers 3 and 8 represent the smaller part and the whole in the historically more recent approximation $3:5 = 5:8$. Hence the essential feature in this: the proportion $(2:3 = 3:5)$ suggested by the absolute numbers 2 and 3 is not completed; rather the larger part (3) in this approximation is used as the smaller part of the other approximation $(3:5 = 5:8)$ so that now it is not the whole (8) but the larger part (5) that remains unexpressed. Thus we have one and the same proportion, but not represented by one form; rather it is represented by two forms by way of a leap. The symbolic interpretation is not in contradiction with the aesthetic one, in so far as 2, 3, 8 (or 2^3) express either the union of the earthly dualism with the heavenly Trinity, or (in the formula $2:3 = 3:\ldots 8$) the gap over which this union of earthly with celestial substances must take place, a union which of course excludes any pantheistic-mystical identity. (The numbers 6 and 12 are obtained by multiplying the basic numbers 2 and 3: 2×3 and $2 \times 2 \times 3$.)

Our analysis of the seemingly "extraneous" factor of the frame thus has yielded the following results:

1) The frame as such has a double structure: the first is rigid, material, and mathematical; the second is immaterial (light and shadow) and vibrates. The two factors of mathematics and light—the most universal creation of the human mind and the most immaterial of cosmic matter—are here united as a sphere situated between heaven and earth.

2) The function of the frame is twofold: it endows the painting with an articulation which is simultaneously transcendent and immanent and as such serves as a visual symbol of the Catholic relationship between creatures and their Creator.

3) This representation of the theological relation between finite substance and infinite substance is underscored by the fact that the same divisions are employed for the horizontal and vertical parts, although the former are longer than the latter. At the same time the rectangular format comes close to being a square, the form of absolute repose. This yields a concrete expressive value by setting up tension between uncertainty and certainty, aspiration and fulfillment.

The significance of the frame is confirmed by the fact that the great changes in the later work (after 1317) also affected its frame (Plate XVI). In format it is a horizontal rectangle in the ratio of the golden section, the horizontal standing for the whole, the vertical for the larger part (5 : 8). This means a balance between the static tendency of the square and the dynamic quality of the oblong. By virtue of these proportions the picture surface has acquired greater firmness. This enhancement of the autonomy of the painting, in relation to the powers that condition it by transcending it, accounts for the unequal number of subdivisions, 8 on the horizontal and 5 on the vertical. Thus the proportions of the sides are expressed in the numbers of the subdivisions, now all of equal length—i.e., a unified measure is employed, which makes possible the rational conception of the external composition of the picture.

In form the frame is utterly different. Where before there were three bands, there are now two. The unornamented middle band has been eliminated. In the *Lamentation* the emptiness mediates between a single and a complex ornamentation, separating them and measuring their distance. So does absolute silence measure the labor of the mind between beginning and end, or sleep man's effort between intention and fulfillment. In the early work this void (without ornament) was important, for Giotto was unable to realize voids within the painting, as we have already seen. In the later painting voids appear as a motif between the figures, and have to be eliminated from the frame to avoid unnecessary competition. The positive meaning of replacing a triple division by a double one lies in the substitution of the contrast between unity and plurality for the idea of the Trinity. The relation between unity and plurality appears in both bands of the frame of the *Death of Saint Francis*. The inner band now consists of a group of moldings of which the innermost shows a design of quoins in alternating colors, and the outermost, one of bead and reel. It is true that we may pick out the individual elements within each pattern, but they are so narrow that the effect is one of an infinite number of parts, though they can be counted: a rational basis in interaction with an irrational appearance, the latter being born of the former by the perpetual repetition of the same unit. In addition, we must note that the quoining is not uniform all the way across at the top and bottom, but comes to a center, in each case, where the two directions of movement meet and repel each other (> <). Not only does the row acquire a center, it acquires a centrifugal movement about an axis of symmetry. Generally speaking, the dimension of width has been broken up into a leftward and a rightward movement, and the interplay of the two emphasizes the autonomy of the dimension. With this element of spatial figuration the earthly sphere is given greater importance; in the earlier painting the theological content was decisive. This new point of view is still very limited: the opposed directions of movement do not appear in the quoining of the shorter vertical borders; and the bead and reel molding does not even provide a formal pretext. This, too, is significant for the quoin pattern was no doubt taken over from North Italian brickwork, whereas the bead and reel molding was of classical origin. Thus the juxtaposition of Christian with Greek motifs has the same significance as the combination of real numerableness with the impression of infinity, the combination of continuous sequence with the presence of a center, the combination of an unbroken dimension with one broken up into opposing movements.

The greater influence of Greek rationalism on Christian theology also entailed a change in the form of the outer band. This fact is all the more noteworthy because the new form is merely a variation of the old one: the same indented narrow rectangles occur again now separated by simple hexagons instead of by the complicated system of squares. Once again, each rectangle is subdivided and each two adjacent subdivisions overlap. But now the tripartite combination of two hexagons with one dodecagon between them has been replaced with a sequence (also tripartite) of a square inscribed within a square—the corners of the inner halve the sides of the outer—and a sixteen-cornered figure around them (thus $4^2 = 16$). The overlapping does not result in a rhombus ($\Diamond$) but takes on the form $\Join$ at the top and the bottom of the frame and the variant ($\bowtie$) at the vertical sides. These figures go back to the Neolithic Age, and even to the Paleolithic Age, as magical signs of rebirth. To Giotto they may simply have been a transformation of the cross-stitch pattern into a limited unit. He has not abandoned the play of light and dark or, more accurately, the play of color; spatial differentiation within the outer band is achieved in painter's fashion, while the inner band gives an illusion of relief.

If we were to examine the later painting without reference to the earlier, we would not be at all inclined to begin at the frame and its metric division by hexagons. The effect of the picture's own internal articulation—the six vertical bands separating the five panels on the wall—is very strong. The articulation of the frame is in a complicated relation with that of the picture. Only the first vertical from the left approximately coincides with the middle axis of the hexagon (in imaginary extension); the further verticals no longer meet the hexagons, and as we move to the right the intervals become increasingly greater. Because of this discrepancy, the middle axis of the middle hexagon divides the middle panel of the wall into two unequal parts; from there on the corresponding intervals between the axes of the hexagons and the articulation of the wall become smaller (rather than greater as before), until the middle axis of the hexagon at the extreme right passes through the far edge of the open doorway. Thus we now have two articulations, the outer and the inner one—two voices, as it were—connected only near the two corners, and elsewhere either diverging or converging, since the number of main articulations is different in frame and picture. This obviously makes it easier to illustrate the dualism which obtains within the unity of aesthetic feeling and pictorial form.

The inner articulation gains in significance, too, because its relation to the figures is easily grasped while, to the contrary, its connection with the axes of the hexagons is less directly perceived. But if we were to extend a grid from these axes, we would see their significance. Without going into such details as before, it is possible to summarize their function: The vertical lines of the grid emphasize—with variations and with the stress on symmetry—the struggle between the static and the dynamic, between repose and movement, both for the individual figures and for the composition as a whole. As for the horizontal lines of the grid, they bring the two systems of articulation together—the frame and the painting. Each system serves the same purpose, in a different way, by introducing a strongly emphasized stability into the dynamism. The latter consequently develops from an expansive, explosive movement into a deep, more controlled one that vibrates between limited areas.

In Giotto's later painting the tension between the transcendent geometry of the frame and the autonomous geometric life of the painting has become greater. The two are more independent but the relation between them is more complicated; of unequal value, they nonetheless do not fall apart. We must not overlook one feature the later painting has in common with the earlier one: the simultaneous connection and separation between inner and outer, between transcendence and immanence, which brings to mind the conceptual world of Thomism. But this makes the tendency toward autonomy of the geometric life in the plane of the painting all the more significant. Here we shall confine ourselves to pointing out only the most striking difference: in the earlier painting all the verticals and horizontals—i.e., the structural lines of the surface—deflect into curves, and the diagonal plays the leading role; the surface itself has no constitutive significance. In the later painting the verticals and horizontals are strongly accentuated, all the curves have the effect of being in tension with them, diagonals are much less prominent, and the pictorial space is articulated by a succession of parallel planes, a feature that is another link with Greek art, especially with reliefs.

It would be presumptuous to attempt to draw general conclusions about the relation between Giotto's biological and artistic development from this analysis of only two works. The diversity of world views and world syntheses is too great and our knowledge of them too modest to make this possible. Giotto's progress in enlarging and deepening his subject matter, in acquiring objectivity—in other words, the growing dematerialization of his materials and the growing concreteness of his forms, ever greater unity in ever greater diversity—these main features of his development are so many criteria for evaluating works of art. What we have here is the frequent (but far from regularly occurring) case of biological and artistic development marching hand in hand. But how a work of art is to be evaluated is a question that must be answered independently of biological, psychological, and historical considerations. The creation of supratemporal values takes place at another level, an epistemological and logical level. The two levels may coincide (as in Giotto's case), but not necessarily, and they will rarely do so if the artist's method is directed toward their separation rather than toward the unification of form and meaning.

IV. THE LITERARY MODEL AND THE WORK OF ART

Rembrandt: *Joseph Interprets Pharaoh's Dreams*

(PLATE XVIII)

Amor Dei intellectualis.

SPINOZA, *Ethics*, V

XVIII Rembrandt. *Joseph Interprets Pharaoh's Dreams*. ca. 1655. Drawing in pen and bister wash, 7 × 10 in.

And it came to pass at the end of two full years, that Pharaoh dreamed: and, behold, he stood by the river. And, behold, there came up out of the river seven well favoured kine and fatfleshed; and they fed in a meadow. And, behold, seven other kine came up after them out of the river, ill favoured and leanfleshed; and stood by the other kine upon the brink of the river. And the ill favoured and leanfleshed kine did eat up the seven well favoured and fat kine. So Pharaoh awoke.

And he slept and dreamed the second time: and, behold, seven ears of corn came up upon one stalk, rank and good. And, behold, seven thin ears and blasted with the east wind sprung up after them. And the seven thin ears devoured the seven rank and full ears. And Pharaoh awoke, and, behold, it was a dream.

And it came to pass in the morning that his spirit was troubled; and he sent and called for all the magicians of Egypt, and all the wise men thereof: and Pharaoh told them his dream; but there was none that could interpret them unto Pharaoh.

Then spake the chief butler unto Pharaoh, saying, I do remember my faults this day: Pharaoh was wroth with his servants, and put me in ward in the captain of the guard's house, both me and the chief baker: And we dreamed a dream in one night, I and he; we dreamed each man according to the interpretation of his dream. And there was there with us a young man, an Hebrew, servant to the captain of the guard; and we told him, and he interpreted to us our dreams; to each man according to his dream did he interpret. And it came to pass, as he interpreted to us, so it was; me he restored unto mine office, and him he hanged.

Then Pharaoh sent and called Joseph, and they brought him hastily out of the dungeon: and he shaved himself, and changed his raiment, and came in unto Pharaoh. And Pharaoh said unto Joseph, I have dreamed a dream, and there is none that can interpret it: and I have heard say of thee, that thou canst understand a dream to interpret it. And Joseph answered Pharaoh, saying, It is not in me: God shall give Pharaoh an answer of peace.

And Pharaoh said unto Joseph, In my dream, behold, I stood upon the bank of the river: And, behold, there came up out of the river seven kine, fatfleshed and well favoured; and they fed in a meadow: And, behold, seven other kine came up after them, poor and very ill favoured and leanfleshed, such as I never saw in all the land of Egypt for badness: And the lean and the ill favoured kine did eat up the first seven fat kine: And when they had eaten them up, it could not be known that they had eaten them; but they were still ill favoured, as at the beginning. So I awoke. And I saw in my dream, and, behold, seven ears came up in one stalk, full and good: And, behold, seven ears, withered, thin, and blasted with the east wind, sprung up after them: And the thin ears devoured the seven good ears: and I told this unto the magicians; but there was none that could declare it to me.

And Joseph said unto Pharaoh, The dream of Pharaoh is one: God hath shewed Pharaoh what he is about to do. The seven good kine are seven years; and the seven good ears are seven years; the dream is one. And the seven thin and ill favoured kine that came up after them are seven years; and the seven empty ears blasted with the east wind shall be seven years of famine. This is the thing which I have spoken unto Pharaoh: What God is about to do he sheweth unto Pharaoh. Behold, there come seven years of great plenty throughout all the land of Egypt: And there shall arise after them seven years of famine; and all the plenty shall be forgotten in the land of Egypt; and the famine shall consume the land; And the plenty shall not be known in the land by reason of that famine following; for it shall be very grievous. And for that the dream was doubled unto Pharaoh twice; it is because the thing is established by God, and God will shortly bring it to pass.

Now therefore let Pharaoh look out a man discreet and wise, and set him over the land of Egypt. Let Pharaoh do this, and let him appoint officers over the land, and take up the fifth part of the land of Egypt in the seven plenteous years. And let them gather all the food of those good years that come, and lay up corn under the hand of Pharaoh, and let them keep food in the cities. And that food shall be for store to the land against the seven years of famine, which shall be in the land of Egypt; that the land perish not through the famine.

And the thing was good in the eyes of Pharaoh, and in the eyes of all his servants. And Pharaoh said unto his servants, Can we find such a one as this is, a man in whom the Spirit of God is? And Pharaoh said unto Joseph, Forasmuch as God hath shewed thee all this, there is none so discreet and wise as thou art: Thou shalt be over my house, and according unto thy word shall all my people be ruled: only in the throne will I be greater than thou.

Genesis 41:1–40

The main possibilities for pictorial representation offered by the preceding text are three: Pharaoh's dream, Joseph's interpretation of it, and the interpreter's appointment to high office. To understand Rembrandt's choice we must first study the Biblical text in some detail.

"And it came to pass . . . that Pharaoh dreamed." The text contains no description of the act of dreaming, of the dreamer's behavior, the position he was lying in, what he looked like, etc. We are, however, told the content of his dream: the things he saw, their distinctive features, and their effects on each other. After the dreamer has awakened and gone back to sleep, he dreams a second dream, involving other things in similar relations. Thus we are given the description of a specific state of existence (a dream involving particular objects of various properties and clearly specified relationships); after it is interrupted we are given the account of a second, similar state, in the course of which other things, with the same various properties and relationships, appear. One state, though interrupted, is broken down into a time sequence of things, properties, and relationships, some of which remain constant and some of which change. This succession of words constitutes, on the one hand, a formally complete word picture in which the mind finds a unified meaning concentrated as if at a single point; on the other hand, the events narrated demand further events to follow in time.

To begin with, the dream affects Pharaoh: the emotional tension it creates in him inspires certain actions on his part. These actions fail in their purpose (the magicians are unable to interpret the dream); and this leads to another pause in the action and the words create a corresponding state of mind. Now the dream begins to bear upon Pharaoh's entourage. Joseph's name is brought up in a specific connection. Another narrative is interwoven with the first, one referring to past events but starting a new chain of events. It plays the part of the device in classical drama that delays the denouement and heightens the tension. It makes Joseph briefly independent, and serves as a bridge linking the past to the future.

The appearance of Joseph marks a new point in time and a new state of existence. The style of the narrative changes. Up until now the anonymous chronicler has merely *narrated* the events, addressing no one in particular; but now Pharaoh himself *speaks*.

Though he refers to the past, he addresses Joseph personally. This change invests the same words with new resonance; a tension is aroused that was not present before. At the formal level the narrative moves forward, although there is no new content for the time being; but the same meaning takes on greater reality and we are made more aware. Moreover, it is noteworthy that Joseph, the other important character to be introduced, is not described in terms of personal appearance, stature, demeanor, clothing, etc., but solely in terms of his relationship to God—"It is not in me: God shall give Pharaoh an answer . . . "—i.e., by the single feature that makes him significant in this story.

We have been stressing characteristics of the literary art: the narration of an event in terms of objects, their properties, and their relationships, all represented as they occur in time, either as successive events involving persons, things, and motives, or as a recurrence of past events, arousing images in the reader and modifying his level of awareness by changes in the style of the narrative. In pictorial art, however, things and mental states cannot be shown in time sequence, but only in spatial juxtaposition. The body, the attitude, the proportions, the articulations, which are not referred to at all in the literary text, must now be provided as the elements of representation and, as such, as vehicles for conveying the state of mind. Every event in time must be rendered in spatial terms; thus, the artist must make a definite selection from among the events. The one Rembrandt chose to depict[1] was the act of interpreting the dream; and into it he had to concentrate whatever other elements seemed important to him in the rest of the narrative. Although he could not depict the events as they occurred in time, he still could make use of time as a dynamic inner possibility in his shaping and structuring of space.

If it is granted that the artist has to replace time and occurrence with object and space, we might expect Rembrandt to have rendered the objects mentioned in the text. But there are no kine and no ears of corn in his drawing, either fat or lean. In Rembrandt we find only light and shadow—that is, the medium in which the things named by words have their being—not the things themselves in their verbal clarity, despite their sensuous perceptibility. On the other hand, we find that things not mentioned in the text are prominent in the drawing: the throne room, a covered arcade to reach it, a council table, and the throne itself, protected by a guard. This room, where the king holds audience, is a surprising setting for the interpretation of a dream which leads to the most irrational roots of our being. What was Rembrandt's purpose in so transforming the concrete objects mentioned in the Biblical tale into something immaterial, and in introducing quite other objects, no less concrete? How did this serve his aim of rendering the story of the dream and its interpretation?

1. [Not all art historians agree in attributing this drawing to Rembrandt. Valentiner accepts it, Benesch omits it from his corpus of the Rembrandt drawings, and Hofstede de Groot lists it with the remark "not absolutely sure." In the opinion of Professor Jakob Rosenberg, it is a copy of a Rembrandt original of the time and reflects Rembrandt's style of about 1655 (private communication).]

Our first glance at the drawing tells us that Pharaoh has already had his dream and spoken of it: he sits dejected on his splendid throne, listening to Joseph's interpretation. Rembrandt makes no effort to depict the dream itself or the mental state produced by it (as he did in the early picture *Mene Tekel Upharsin*[2]); he does not show Pharaoh telling his dream nor the content of the interpretation. All he shows is the act of interpreting and the manner in which it is received; what he depicts is not objects or a specific state of mind but an event. This event involves not only Pharaoh and Joseph; the king's councilors are present. In consequence, the purely individual character of dreaming and interpreting dreams becomes suprapersonal; the event has been made social and objective. The space in which this more broadly conceived event takes place is a council room in Pharaoh's palace, to be sure, but it has been further characterized by a use of light and shadow, elements at once atmospheric and cosmic, which enlarge the personal relation between Pharaoh and Joseph to a scale beyond the social—into the realm of nature. The figures are quite small in relation to the room; they are part of it and yet subordinated to it. In this way Rembrandt has managed to introduce the element of fate. The artist has not depicted the contents of the dream or its interpretation literally, but by more indirect means has expressed the forces involved and the characters of the chief actors. By so doing he has retained the whole range of the dream without stating any of its content.

Rembrandt does not, however, confine himself entirely to the episode of dream interpretation. He has characterized Pharaoh as spiritually impotent despite his worldly power. The latter is suggested by the pompous throne, the man next to it, the colonnade, the limitless height of the room; the spiritual impotence is suggested by the king's posture (note how he holds the scepter!), the shadow on the back of the throne, the king's physical debility in contrast with his rich turban and throne, his distance from his councilors, the way he bends toward Joseph to indicate his dependence. In contrast to the Pharaoh, Joseph is characterized as a man of great spiritual strength for all his physical helplessness. His poverty is indicated by his emaciation, his shabby clothes, by the way the others are looking at him; his inner strength can be seen in his animation and in the shadow that descends down to him like a suprapersonal power and makes him capable of interpreting the dream. Thus the episode of interpreting the dream serves Rembrandt as a mere pretext for disclosing a deeper level of meaning: the opposition between worldly power and spiritual power or, more accurately, the opposition between the spiritual poverty of the mighty and the spiritual force of the physically weak. Both elements are implied in the Biblical narrative: Pharaoh, the mighty king, looks for a wise man and cannot find one; Joseph, the imprisoned slave, is in reality God's chosen vessel. In the Bible, too, Pharaoh's dream is only an occasion for bearing witness to the power of the man who is blessed by God.

2. [Also known as *Belshazzar's Feast.*]

Is this duality, each term of which implies the other and is in reverse relation to the opposing pair of terms, Rembrandt's last word? Just as the ideal meaning is more effective than the content of the events, unity is more effective than duality. Even in the Biblical account the most important thing is not the contrast between Pharaoh and Joseph, but the infinite God working through the finite medium: Joseph. We must not assume that Rembrandt meant to render this level of Biblical reality or that any artist could; here we may be confronting one of the boundaries between art and religion. The artist does not show God's intervention, but we feel quite clearly that it was not Pharaoh's power that brought Joseph's prophetic trance and that Joseph's power is not rooted in himself, but in subordination to a higher power as its willing and obedient vessel. This is the deepest level of Rembrandt's theme: the one infinite substance using a finite substance as its instrument against godless matter in need of God.

Let us summarize the results of our analysis so far: one mode of reality, namely, the substantial mode; one opposition, namely, the self-posited conflict between spirit and power; one content (subject, narrative), namely, the dream interpretation with all its social and cosmic implications and its hint of fate. These components—a mode of reality, a conflict, and a content—are brought into systematic unity. They appear progressively more concrete when we start from the mode of reality, and progressively more dematerialized when we start from the narrative; the subject is the realization, and the mode of reality is the foundation, of the work of art. There are other possible types of reality and of conflict, as well as other subject matters and methods; but in each case they form together the ideal content of the picture—in contradiction to the content of the narrative, to the physical subject matter.

Rembrandt treated dreams and the interpretation of dreams at various times. The complex relationship between dream and reality must have held a quite special fascination for him. But only once, in this late drawing, did he succeed in communicating to the viewer, with compelling force, the mood of dream interpretation. Just how did he do this —in so far as it is intellectually controlled?

In this drawing Rembrandt very clearly distinguishes between currents of living energy and heavy masses. The first current of energy is given in terms of light and shadow. A heavy shadow comes down from the top of the drawing and gathers above and behind Joseph; a light rises from the floor and is concentrated above and behind Pharaoh (at the edge of the canopy on the throne). The light and the dark areas are separated by a slanted line that runs across the drawing and on which, as we shall see later, the composition is balanced. In this way a pictorial space is created, light in weight at the bottom and heavy at the top, i.e., a space in contradiction to the law of gravitation. This pictorial space is a kind of miracle in itself, within which we are quite prepared for a miracle to occur. Such a miracle would utilize the spatial motif rather than destroy it.

The second current of energy is defined by the spiritual relationship between the two principal persons. Both are, to begin with, centers of energy. The energy of his surroundings is focused upon Joseph, most clearly in the wedge-shaped dark area above him. The rigid, imposing masses of the throne and the standing man next to it are concentrated upon Pharaoh. Joseph is in an unstable position, as though pushed forward by the columns and the shadow, but he requires no external support because his body is balanced in itself. Pharaoh, who is leaning forward slightly, acquires a static weakness which is projected into the phantom shadow cast on the back of the throne. Thus the two centers of energy relate to each other, attracting each other over a distance. This second current of energy takes the form of an imaginary geometric figure—a fairly flat ellipse pointing obliquely upward; its ends are strongly connected by various horizontals. The major axis of this ellipse is not as long as the drawing is high. Thus it is securely placed within the composition, and this placement is supported and enhanced by moving the group inward and away from the lower edge and by other factors.

The first current of energy prepares the pictorial space for the miracle, while the second prepares us for the miraculous occurrence between these men. The slanted line, which is not clearly stated, is answered lower down by the ellipse. The two reinforce each other.

This elliptical figure, expressive by virtue of its special position in terms both of surface and of pictorial space, is repeated with variations: at the left, in the perspective passageway; at the center, in the group at the table; and at the right it occurs several times in the throne and in the man standing by it. It is important to note that in all these variants the slant is replaced with a vertical or a horizontal, i.e., it coincides with the structural lines of the surface, in the narrower sense. In this way the following important results are achieved:

1) The verticals delimit the ellipse and thus give a character of privacy to everything within it, an expressive device which serves the interpretation of the dream.

2) Thanks to the horizontals, we clearly see the rising movement of the ellipse, and thus the difference in terms of power between Pharaoh and Joseph becomes visible.

3) The horizontals provide a transition from the currents of energy to the heavy masses, from the dynamic to the static. In this way internal boundaries are created. As the currents of energy are made visible, a self-sufficient structure comes into being. In terms of subject matter this is expressed by the fact that the figures at right and left are mere spectators, whereas Pharaoh and Joseph are in a tense relationship.

4) The character of the work thus fundamentally determined, attention is directed to the problem of balance. The vertical axis of the picture divides the ellipse into two unequal parts which are *approximately* in the ratio of the golden section (i.e., the smaller part is to the larger as the larger is to the whole). This separation of Joseph from Pharaoh

is moreover stressed by the fact that Joseph, although he is below the horizontal axis, is less far from it than Pharaoh, who is above it. For all the expressiveness of this distribution, it does not produce balance at the picture surface; rather, balance is produced by the spatial diagonal, which separates light from shadow. This once again stresses the special importance of the spatial motif (which negates the law of gravitation).

The further figurative concretization of the motif will be discussed below. Before that we shall examine the relationship between the ellipse as optical motif for the individual conception and the structural lines of the picture surface. The surface measures 17:25.5 centimeters, i.e., it is a horizontal rectangle, the sides of which approximate the proportion 2 : 3, the division of the golden section. The delicate balance between the static and the dynamic expressed in this proportion was found by Rembrandt to be particularly suitable for effecting transitions between the currents of energy and the heavy masses, for stressing the process of becoming a finished work and, in addition, for maintaining the suspense.

The role of the middle axes has been mentioned. Now we can add that the vertical axis passing through the councilor at the left finds expression in his eyes. One of his eyes seems to look mistrustfully in Joseph's direction while the other takes in Pharaoh; his uncertainty is in marked contrast to the massiveness of his body. The horizontal axis just touches his head covering. The extension of this line (to the right) shows its importance to the arrangement of the figures: it touches a curving line (perhaps a decorative chain) on the Pharaoh's body and falls between the head and body of the man standing in the right corner—which circumstance brings out the shortness of his neck.

Further, the two axes make themselves felt in repeated bisections over the picture. In either dimension there are eight (2^3) divisions, the third and fifth of these coinciding approximately with the divisions by the golden section on each side. This built-in grid codetermines the filled-in areas on the surface and, by the same token, the linear composition. The first division from the left runs through the third ornamental line of the entablature and the highest point of the outer archway. Then it touches the inner edge of the left foot of the man coming in and approximately coincides with the short perpendicular of the parallelogram on the floor, which is of the greatest importance for the structure of the whole by virtue of its position and its similar proportions. This first division separates the objects into unequal areas, the larger of which is at the right; it prepares the over-all shift of the motif to the right. In contrast to the first dividing line the second (vertical) line is not at all emphasized in terms of objects: it lies in the shadow of the column and in the light area at its pedestal, but thereby indirectly underscores the fluctuation between light and shadow and separates Joseph from the outside world. The third vertical, which is also the first division according to the golden section, extremely is important; it is technically emphasized by the black stroke of the pen in the dark area. It runs through the

back of Joseph's head and coincides with a black line on his near arm, whereas his right
knee and the end of the dark area at the lower edge reach just a little beyond it. Joseph is
thus divided into two very unequal parts; the larger part, which is however less important
in terms of expression, is situated at the left, where it sets up a countermovement to the
principal movement of the oval. In addition to so animating the movements in the horizontal dimension, the third vertical isolates the actual vehicle of expression—the narrow
part of the face and hands—from the rest of the body, thus stressing Joseph's groping gesture and at the same time giving it the effect of internal inhibition. As for the fourth
vertical—the vertical axis—of the grid, we have already said that it makes the councilor
seem to be cross-eyed; thereby it concentrates the movement and its countermovement
in the horizontal dimension, and it divides the distance between Joseph and Pharaoh,
which clearly shows all the internal and external oppositions between them, into two unequal parts. This vertical is scarcely realized, so that we have a continual alternation of
grid lines passing through filled-in and empty areas, which introduces a differentiating
accent into the rigid metrical system. The fifth vertical—very nearly the same as the
second division according to the golden section—almost touches the far corner of the
throne canopy and, below, the far corner of the dais; in the middle of the picture it
separates the second councilor from the third. Thereby it moves Pharaoh farther away
from Joseph, accentuating the dynamism of their separation. The sixth vertical of the grid
checks the current of energy; at the top it is more or less identical with the vertical line
that almost touches the edge of Pharaoh's turban, then falls over his lap, leaving his legs
to the left of it, and divides the ruler just as the third vertical divides Joseph—with this
difference, however, that in keeping with his spiritual situation, he turns the inexpressive
lower part of his body toward Joseph, while Joseph turns his expressive hands and face
to the troubled king. It is as though the artist, by thus splitting his principal characters,
wanted to reveal the inner conflict within each and at the same time to suggest that the
relationship between them, for all their intense absorption with each other, is but partial
and momentary. The last vertical of the grid touches the capital of the near column of
the throne on the inside and then runs down along the cloak of the man standing in the
corner. Thus it emphasizes the emptiness of space between these corner pillars of the
composition and Pharaoh—in his isolation and impotence.

Our analysis shows that the rigorous metrical system of the grid performs three main
functions: it animates the space, delaying movement; it connects or separates the figures;
and it splits some of them internally into unequal parts which yet are in fluid balance.
The contradictions implied in these functions are alternately emphasized or left unem-
phasized by the filled-in or empty areas through which the grid lines pass, thus bringing
an element of rhythmic and functional freedom into the metrical scheme.

The reader may now trace for himself the horizontal lines of the grid, noting especially the lines that coincide with divisions according to the golden section (which can be calculated by multiplying the total height by 2/5 or 3/5 or, more accurately, by .618). In this way he will discover a number of interesting facts:

1) Rembrandt repeatedly employs the smaller division of the golden section found in the dimension of *width* to determine the *height* of objects: he uses horizontal measurements for purposes of vertical articulation. See, for instance, the height of the man standing at the right, the passageway at the left, the column at the extreme left (disregarding the pedestal), the throne from the armrest to the lower edge of the canopy. Conversely, the smaller division of the golden section in the vertical is equal to certain important intervals in the horizontal dimension—for instance, the distance between Joseph's fingers and Pharaoh's knees, between the left edge of the drawing and the right edge of the pedestal supporting the nearest column of the passageway, the greatest width of the steps to the throne, etc. Rembrandt often used such equivalences, probably in order to reintegrate the dimensions within the pictorial surface. To assert surface properties against the pull of space was so crucial a problem for the early Rembrandt that he studied the Italian Renaissance masters to solve it. It should also be noted that $3 \times 1/8$ of the height is approximately equal to $2 \times 1/8$ of the width, so that infinitely small differences appear in the measurements. Rembrandt no doubt deliberately made use of such differences to give life and vibration to his articulations; infinitely small differences—in chiaroscuro, for example—are an essential feature of his art.

2) The lower horizontal and left vertical divisions according to the golden section pass through Joseph's head; the upper horizontal division according to the golden section and the sixth vertical grid line intersect in the edge of Pharaoh's turban. The distance between the two points of intersection is equal to the larger part of the golden section in the dimension of height and forms the diagonal of a rectangle whose sides measure 2/8 of the height and 3/8 of the width of the picture—a striking and highly instructive relationship between important points of the ellipse and the dimensions of the picture surface.

3) Obviously the division into eight is not the ultimate unit of measurement. Objects such as the stressed pillar at the left or the canopy over the throne not only suggest a further subdivision into sixteenths, but also show that these smaller units are less strictly measured than the larger divisions and tend to be intermediate between the horizontal and vertical units. A further advantage of this subdivision is that new comparisons become possible. Thus, Joseph's height comes to about 5/16 of the picture height and Pharaoh's to 7/16.

The more systematically we explore the bisections, the greater the freedom we discover as we see how the rigid surface requirements are combined with the more fluid ones of the motif. Only when the artist brings the two into unity does he achieve that freedom within necessity which is the hallmark of great art.

Mathematics—both in its geometrical-figural aspect and its arithmetical-proportional aspect—is a middle term, so to speak, a bridge between the inner image and the outer visual perception. But it provides no more than the scaffolding for such a bridge; the gap is closed only by the sensual actualization of the artistic potentialities of the artist's materials. This drawing is an example of a mixed medium: India ink wash, charcoal (or is it crayon?), and pen.[3]

Besides the brightest and the darkest areas, which are sometimes in adjacent contrast, there are intermediate tones. These can be divided into two groups: those which illuminate a dark area and those which darken a light area. Rembrandt has so organized these that they create an illusion of infinitely many tiny gradations. There are no clear-cut demarcations between them. Light and dark areas are never completely separated. The shadows permit light to shine through them, and the light areas are nearly all touched by a thin film of shadow hinting at potential darkness. He also employs quite subtle contrasts. He sets off light tones against intermediate tones (Joseph), intermediate tones against light tones (man in the passageway), and light tones against light tones (Pharaoh). Rembrandt uses extremely strong shadows to emphasize finitude but, thanks to the different spatial functions of his graduated tones, their hovering, fluid, transitional character is preserved. The two methods—contrast and transition—result in a highly animated tonality that unifies the many aspects of the picture. It is gentle and weightless, being more light than dark in total effect. The extremes of light and dark we find at the edges are seemingly the result—spatially both internal and external—of a polarization of this tonality.

Much the same may be said of the warm-cold scale: extremes punctuated by intermediate degrees, and an over-all effect somewhat closer to coldness than to warmth. This expresses the hostility surrounding Joseph; it also helps to create an effect of dream-like remoteness. Here, too, we find both contrast and transition. For instance, in the V-shaped shadow there are transitions between warm and cold, while there is a contrast between Pharaoh's cold shadow and the cold light on the back of the throne. Similarly, we find cold light set against cold dark in the near column of the passageway. And so on.

The two scales—tonality and warmth—frequently overlap. There are light areas which are cold as well as dark ones; and there are gradations of these. The hovering transitional passages tend to warmth, the contrasting passages to coldness.

In quantitative terms we have here relatively large coherent planes, occasionally interrupted by small areas that serve as striking accents. The half tones in the clothes and the faces of the councilors serve as such accents in the light area of floor, table, and wall; the V-shaped shadow at the right of the passageway is similarly interrupted by the

3. [The Budapest Museum describes the medium as "bister wash drawing." Professor
Rosenberg says: "pen and wash (in bister)."]

slitlike progressively narrower shafts of light on the front of the columns. The over-all effect is one of intensity, perhaps necessary to give firmness to the reality of both the throne room and the interpretive action. But there are many gradations between the subtlest and the most emphatic treatment. The tempo varies between steep rising and falling and occasional local vibrations. The strongly dramatic contrasts are balanced by an over-all effect of repose.

To sum up: the values are organized in large planes; they are vigorously dynamic and richly nuanced in terms of light and shadow, warmth and cold, as well as in degrees of intensity—now sharply contrasted, now softly merging in a tonal unity.

Next, let us consider the use of line. Although it determines effect to a far lesser degree than light and shadow, it is quite varied. There are straight lines (vertical, horizontal, and slanted—both on the surface and in depth) and there are curved lines (on the surface, to the left; in depth, in the throne). The link between the poles is effected from either. The straight lines are not rigorously geometrical; they may be broken (for instance, at top and bottom of the tablecloth), and in such cases the components are only approximately straight—i.e., there may be slight curvings, sometimes in opposite directions (the right edge of the pillar at left). They may be shot through with curves (Pharaoh's thigh). They may end in one and the same curve (leg of councilor at left) or they may turn into curves at their ends. Nor are the curves rigidly geometrical. True curves are at a minimum (top of the throne); curved lines may be rendered as a number of small curves (the arch over the passageway); some curves are only due to the blunting of angles. Such variety creates the effect of a line that hovers between the straight and the curved without the slightest tension (such tension as we encountered in Giotto). The lines run parallel at a distance but, unlike Degas, Rembrandt does not use individual parallels in relation or tension to the mass which they form. Sometimes two lines run toward one point, sometimes they form harsh angles (as at the foot of the throne), sometimes gentler joinings.

Most of the lines are short, but those that give the effect of length are actually composed of many short ones or of complementary curves. The lines suggest finitude, limitation, measurability. There is remarkable range of intensity, from the vigorous lines in the man at the right to the barely indicated ones between the columns. Note the variety at the upper part of the throne. The tempo is for the most part pronounced. Even horizontals have a great deal of directional movement.

Line, characterized by lack of both mathematical structure and tension, by freedom, by its limited dimensions, and by rich gradations in intensity and movement, must now be studied in relation to the use of light. There is a fundamental difference between light —immaterial, hovering, formless, boundless, marked by strong contrasts and large effects—and line—measurable, fragmented, differentiating, form-giving. This difference is the more apparent because light seems to be the dominating element here and line secondary to it. But there is no real contradiction: each line is part of the light-and-shadow scale as well as the scale of warmth and cold; it is largely determined by both scales. Because it is without tension, although it never submits to pure ornamental play, it participates in the hovering quality. On the other hand, the organization of light and darkness, with its sharp contrasts, helps the linear composition. Lights and shadows contribute to the definition of objects conceived of as concrete parts of an entire cosmos. Thus it can *not* be said that line arises from light, or physical-psychic delimitation from the unlimited. Here line has another origin. Its nature and the manner in which it performs its task is largely determined by the same cause as light (though it does not serve the same purposes).

If now, after the means of representation, we turn to the material qualities, we find that Rembrandt respects the properties of his medium (paper, India ink, crayon), and that despite the varied uses which he elicits from them, he has an objective attitude toward their concrete requirements. The material qualities of the objects represented are subdued. To be sure, we can distinguish stone, linen, wool, etc., but certain over-all factors, such as transparency, heaviness, reflectivity, are more important. The material rendering of the spiritual meaning is still more important: the mode of reality (which is substantial) and within it the mood of dream interpretation are strongly and sensually expressed. Within the over-all mood each person's individual traits and function are carefully detailed. Note, for instance, how the tip of Joseph's foot touches the floor, how his knees do not firmly rest on it, and how his hands feel the air around them. The three aspects of matter are combined, with the spiritual one dominant. For example, the texture of Joseph's clothing vanishes almost completely behind the state of mind expressed by his body; only the specific quality of the line keeps this pure spirit tied to the surface of the picture. At the other extreme—the man at the right corner—the heaviness and texture of the material are rendered with the subtlest differentiation; but here, too, this is done not for its own sake but as a consequence of the compositional function—that is, for a spiritual reason. "Thinking" takes precedence over "being," if we may use the scholastic language of Spinoza, appropriate in this context; but there is no "thinking" without "being," even though the being of the medium is at least on a par with that of the material quality of the objects represented and both are subordinated to the means of representation.

So far we have shown how light and line are interwoven to constitute the means of representation and how the picture's materiality is constituted out of three essentially different material factors. Now we must stress the fact that the means of representation are interrelated with the material factors in extremely differentiated ways. Fused, the two elements are inseparably linked both in range and in definition, so that the viewer may alternately lose himself in profound contemplation or concentrate on the richness of physical detail without ever suspecting that the two elements have different sources. We shall call this created unity the material of figuration.[4]

There is an inner tension between the picture surface, its format, and its vertical and horizontal divisions on the one hand, and the material of figuration on the other, because the latter has primarily spatial functions. They are due partly to the differences in the light–dark and warm–cold scales in intensity and quantity, and partly to the variously directed slanted lines. The artist must bring this tension to a head because only thus can he achieve order in the spatial functions within the surface. Otherwise he would eliminate depth in favor of the surface, or surface in favor of a space open to infinity. Furthermore, the objects represented possess depth, and their positions in depth are revealed in the way portions of themselves overlap each other or other objects. This contest between space and surface is what we call modeling, and it is only through modeling that the artist can give form to his material of figuration. Now, Rembrandt has opened up a space of indefinite depth, yet he has not broken the surface in terms of over-all effect; he has not really made a hole in it. Rembrandt learned how to do this from the Italians (as we see in his drawings after Leonardo, Raphael, Michelangelo, etc.) and from Persian miniatures. He applied these lessons, however, in his own way; there are, after all, as many methods of modeling as there are great artists. What then was Rembrandt's method?

We see at once that there is a foreground plane and a background plane in the pictorial space, between which everything is contained. The two differ in essential respects. The foreground is contiguous with the edges, while the background plane lies at an indefinite distance behind the objects. This is done deliberately, for if the warm shadow comes forward from the back wall and the cool light recedes, there is still light lying in another plane behind both at the end of the passageway. Nonetheless, the picture has a back plane, terminating it in depth and contrasting with the frontal plane. Connection between the two is established by quite different means: first, by discontinuity—parallel planes set in successive strata; and second, by continuity—planes and lines at an angle to the picture surface. The first is to be found mainly in the middle, the second at the sides. These methods are closely linked.

The parallel planes are constructed by the viewer's eye, sometimes from horizontal lines, sometimes from relatively small bits of vertical planes. The illusion of their presence is evoked by small indications: the horizontal prolongation of the dais, for example, Joseph, the side of the throne, the wall above the passageway, the table drapery, the man in the passageway, etc. One of these planes is pivotal—it serves as the center to the foreground and background planes in depth. Centripetal energies flow to it from these

4. [For "material of figuration" (*Gestaltungsstoff*), see also the Appendix, p. 211.]

two directions. Thus, it has a constitutive significance in the figuration of depth. In the drawing this part is played by the table drapery.

The continuous means for figuring depth is the plane at an angle to the picture surface. In the form of the man at the right we easily discern a kind of ridge which has the effect of an extremely narrow plane parallel to the picture surface. On either side of it we see a plane receding into depth, each to a different degree yet not to the point of losing all relation to the other. Together with the contrast of values and the spatial functions of the lines, this produces the impression of a figure fully in the round. Another interesting illustration is found in the area where the councilor at the left and the councilor at the center overlap. They form an angle, the vertex of which points into the picture, not out of it.

An extension of this principle is illustrated by the positions of the objects at the far right and left, i.e., the throne and the passageway. Here we fully realize the significance of the fact that the two objects are shown in different degrees of three-quarter view. For one thing, they are intrinsically tied to the surface; for another, they do not recede to an equal depth, so that the point where the planes would meet if extended—there is no actual vertex as in the two illustrations above—is displaced far to the left of the vertical axis. Thus, the eye is led in a direction opposed to the movement of the ellipse; this enhances the contrasts inherent in the spatial dynamism. Because of this activation of the dimensions and directions—fundamental in any nonacademic type of modeling—the passageway and the throne, though receding unequally in depth, seem to be strongly related to each other. The central plane parallel to the picture surface, with the group of the councilors, makes its own contribution to this effect, for it ties together the spatial movements starting from each side of the picture and at the same time emphasizes the middle of the surface in the dimension of width.

Thus the pictorial space has a three-dimensional character. It gives the effect of openness almost to infinity and yet is rigorously bound to planes. All modeling and modulations of the objects are at the same time modulations of the pictorial space. We shall now analyze the methods used in the figuration of space, in greater detail, in relation to individual figures.

Joseph is shown in profile. Any figure shown in profile can be divided by an imaginary plane, defined by the outline, which separates the part actually shown from the part suggested. What such a silhouette involves is elimination of the third dimension, first in terms of the figure itself, then in terms of its relation to the pictorial space. Joseph's profile is distinguished from such a silhouette by its many levels of depth and the ordering of these into a serene aspect. How has Rembrandt achieved this effect? Certain lines seem to run obliquely into depth, sometimes cutting across horizontals (legs and forearms) and sometimes across verticals (thighs, back, chest), beginning as they do at different depths and extending as they do to different depths. The different parts of the body, themselves located at different depths, are thus made to form a *single* figure, and invisible elements are made visible (nonnaturalistically). Further, it is by this means that the figure is detached from the surface, with the additional aid of varying intensities of line and varying values of light and shadow. Rembrandt has not been content to assemble all suggestions of depth in a *single* continuum: the lines are now bent, now broken, and they constitute inhibiting influences that recall the eye to an ideal plane. He has varied the inclinations of the various planes (lower part of the body, torso, shoulder). As a result, the entire movement in depth is relativized so that sometimes it can also be seen as a forward movement, and within the movement modulations appear which are variants of the modeling. These modulations in turn refer at once to an ideal frontal plane parallel to the picture surface and to an indeterminably distant background plane, itself internally modulated. The simultaneous reference is such that the contrast between lighter and darker tones suffices to set off the figure, to surround it with air, and to create an impression of a depth far greater than the actual depth. In this area the space conveys many tensions. There are the opposing movements of the hands, of foot and knee, elbow and head; there are the differing amounts of space in front of Joseph and behind him. All this brings out Joseph's significance in terms of subject matter. Space and idea are treated as two aspects of a single artistic reality.

We seek the active collaboration of the reader in making a similar analysis of a full-face figure (the man in the passageway) and of figures shown in three-quarter view. What will be found is that the same means have been used throughout: concentration of depth values around an imaginary central plane (depth axis); activation of all dimensions and directions of movement; figuration of depth by indirect methods; different degrees of continuity and discontinuity in depth; combination of several not simultaneously visible depth strata in one figure; overlapping; contrasts between light and dark; variations of intensity; reference of three-dimensional values to ideal foreground and background planes situated at different distances from the central plane and enclosing a self-contained space. The artist's purpose, too, is everywhere the same: precise arrangement in depth, combining richness and simplicity; impression of greater depth than the depth shown, so that the tension between the surface and the third dimension represents both freedom and necessity.

So far we have analyzed the philosophical content and its figuration in the motif, the material of figuration, and the modeling. As we now pass to the formal construction, we must presuppose the concept of a "work typology." There is no such thing as an external or internal composition that is merely an accretion of individual elements or mere differentiations of a unity. All relations—those between elements as well as those between elements and the whole—are determined by the structure of the type (which, in most works of art, is identical with the structure of their elements). The type of *this* drawing might be described as quasi-organic, inasmuch as all the conditions of its structure are immanent, each part being determined by its adjacent part, and the purpose of the whole determining the function of each. Thus, causality and finality join hands to produce an entity at once architectonic and musical—self-sufficient, a product of logical thinking and spontaneous growth, as independent of the artist's subjectivity as of the world outside.

The development of the motif (i.e., the internal composition) is more essential to the structure of the type than the organization of the external composition. The motif is bound to the three dimensions of space which, for purposes of analysis, we shall take up one by one, although of course they never appear separately. Each of the three dimensions has a character and expressive value of its own, and it is very important for our understanding of a given artist to ascertain whether he submits to this character (in which case he is an artist of the objective type) or ignores it (subjective type). Height, the vertical, starts at the bottom, i.e., from weight, dependence, unconsciousness; it passes through our body and reaches beyond the head, i.e., beyond our consciousness. Width, the horizontal, lies parallel to the axis that connects our eyes; as long as we see in the horizontal we remain in the realm of the earthly, and as we move from one side to the other, we observe the sequence of earthly objects and events. The dimension of depth starts at ourselves and leads away from ourselves; it liberates us from ourselves, confronting us with air and objects, with physical realities which we may feel more or less strongly than our own. In architectural terms we may liken height to elevation, width to transverse sections, and depth to the ground plan.

To begin with the dimension of height, we divide the drawing into three loosely distinguishable sections. The lowest extends upward as far as the horizontal prolongation of the dais. The second section extends to the upper edge of the pedestals of the hall columns (to the level of Joseph's head). The third section consists of the remaining three-fifths of the drawing—a disproportion that emphasizes the importance given to air and space. In the first section—a shallow rectangle—verticals occur only at the sides, and there only in the upper half; the vertical at the left has an upward movement, while that at the right moves downward. From the very outset Rembrandt suggests the two movements in the dimension of height, although the full width of the picture separates one from the other. The two verticals enclose another contrast, that between light and dark, with a movement from left to right across the drawing. Thus the two main contrasts occur together, but they remain external to each other, unrelated. The second section is about twice as high as the first and bounded not only by two verticals but also by two horizontals which are quite different in character. The lower horizontal is actually traced as an almost unbroken line; only at one place, where Joseph kneels, is there a break. The upper horizontal is almost entirely imaginary, except at the left edge, and not only broken but at many places cut by verticals. The latter are straight lines only at the far left and far right—and again offer opposing movements. In the area between we have, instead of verticals, pairs of slanting lines pointing in opposite directions (Joseph's back, the corner of the tablecloth, Pharaoh's knees, etc.). Within this frame the downward verticals seem crushed and, conversely, the rising verticals seem to break up the horizontal line at the top of the section—as though a struggle were taking place between verticals and horizontals, each winning and each losing. Significantly, where the horizontal is most completely broken through we find the most defeated figure (broken verticals) —Pharaoh; where the horizontal is least broken we find the victor—Joseph. The councilors, least involved in the struggle, are formally rendered by way of an ellipse extending over their heads; here the second section definitely reaches beyond the enclosing horizontal into the third section—a flowing transition, typical of Rembrandt, which contrasts with the clear-cut division between the first and second sections. In keeping with this, the upper section shows free and simultaneous upward and downward movements, side by side and interlocked, the full realization of the two-way movements already indicated in the lowest section. But here we have no struggle between opposites; rather, they have been brought into balance, a state of suspension, in which the greatest opposing forces are resolved. This state of suspension remains *inside* the drawing, being bound at the upper edge by the canopy over the throne and by the small dark area in the middle; it does not go beyond the top of the drawing. Rembrandt does not recognize anything supra-earthly (in the literal sense) to which the picture might refer.

The division of the drawing into three sections of unequal height ($1:2:4+$) has, in addition to this formal spatial function, a spiritual function, which Rembrandt develops over the range from uncomprehending, dull weight to consciousness. The two extremes are so closely co-ordinated that their exfoliation coincides with the division into three sections. The lowest is not instinct or undifferentiated unity but cold, unawakened reason as yet unaware of itself. Such a beginning is in contrast to the over-all mood of dream interpretation, a springboard to it. It is in keeping, however, with Rembrandt's reversal (mentioned above) of the customary relation between heaviness and lightness, gravitation and flight, which makes the miraculous spatially visible. A higher form of consciousness prevails in the second section, in the expression of the three councilors and in the lucid architecture of throne and passageway. There is emotion here, but of a kind that is aware of itself—and hence a heightening of consciousness, for all that rationality has yielded to emotion. In the third section both have been elevated to the suprapersonal, the cosmic; it is dominated by a world-consciousness at once animated by the highest emotion and yet ordered by clarity and comprehensiveness. Between the two extremes lies the narrow range of ordinary human consciousness; Rembrandt does not denote a conflict between the extremes, but simply a region where they overlap. Such struggle as remains occurs between human beings or, more accurately, between individual impulses of the human soul. Rembrandt's theme throughout his handling of the dimension of height is the struggle to control human passion, conceived of as a region between the rational-impersonal subconsciousness and the emotional-suprapersonal world-consciousness.

Analyzing the dimension of width we note that it, too, is divisible into three sections—three vertical rectangles within the horizontal one of the drawing—but the results will differ according to whether we divide at the innermost architectural elements left and right—marking the division according to the golden section—or whether we make the middle section broader, to extend from the inside pedestal of the first column at the passageway to the inside of the throne column at Pharaoh's right. Were we to follow the first method of division, allotting one-fourth of the width to the middle rectangle, we would bring out the underlying symmetry and, by the same token, the concrete asymmetry of the slanting side rectangles, as well as the void between Joseph and Pharaoh, the great hiatus across which an action-at-a-distance occurs. Were we to follow the second method (middle rectangle = one-half) we would point up all the elements of the motif: the fact that Joseph and Pharaoh are linked in the ellipse (note that Joseph is turned into, Pharaoh out of the picture), and the diagonal that separates light from shadow, upward movement from downward movement, lightness from heaviness. Static symmetry is now replaced with rhythmic dynamism, for the middle rectangle is larger than the first whereas the third is smaller than the first. Thereby the movement of the eye from left to right, as it follows the movement of the ellipse, is checked and carried back toward the middle in slower, shorter stages. The two methods of division are so strongly interlocked that it is impossible to choose between them. Together they produce interaction of the static with the dynamic, as well as transition between them in terms of space, along with simultaneous, reciprocal attraction and separation among the human figures. Nevertheless, unification dominates. Figuratively, the most visible expression of these twofold tendencies is the councilor at the left. Of pronounced massiveness, not only is he looking in two directions, but his body turns, comes forward, one of his elbows is pointed at Joseph as though to shut off communication from Joseph to Pharaoh; and yet he must help to provide a bond between them.

The formal development linked with this division in width can best be clarified by comparing the corner pillar at the left with the man and the column at the right. The pillar, with its shadow, its upward movement, and its frontal view, is all of a piece. In the man, however, light and dark areas are separated; various tendencies—rising, standing, falling, and weighing down—interpenetrate, merge, alternate; instead of the frontal view we find diagonals leading in opposite directions; only the division of the height into a smaller and larger part according to the golden section is approximately maintained, though it is reversed. The viewer is led from simplicity to complexity, from the single to the multiple.

The development in the dimension of width governs the action—both in Joseph as a single figure and in the drawing as a whole. The path leads from the open (back left) to the closed (front right); from those who are not yet participating to the active participants and to those who are no longer participating; from the atmosphere of landscape to the mood of dream and on to blocklike rigidity. We move (methodologically speaking) toward the concrete: from an external movement through immaterial air, through a self-contained current of psychic energy at whose poles psychic and physical elements have completely interpenetrated, to a physical reality which is characterized as the least spiritual. (Compare these degrees and modes of reality with Giotto's.) Time and again we are confronted with the Spinozistic opposition of thought and being in the unity of substance.

The participants themselves are so arranged that the eye is led first to the active giver and then to the passive receiver. As a result, our curiosity about the content of the dream is eliminated: dreaming is conceived of abstractly, as an ordinary psychic need common to all. The viewer is not given occasion to speculate on dreaming, let alone on this particular dream. A viewer who might wish to offer his own interpretation is forestalled; by this means we are made more receptive to the miracle of Joseph's prophecy. Interpretation in intellectual terms is effectively excluded by our enforced ignorance of the dream material. Only by intuition can we approach this theme; it took Rembrandt himself some time to arrive at this arrangement.

At this point we must say a few words about the temporal setting of the scene. It depicts a phase of the human condition embodied in relations between men (and between men and suprahuman powers). It is essentially a timeless conflict which is brought to reality among mortal men. (In the same sense the witches or the ghost in *Macbeth* are plausible only as projections of the hero, and Macbeth and Lady Macbeth are figured as two aspects of a single idea.) Or, seen from another angle: the succession of events is compressed in a single moment, as a visual confrontation of persons, an activation of their relationships in terms of energy, an exploration of past and future. Instead of viewing events in succession, we see them all together in a single moment of energy whose pure duration is indefinable because the action repeats itself continually and because its present includes past and future. This moment, which is both in movement and at rest, all encompassing and in process of becoming, differs considerably from the Biblical text. The latter gives us the interpretation in a temporal sequence: first we are told that the two dreams are identical; next, that the kine and ears of corn stand for years; then, that the years mean years of plenty and years of famine; the events are then located and dated and, finally, advice is given on averting the evil consequences of the events foretold. To be sure, the sequence is held together by a central motif: God tells Pharaoh what He intends to do —a motif Joseph has to repeat three times before Pharaoh understands and acts upon it. An element of timelessness is thereby introduced into the temporal sequence, and it is this conjunction of timelessness and time that Rembrandt tried to record—albeit by different means.

As for the dimension of depth, we need not add much to what was said before about modeling. Here, too, we may distinguish three sections. The first is the relatively shallow, nearly empty foreground, notable for its distinct horizontal boundary at the back. Next comes a middle ground which is itself articulated into three strata, the middle one clearly ending at the table drapery. The action proper takes place in this middle stratum of the middle ground; its placement at a depth between the near and far images gives the scene both actuality and remoteness. Two broad curved spaces frame it: one leads out of depth (at the left) to the foreground and runs along the latter to the right; the other begins at the front right and runs along the back of the throne into depth, then comes forward again in the cloud and the columns of the passageway. The result is not a closed curve but a centripetally-moving spiral; and it is from the end of this curve in space that the oval curve on the plane is developed as a variation upon the former. The movements of the two main characters follow the opposite thrusts of this spatial curve—Joseph that coming from behind and Pharaoh that pushing back. The third section of the depth dimension is not occupied by human figures, but solely by contrasting light and dark areas. These contrasts are not harsh like those in the foreground, but vaguer, hovering indefinable in the distance, with the merest hint of a terminating limit—finite in so far as it is parallel to the picture surface but infinite in so far as it eludes the eye. Nevertheless, the effect is one of a closed pictorial space, for the movement into depth is counterbalanced by a movement out of depth.

As the eye moves into the picture depth, it passes from a terrifying void to a promising fullness and, at the same time, from materiality to immateriality, from the finite to the infinite, from the particular to the universal. Between the two extremes we find man conceived as both body and soul, as both individual and social being, as a natural organism and as related to God. But for all his complexity man is merely a bridge between two poles, a stage in the process of dematerialization (and fulfillment). The idea of a transcendent God is not present here; the deep religious feeling expressed in this drawing has nothing in common with the Catholicism of the Middle Ages. It reflects an immanent faith, yet without claiming the identity of God and the world. This is a Protestant mysticism; it endows God with an almost exclusive efficacy and reduces man to the status of an individual point of passage in the cosmic flow of the infinite substance, which comes into being and passes away without ever losing its substantial character.

Let us sum up our analysis of the pictorial space. We see a council room in Pharaoh's palace, a real space with a well-defined social function. This space is taken up with im-material-cosmic and inner-psychic processes to such an extent that they entirely over-shadow—indeed, almost submerge—the social-realistic elements. On the other hand, seen from its limits we have a static, spatial structure in which all the dimensions and move-ments are in tension with one another in such a way that only a diagonal in depth can establish balance among them. Does the psychic-spiritual content create the appearance of its space? Or is it this content that reduces the reality of the space to appearance? Do the currents of energy attain repose or is the static structure of the space merely a vessel of dynamic process? Detailed discussion will show that neither alternative is altogether correctly stated.

Let us take a closer look at Joseph. Above his knees the edges of his cloak are formed by slanting lines which run parallel to each other first toward the left, then toward the right, up to a point below the neck, where they merge. An approximately vertical line, which passes through the shoulder, balances the opposing movements of the projecting extremities. These few lines create a great many things for our eyes: an articulated clothed body, balanced despite the angle at which it leans; a state of mind as concretized in a gesture; a physico-psychic form as a light area against a dark one, that is, in space. How are these elements connected? At first it might seem that body and garment are without significance in comparison with the inwardness of Joseph's spirit, the burning ardor of which has, so to speak, melted away all such externals. But we soon become aware of the very individual character of Joseph's attitude, how his knees grope at the floor or his hands fumble the air; how his arm is joined to his shoulder, or the point of his elbow. The transparency of his garment seems less a physical characteristic of the material than an expression of his spiritual animation; the gesture, similarly, seems no less a personal act of will than a necessary—and hence limited—resolution of the formal conflict im-plied in the structural lines. But what is it that brings about this unity of body and soul, of gesture and state of mind? Is it the body that forms the soul, or the soul the body? The lines seem to trace both simultaneously, separating them from the background and detaching them from the space that belongs to them—not as a space but as a shadow that is made space and mood (i.e., again body and soul, extension and thought) only by virtue of these traced lines. What we have here is the *concretization of a single substance*, which the viewer sees as body and soul.

If we now compare Joseph with the other figures, each has individual being—in-dividual because of a different state of mind, to which corresponds a different corporeality and, of course, a differing linear technique for constructing it; and being, for over-all character has become more important than individual gesture or attitude. Pharaoh, the mighty king, sits there, a heap of patched-up fragments. It is not that he *has* a dreamy or reflective attitude, but that he *is* a broken man, broken by his dream and his inability to understand its meaning. His body cannot conceivably assume a different posture, nor can he hold the scepter differently than he does.

Note, further, the differences in the three councilors' attitudes toward Joseph, Pharaoh, and each other. It might almost be said that their characters are embodied in the three different headpieces. Each councilor is an individual concretization of a single substance. What the viewer distinguishes as body and soul are two aspects of an underlying unity.

We have already mentioned the great diversity of the individual concretizations. It is enough to compare Joseph with the man at the right. Nevertheless, all men have something in common apart from the fact that they are born: individual concretization does not mean isolation from spiritual contexts, the exaggeration of uniqueness at the expense of personality, the abolition of communal bonds. This common element is man's being in the image of God, his immortality, his freedom of will. The three are inseparable and can be understood in terms of relations between three groups of categories: being and nonbeing, being and becoming, and being and consciousness.

Each thing takes its form by negation, through the fact that it not only passes through its death as something external to it but also lives in it. In a sense, all Rembrandt's human figures partake of nonbeing—not because they are incomplete and have not yet come into being: but precisely because they are separated from that which they no longer are, from that which has died. They are all aware of the relativity of their existence; Joseph is well aware that even his link with God is relative. But Spinoza's theorem that every determination is a negation is only partially valid: it is necessary to add the constitution of the remaining being as the core to which all determinations apply, the essential determinateness of the being that has not been abandoned. We need not digress into philosophical speculation here, but we may say this much: all individual men are expositions of the same fundamental mood in its immanent diversity, and each individual man therefore reveals some portion of the other's inwardness. We have justified this proposition with respect to Joseph and Pharaoh. The moment we add that Pharaoh, after all his earlier failures, was incapable of unconditional faith in Joseph's abilities, we have explained the poses and gestures of the councilors. But the man standing at the right, too, is no more than an aspect of Pharaoh: he represents the royal dignity which the man on the throne so plainly lacks. A single individual idea projects its existence in all its multiplicity, and when all multiplicities have been added up, the total again comes to a self-contained whole.

We have already shown how each figure is wrested from the surface as though from the primal ground, how it comes into being and is constructed before our eyes. This process leads to a particular being. But the lives of the men in this drawing are not fixed forever in the conventions of habit; they carry their pasts with them, as pure intensity, into a future far from this present yet very close to their primordial past, their common origin. Existence is only a transitory moment in an act of continuous procreation that extends beyond all present particularities to the totality of personality and its conditions. And still further beyond, to the primordial oneness of Substance. The latter manifests itself in the viewer's certainty that the dream will be interpreted and that the interpretation will have consequences. We can imagine that Pharaoh's dependence on Joseph or Joseph's need of Pharaoh is momentarily interrupted or changed in intensity, but we cannot imagine that this relationship will ever come to an end (save by death). Despite the relativity of being between becoming and ceasing to be, it has a fullness that far surpasses one-sidedness and uniformity.

The relation between being and consciousness lights up existence; it expresses the process by which being attains self-awareness. In the three councilors, being, instead of including consciousness, is split off from it. It is consciousness that watches being, and this is why each individual's consciousness varies and resembles no other. Rather, we see here various degrees of consciousness, ranging from subconsciousness in the lower parts of the bodies to consciousness proper in the heads and, in between, the struggle against passivity for full, active consciousness. Accordingly, some bodies are heavier at the bottom than at the top, and vice versa. Often the figures are least heavy somewhere in the middle and heavier at the bottom and the top.

Connected with man's consciousness is his freedom of will, his autonomy and responsibility. We have already emphasized, in our discussion of how Rembrandt represented and particularized his figures, to what extent they are determined. Such lack of freedom as they show has thus been imposed from "above," not from "below" (i.e., by influences, circumstances, etc.). They are not the product of the workings of any fate, but momentary manifestations of an eternal substance. They justify the moment in its passing because it reveals more than their individualities and more than their specific function within a social reality—the innermost, inviolable axis around which everything takes shape—the axis which we may with equal propriety name resemblance to God, freedom of will, or hope of immortality. These three terms are merely aspects of one and the same ultimately ineffable reality, from which we emerge for a fleeting moment and to which we return.

The men Rembrandt created in this drawing are in essence persons—i.e., both particularity and totality. The form of their empirical existence is neither portrait nor type, but a unique yet universally human determination of the whole man. Here, in terms of psychology—or, more accurately, with respect to what Rembrandt regarded as essentially real in man—he most resembles Shakespeare even though he did not, like Shakespeare, carry particularity to the point of *hubris*, i.e., he did not create comic or tragic figures. The relation between unmistakable particularity and human universality varies according to each figure's significance. The greater this is, the greater the contrasts and the tension between the particular and the universal; the result is a correspondingly greater unity of the mental state which may tend toward the active or passive side. In all this Rembrandt is fond both of contrasts (Joseph–Pharaoh) and of transitions (the councilors become progressively more relaxed, more passive, starting from the left).

When we examine the psychic functions more closely, we are struck by the predominance of inwardness and wisdom. These men live from the inside out. They are absorbed in themselves. The dark spots in place of their eyes suggest that their inner vision is stronger, more assured, than their divided outward vision. What goes on inside them matters more than what is going on around them. The external senses are the means of revealing inner experiences; this is true even of the sense of touch, customarily our means of closest contact with the world. In this drawing the sense of touch is emphasized in various ways. I have already discussed the figure of Joseph; now let us look at Pharaoh, at how he sits, sagging, how he holds the scepter. Or the way the councilors touch themselves. Sounds, too, are distinctly to be heard in this silent drawing. Every viewer will hear the rhythm in which Joseph speaks: searching but sure; with pauses, because he must listen, because the words do not flow from him mechanically but carry the weight of divine revelation. We can also distinguish types of listening among the other figures. These men are, on the one hand, endowed with the keenest sensibilities and, on the other, with an unmovable core of existential wisdom. They are not thinkers or questioners; they sense their own needs and abilities. They understand, indeed they solve, their difficulties by assisting or by restraining themselves.

In their social relationships these men do not rely wholly upon their own wills or purposes. They are individuals within a group context which is conceived of as a category more basic than and superior to themselves, the first stage in the development of substantial being. The more individualized they are, the more closely they are bound up with the group, for one and the same principle governs both—the emphasis throughout is on meaning and on composition. This principle creates the group and endows it with an organic hierarchy of social values—i.e., the group does not smother individuality nor is it a mere sum of individuals. These men are complete beings (in the sense just defined) within the group; they form a social unit for all their individual diversity because this, too, is merely a single aspect of a spiritual substantial unity. (Compare the group enclosed within the ellipse with that of Giotto.)

Not only the figures *in* the drawing but also the viewer *in front of it* has acquired greater concreteness. The picture imposes upon the viewer a specific attitude and mode of being. To mention the obvious first: Rembrandt has put us at a certain distance from which alone we can contemplate the drawing alertly and objectively. The line of vision he has provided is also the guiding line.[5] This line is the horizontal at the top of the pedestals of the columns; beginning at Joseph's head, it continues as a curve above the other heads. Furthermore, he gives us a meeting line which divides Joseph's body at the point of the golden section (smaller part from the left). Where the line of vision intersects it, the two main linear motifs meet: the ellipse around the figures and the diagonal that separates light from dark areas. When we have followed them both to the end we realize that a change has occurred. There is no longer *only* a point of view *from* which to look at the drawing. Some part of us—some immaterial part—has been drawn into the work and merged with it. Detached from us, it now soars beyond all determinations of space. Now we are freed from the subject matter, now we are confronted with the specific content, and all that remains to us is consciousness of a creative power which has made the invisible visible—and not only this, but mystery and miracle as well—and subjected them all to a new order. When we now look away from the picture at the world around us, it does not much resemble the drawing, but we know that it *is*, nevertheless, like it. We are convinced that its essential order, its purity, its holiness, and the inner beauty of its soul are merely veiled by chaotic accidents. When we see how spiritual breadth in a barely outlined body may be transformed into spiritual narrowness within a fully realized body; how currents of energy are metamorphosed into heavy masses; how relative finitude may be made to approach the infinite and the absolute—when we have seen all this, we realize at last how Rembrandt, starting from an intuitive idea (conception, motif), following a method of continuously concrete deduction, has brought all opposites into unity within the work of art. For a moment the source and substance—eternally one—shines forth.

5. [For "guiding line" (*Führungslinie*), see Pl. XXV and the Appendix, p. 223.]

V. DISCORD BETWEEN FORM AND CONTENT

Picasso: *Guernica*

(PLATE XIX)

Those trying to explain pictures are as a rule completely mistaken.

PICASSO

Allegories are in the realm of ideas what ruins are in the realm of things.

WALTER BENJAMIN

As often happens in Chinese poetry, there are varying depths of meaning, yet these different meanings meet at a point of fusion, and the implication is clear—there is a compact with the past for the sake of future inheritance, and a proud belief that the time has come when the Chinese will be masters of their own land.

ROBERT PAYNE

At bottom we are all collective creatures, whatever airs we may choose to put on. . . . Even the greatest genius would not get far if he were determined to owe everything to his own inwardness. But many good people don't understand this, and grope in the dark half their lifetimes, dreaming of originality.

GOETHE, *Conversations with Eckermann*

XIX*b* Picasso. *Guernica* (first stage). May 11, 1937

XIX*a*   PICASSO. *Guernica*. 1937. Oil on canvas. 11 ft. 6 in. × 25 ft. 8 in.

The four works of art we have so far discussed have this in common, that in them form and content have been brought into unity, although by different methods. The artist's creative method is thus the essential subject of any analysis of art, whether theoretical or historical. But failures to achieve this unity have occurred, not only in the case of individual works and individual artists, but also in the case of whole epochs and over great areas of the earth's surface. There may be different causes: failure of artistic power, irreconcilable conflicts within the content, rigid religious dogmatism, or violent changes in the social and political structure. Accordingly, the breakdown of unity may take on a variety of forms: pure formalism, one-sided mannerism, propaganda art, imitation of fixed patterns, etc. In this essay we shall analyze a single instance of discord between form and content: Picasso's *Guernica.*

This work differs from all the artist's other works in being a historical painting. Paintings treating historical events existed in Spain as far back as the paleolithic era: the painting on the ceiling of Altamira, for example, which has been interpreted as a historical work,[1] is by no means the most ancient portrayal of wars between totem clans or between male warriors and female sorcerers of a single clan. Such works depict more than single events; they represent an epoch, as Velázquez' *Surrender of Breda* does, or Goya's *The Third of May, 1808.* While the latter two works are objective portrayals based on ideas—*the* idea of an epoch in both cases—El Greco, in his *Laocoön,* drew upon Greek mythology to express a protest against the Inquisition's extermination of the Moriscos (if the view of Stephan Bourgeois is correct).[2] El Greco seems to have compromised his conscience and concealed this reality out of his own fear of the hangman.

The nineteenth century produced an especially large number of historical paintings. Some artists confined themselves to the past of foreign peoples, for the most part treating it romantically or anecdotally, though a significantly large number of the portrayals of decline may have been allusions to the contemporary situation. Other artists treated the passionate revolutionary struggles of their own times and their own nation, as Delacroix

---

1. [Cf. the author's *Prehistoric Cave Paintings.*]   2. "El Greco," *Byrdcliffe Afternoons* (Woodstock, N.Y., 1939), pp. 74–103.

did in his *Liberty Guiding the People* (1830), in which he "raised" liberty and the French nation to the rank of allegories. Historical painting, then, by no means demands, let alone imposes, one style only—namely the objective one. Indeed, this style at its purest, as in David's *Coronation of Napoleon I* and Menzel's *Coronation of Wilhelm I in Versailles*, degenerated into a Byzantine portrayal of court scenes, devoid of intellectual content. Such works are neither art nor history because the historical power of the nation takes no active part in these events. The objective style of historical painting that served as a vehicle for ideas had become inadequate because new powers had arisen to dominate both society and the individual—capitalism and technology. Technology put to capitalist uses led to a new alienation of man from himself and from his group, an alienation that could not be overcome but only camouflaged by hollow concepts of nation, freedom, equality, etc., or reference to dynasties still claiming to rule by the "grace of God" but actually existing by grace of profits and surplus value. Behind all these masks a transformation took place in the ultimate resource of politics: warfare. In modern wars man no longer confronts his fellow man but, rather, the abstract powers of money and the machine, powers which serve his progress only for a time, the better to destroy him in the end. No representational style is adequate, perhaps, to portray these new powers which have degraded mankind to mere material and have elevated bombs to the metaphysical status of a new omnipotent devil; at all events, no such style has as yet been invented.

When Picasso set to work in Paris to give expression to his feelings about the bombing of Guernica, he hoped to create a new form of the ancient, eternally changing tradition of historical painting. Doubtless the facts are still fresh in everyone's memory. Spain was in the throes of a civil war which pitted the old moribund Spain, still dominated by the dead hand of the Church, against the new Spain striving to live—a struggle between reaction and democracy. While the Western democracies talked on and on about non-intervention, the Italian Fascists and the German Nazis sent troops and the most modern weapons in order to deter progressives all over the world by a decisive defeat. A bombing squadron destroyed the Basque town of Guernica and seven thousand people lost their lives in a single night's raid.[3] There had been no previous declaration of war. After Hiroshima this may seem a bagatelle, and had it not been for Picasso's painting, the episode might well have been forgotten by now. At the time, however, it revealed more clearly than any other the disintegration, barbarization, and dehumanization of the epoch and of the class responsible, which was no longer capable of surviving save by destruction. The general horror and indignation, and the determination to resist the forces of destruc-

3. [At the time Raphael wrote this chapter, little research on the events was available, but the following facts have by now been recorded: Guernica had about 7,000 inhabitants, but not all of them were killed, and the raid took place in the daytime, beginning at 4:30 P.M., on April 26, 1937. The center of the town was destroyed; 1,654 people were killed and 889 wounded. See Hugh Thomas, *The Spanish Civil War* (London and New York, 1961), p. 419.]

tion and to struggle for a better future, stood behind Picasso. He then began a painting which was to expose the true face of Fascist madness and barbarism.

The composition of the painting clearly shows a division of the surface into three parts: two more or less equal at the sides, and a central area about three times as wide. This scheme would be even more like that of a medieval altarpiece than it is had Picasso not placed a triangular form in the center, leaving empty areas between it and the rectangular areas at the sides. Thus, what we have here is more a kind of revolt against the medieval form than a revival. The triangular form in the middle connects the two bottom corners of the picture surface with its center at the top. But the effect of the two equal sides is played down because the right side of the triangle runs on the surface, while the left side runs into depth; moreover, before they meet, both sides are interrupted by forms that shift the center of gravity out of the triangle to the left of its apex. While the ancient form of the pediment is suggested, it is not carried through; this shows even more clearly in the first version of the painting (Plate XIX*b*), where a standing rectangle with the raised arm of the dead warrior prevents the meeting of the sides and breaks the triangle apart in a wide gap. Again, a traditional form has been suggested, only to be destroyed by a rebellious spirit. The Christian altarpiece and the Greek pediment negate each other as the artist searches for a still older form—the acute angle open either at the top or at the bottom.

The first stage of the mural clearly shows how Picasso employs this angle. At the right we find two such angles, which start at the same vertex at the bottom, and open upward with their three sides; in the middle there is an angle pointing to the top, the two sides of which are on the surface and would, if prolonged, meet above the picture at the top. At the left there is another angle opening upward. The final version has only two departures from this arrangement. The angle at the left is almost eclipsed by one opening downward that connects the figures of the mother and the bull. Further, in the middle area the left side of the angle is projected into depth, whereby the breaking up of the pediment takes on its full plastic value. In the first stage the combination of these parts has produced a W-shaped figure which does not appear in the final version.

This scheme of a group of angles is not related either to the structural lines of the picture surface or to the main lines of orientation,[4] determined by the body structure of the observer; it has been imposed on the picture and the viewer by the artist himself. In the first stage Picasso had traced out the vertical axis of the painting in accordance with its specific function, namely, to separate the unreasoning panic at the right from the calmness of death and life going on at the left. In the final version this axis is not visible; it has been broken into many parts by the thrust of the horse's head. But though it is less directly emphasized, its function seems enhanced in an indirect way: its parts create measurable

4. [For "structural (or "privileged") lines" and "lines of orientation," see the Appendix, pp. 222, 223.]

intervals between the hand with the lamp at the top (pointing to the left) and the hand with the broken wooden sword at the bottom (pointing to the right), as though Picasso had meant to contrast the "spiritual" with the "physical" weapon. In both versions the middle axis is the only immanent line of the picture plane used by Picasso.

The viewer no more determines the composition than do the structural lines of the surface. There is no over-all line of vision to make all the figures visible from one height. The missing meeting line and meeting point may have been replaced with a meeting plane situated in the horse's stippled body; as we shall see, this plane is the vaguest of all in the picture. There are some guiding lines, though only for certain parts of the painting; sometimes they coincide with the emotional lines of the figures' movements, sometimes with parts of the compositional scheme, and they end—or should we say "begin"?—in the same jagged form at the top. The latter might be regarded as the point of vision (and meeting point) from which the entire composition flies apart, were there no compulsion to look at the painting from the bottom edge and to regard the guiding lines as holding this shattering together (though partly shattered themselves). Moreover, contrary to all our reading and writing habits, these lines lead from right to left. Similarly, the painting considered in terms of subject matter begins at the right and ends at the left. But even so it may be questioned whether the painting should not rather be read from both sides simultaneously. If so, the major emphasis would fall on the triangular composition in the middle, as indeed suggested by its great width; in the former case, however, the left side would be emphasized as the resolution, more important than the content of the middle. Accordingly, our evaluation of the various components of the content will also vary. The effect of all this is to put the viewer in a state of uncertainty and irritation ruling out any easy assimilation of the work. But it also heightens the feeling of isolation, destruction, and seeming disorder for the viewer, who is thus repeatedly shocked out of his habitual ways. At the same time the artist has protected himself against any a priori outside his own personal will and has thus reinforced his control over the painting, the viewer, the subject matter, and his right to be arbitrary. He makes himself the sole creator of order in the midst of chaos.

This raises the question whether so absolute an individualism can create more than a formalistic scheme, an order which has no necessary or immanent link with the representational, emotional, or intellectual content of the painting. Can so absolute an ego achieve more than a merely external unity? In this connection one might regard the mutual destruction of two traditional forms, symbolizing the cultural past, as a parallel to the contemporary destruction represented. But this would be no more than a parallel, to be grasped only by those who knew it already. Three features are particularly expressive: the gap in the pediment, which effectively rules out the aimed-at completeness of a self-contained world; the treatment of surface and depth as symmetrical, so that both cancel each other in romantic irony; finally, the fragmentation of the vertical axis that transforms a potential meeting line into a source of disorientation and uncertainty. As we shall see later, the tripartite composition is matched with a threefold content; this parallelism, however, comes to no more than equality of division: there is no relationship, let alone unity, between the form and content of the respective parts. On the right side, however, we do find a dualism between the rectangle, which is no more than framework, and the angle which is wholly contained within it, while on the left side this dualism is far less marked: one side of the angle serves as diagonal of the rectangle, and the outline of the lighted area of the bull as one of its sides. It is as though here Picasso used at least a close approximation among formal elements, probably compelled by his subject matter. For the bull is no longer, as in the first stage, divided by one side of the middle triangle; by a turn of the head at an angle of 180 degrees, it is now wholly compressed within the left area, so that it belongs only to it and no longer to the world of panic, war, and death. Conversely, the right side of the main triangle passes through the woman running at the right, dividing her head and front from the back, and her right forward leg from the left, trailing far behind. As a result the woman belongs to two parts of the painting. In escaping from the burning house she encounters another victim of disaster—one who has fought valiantly before losing his life. Here the structural scheme is closely linked with the subject matter, and both interact; yet their interaction does not do away with either the merely ordering function or the a priori character of the construction vis-à-vis the individual figures. The form is not an intrinsic expression of the content but is imposed on it from outside.

Despite all this the reproach of formalism scarcely does justice to Picasso's intentions. There can be no question but that Picasso would not have protested as he did against the ancient forms of the pediment and the medieval triptych had not the angles meant more to him than a purely formal means. Picasso had probably encountered them both in prehistoric Spanish ceramics and in paleolithic cave paintings. With his extraordinary empathy for the artistic vocabulary of other epochs he might have sensed their significance as magical signs. If so, the scene of death by fire at the right has been deliberately placed inside the female life form (V), the life-and-death struggle between man and horse in the middle has been placed within the male death form (∧), and, finally, the juxtaposition of mother with child and bull, which (as we shall show later) is an allegory of fertility and procreation, has been set inside a V shape in the first stage and later inside a ∧ shape. In this event Picasso—like the archaic Greek sculptors of the sixth century B.C. and like certain paleolithic painters—would have combined representational art with sign language, the meaning of which would counterbalance any tendency to formalism.

It must be observed, however, that the viewer cannot be expected to know what the signs mean and is probably unaware of their presence; they remain bits of erudition, even when he has learned to decipher them, esoteric knowledge without social or historical roots in our own time. This limitation does not work to the artist's advantage. To be sure, he may arrogate to himself a greater freedom than artists ever enjoyed between the paleo-lithic era and archaic Greece; he is free to associate death by burning with the sign of life and thus to suggest the end in the beginning, the fact of death in the continuation of life. In other words, he can experience life and death, procreation and destruction, as one, and let them everywhere be present simultaneously. However, he can do this only by combining two languages: the representational and the symbolic. What he cannot do is to resolve the oppositions between the two within one artistic form. Furthermore, Picasso failed to discover that there is a synthesis of the two basic signs (X) which denotes sexual intercourse and rebirth and would have been perfectly in keeping with his subject matter.[5] Nor did he use the variant of the X, the combination > <, the meaning of which—struggle—is perfectly suited to the content of the middle area. A pictorial vocabulary as incomplete as this—even if it amounted to more than a mixture of chiromancy, astrology, and historicism—could never serve to liberate the compositional scheme from an essenti-ally academic formalism or to create an artistically legitimate bridge between form and content.

And now we must analyze how the material of figuration is constituted. In terms of means of representation, Picasso has often been criticized for having omitted color in this painting; it could be said with greater justification that he eliminated light. But it would be even more exact to say that what Picasso looked for was the element common to light and color. That is why color is stripped of brightness and why light does not vibrate between light and dark; Picasso retained only a uniform white, black, and gray, without nuances. This is not to say that there are no variations at all. The large planes of cold white are sometimes shaded with a cool blue and sometimes warmed by yellowish-reddish tones, both of which make the pure white appear icy, frozen, coldly glowing. The grays are now darker, now lighter, now cooler, now warmer, without ever vibrating, swinging, or providing subtle transitions. The blacks seem least varied, although they occur in all three pictorial planes. There are only as many variants as are in keeping with the absolute constancy of each color, its self-identity. In other words, the variations are not determined by the position of each color in the pictorial space; the laws of distance and aerial perspective are inapplicable because the idea of an a priori absolute (empty) space—and with it the accommodation of bodies to its infinity—has given way to a different conception of space which we shall discuss later.

Such an unchanging identity of each color with itself is naturally impossible as long as any material characteristics of objects are retained, especially of living objects, whose material surfaces are continually altered not only from outside by the action of light

5. [Cf. the author's *Prehistoric Pottery and Civilization in Egypt*, pp. 76*ff.*]

but also from the inside by the circulation of the blood. Yet what we have here is no mere lack of regard for, or abstraction from, variable material qualities; no art could be created on the basis of such a negative attitude, for art always presupposes a positive point of view. Lack of regard for the material qualities of things is not important when it is a consequence of the search for a specific spiritual matter—i.e., the material expression of a spiritual attitude toward the world. Logically, abstract art should also make abstraction from color; if it did so, however, it would reduce itself to absurdity. But with respect to Picasso's *Guernica* we can only ask: What is the spirituality that fashions for itself a working material so generalized that it is characterized by the element common to light and color after the differences have been eliminated? The answer to this can almost be read from the brushwork alone. Most of the color planes are flat and smooth; they lack the tactile character produced by several layers of pigment. At the same time they have great cohesion and density, for all their thinness, so that they present a wall-like resistance even where an underlying color is allowed to shine through. This resistance endows the colors with a certain corporeality, which at the same time is contradicted by their smoothness. Another factor that makes these colors at once corporeal and incorporeal is their weight or, more accurately, their varying weights; for instance, certain grays have no weight at all, while others are very heavy. These differences in weight depend partly on the emotiveness of the lines delimiting the color areas, partly on their relation to their surroundings—on whether they are supported by the latter or are freely suspended over them—and, finally, to some extent on the color's degree of density: transparency diminishes weight, etc.

But these paradoxical tensions among the color planes or within one of them do not tell the whole story; each of them possesses something else that raises it above the contradictory empirical world and claims for it a deeper, metaphysical reality. The pre-Socratic philosophers spoke of an ἀρχή, a primal principle which is the ground of all the changing, transitory things of the world. They did not try to perceive or understand the world on the basis of empirical data but to express necessary judgments as to its nature, using the ἀρχή as their point of departure. Following a similar method, Picasso found in color identical with itself his own intuitive expression of a primal unity. It may be recalled that Parmenides declared the primal principle to be pure being, while for Anaxagoras it was *Nous*. This metaphysical antinomy between pure being and pure consciousness (spirit) haunted Picasso when he grasped the gulf between personal experience and necessary judgment. Picasso's self-identical color is his most heroic effort to transcend the antinomy and to achieve a unity where consciousness is the purest being and being is absolute consciousness. At the moment of *Guernica*, when he felt the world and himself to be threatened with destruction, he made real his faith in that which is indestructible because it is immutable: absolute unity. Although it is impossible to give an adequate name to his conception of metaphysical reality, we shall call it the unity of consciousness and being or, more briefly, conscious-being. It is particularly his use of white that expresses this phenomenal and metaphysical identity.

There is a difference which is hard to describe, although it is strongly marked, between the expressive values of white and black (this can be seen even more clearly in *Three Musicians*[6]). The two colors have a metaphysical rather than an empirical reality. White produces fullness and density and thereby urges definition—the mere possibility of definition, no specific definition. Black, on the other hand, eludes definition, seems to have a tendency to elude even an attempt at definition. White suggests that any and all things *might* emerge from it, though nothing concrete actually emanates from it, and if anything did its identity as color would be destroyed, just as a distillation from factual experiences can never produce the real experiences themselves. Black, for its part, is the epitome of nonbeing; however, black itself exists, as if to point beyond metaphysical being (as, for medieval Christian philosophers, divinity pointed beyond God). Here Picasso differs fundamentally from Parmenides, who explicitly denied the transcending of being by nonbeing. This difference in character between white and black makes the latter seem an echo of the former whenever the two happen to be superimposed, but an echo of a special kind: of the word *Sein* (being) we hear only the sound *ein*, and are left wondering whether the meaning is *nein* (no) or *eins* (one).

Unlike white and black, the grays—particularly the darker ones—are neutral with respect to definability. They lack the existential plenitude of white and also the almost mystical quality of black, which affirms through negation, creates forms, and steps up the energy of other colors. The grays are indifferent, even inert, with regard to any movement toward the real or unreal. There are at least two different grays in the painting, but it cannot be said that the cooler of them was obtained by darkening cold white or that the warmer constitutes a lightening of black. Despite other differentiations and despite their emphatic spatial functions (the cold gray decreases, the warm increases, the depth), the two do not vibrate like light, nor do they model like shadow; their qualities of repose and of rigidity secure for them the same self-identity that white and black possess. Like the latter two, the grays are unreal in a ghostly way and at the same time highly real. In the colors of *Guernica* Picasso has realized a never-changing conscious-being: for him this is not a self-destructive contradiction in terms but the highest reality.

Now, line contrasts with this metaphysical reality of conscious-being. The painting contains straight lines and curves, intersections at acute angles, and rounded joinings. The curves have a strongly emotional character, being irregular and fragmentary for the most part. The straight lines, however, tend to stress intellectuality, although they point

6. [Picasso painted two canvases of *Three Musicians* in 1921; the author is referring to the one in the Museum of Modern Art, New York.]

beyond geometry into the sphere of signs requiring interpretation. Most of the curves are open, even yawning, but the straight lines often meet. The curves occasionally seem to be hovering, as though seeking to embrace a void in space which nevertheless escapes. The straight lines often set boundaries only on one side or the other and by this very fact open abysses on the unbounded side; they separate delimited forms and an unlimited continuum and confront one with the other by emphasizing the discontinuity. In bodies and limbs straight lines and curves are emphatically contrasted, constituting two boundaries for the same form; in other cases they are used alternately; in still others they form planes of various dimensions and shapes which pierce, overlap, or are superimposed upon one another. In contrast with such crowded accumulations, other outlined planes seem empty. The crowding may be loose or compact and the planes forming it may or may not be distinct, but this orchestral *brio* is invariably effective not only by its variations but also by its contrast to an individual voice.

While the colors are rooted in primal conscious-being, prerepresentational and pre-emotional, the lines are rooted in movement, a movement which is also prerepresentational, yet experienced emotionally. Since they are not determined by the objects, they can diverge where they occur side by side in the object or they can meet where they occur apart from each other in objects. This movement is constituted of directional oppositions, alternations of highly varied tempi, repetitions of equal extreme intensities, and by means of the development of a main direction (e.g., rising lines). This scanning of the movement is prerepresentational, i.e., it does not follow the natural articulations of limbs but determines their size, form, and position. It is itself determined by emotion, however, that is to say, by the specific content of the emotion, and even more by its degree of affect, by its being driven without resistance, swelling to an extreme point at which the movement suddenly stops, pointing to an open, "spurious" infinity without attaining it. This emotional line needs time to get from one place to another but is repeatedly interrupted in its course, after which it begins anew, going on to a climax of tempo and consciousness before stopping once and for all—a scream born of time in the face of infinity. The movement through place and time (and with it, the emotion) either turns back upon itself or attains its terminal point and freezes there, because it is always born of empirical experience and never transformed into an inner development from the possible to the actual, never attached to a personal bearer, never raised to the cosmic sphere of endless coming to be and passing away. The local movement of line scans the emotion which has become affect, the end effect, divorced both from its cause and from the process of its emergence. And it is by this choice of the emotional end effect that Picasso brings the line of movement closest to the effect of his color—the torment of the finite, frozen in its explosion, in the face of absolutely silent conscious-being, none of whose potentialities are realized. This is a world without hope of salvation; mankind is reduced to a scream. Of the nine figures represented in this painting (counting both the human and the animal figures), eight have their mouths open and seven are uttering cries of anguish.

Thus there is no inner connection between color and line. Color originates in pre-empirical conscious-being and never achieves objective or emotional sensuality; it is merely thought, if by thought we mean not scientific intellect but philosophical reason—which posits viewing and thinking, thinking and being, as identical. Line, on the other hand, originates in the empirical life of a specific, measured, rhythmical emotion and, try as it may to surpass itself and leap toward the nonempirical, it never becomes a metaphysical ἀρχή. Color renders the plenitude of primal conscious-being; it lacks the possibility of movement, even of movement toward existence. Line, on the contrary, renders the extreme charge of an emotional movement that cannot possibly achieve being. Hence, neither can be derived from the other nor can both be synthesized in a third term (e.g., Plato's Idea). They are linked neither by inner affinity nor by some outside aspect common to both; all that holds them together is the artist's will, which charges them with equal amounts of creative energy and endows them with very different kinds of formless-ness. If form denotes a reality that is autonomous and self-contained by virtue of its struc-ture, then pure color no longer needs form because, being an expression of the plenitude, density, immobility, unshakability, and impenetrability of the ineffable yet highly real conscious-being, it has gone beyond the realm of form, while the emotional line has not yet attained to form (the form of emotion) but only to its scanned local movement, which turns back upon itself or freezes. What Picasso expresses is the paradoxical gulf between absolute conscious-being and empirical emotional movement, in that he brings them into the closest local contact as outline and filling. This is not to say that Picasso excludes the world of objects, but he transforms it in such a way that it serves to express this gulf between pure conscious-being and experienced emotion.

An analytical comparison between the first and last versions of the painting leads to an analogous conclusion. Even the monumental first stage is the result of a large number of studies in which Picasso emotionally and intellectually assimilated the actual events and gave them pictorial formulation; his medium was drawing. Then he had to go beyond mere emotion or fact, to bring both into relationship with a new metaphysical dimension, thereby giving meaning to the meaningless, isolated occurrence and incor-porating the meaning in the material of figuration. His means are black, white, and gray, and the spatial field formed by their confrontations and overlappings. By blocking in the main agents of the "action"—i.e., the affects—in white against a dark ground (the reverse of this would produce an entirely different impression) and at the same time giving the various grays the power to cover the white of the bodies or break it up into scattered, screaming fragments, he conjures up a picture of wholesale devastation far exceeding the sum total of the individual actions. Or, to look at this from another angle: in the first stage movements and affects are so extreme that they overwhelm man without being borne by him; they are flung over the picture surface rather than assigned their place. With the addition of white, black, gray, and the spatial field connected with them, the affects find their spiritual place. They acquire a panic and demonic character, and man becomes, if not the embodiment, then the passageway of this demonic panic. This also accounts for the collapse of the affect, which in the painting corresponds to the destruction of the external world. But both human panic and bestial fury are only conceptual and emotional façade. If we imagine the colors apart from the drawing, they express the indestructibility and serenity of pure conscious-being; conversely, if we imagine the lines without the colors, it becomes clear that although these lines are born of emotion, they are not themselves emotional; rather, they are aloof to the point of academic coolness. It is a mark of Picasso's greatness that he can compel each of his two means of expression to serve the other; it is the limitation of his greatness that, nonetheless, his theme remained the paradoxical gap between absolute conscious-being and empirical emotion, and that he did not unify them in mutual penetration.

The same is true if we try to interpret the white, black, and gray in terms of light and shadow (although we have shown that the colors are merely the element that light and color have in common—their common denominator, as it were). There is no natural source of light or shadow, either sun or lamp. Light and shadow equally lack the properties associated with natural light: they do not give off warmth, vibrations, or reflections; they do not penetrate each other, but remain absolutely distinct in the degree of their intensity and in their contrasts. Light and dark areas do not set each other off in relief; they are without intrinsic relation to the objects. This is not an empirical but a spiritual light, and it lacks the ability to transcend itself, be it toward the world of the supersensual-unearthly or toward the world of the sensual. This light is absolute consciousness, awareness apart from all else, a light imprisoned in the finite for all its effort to go beyond the merely empirical. In the genesis of the picture, line was Picasso's first means of representation. Light and shadow came after, as though he had always planned to divorce them from line.

Summing up, we may say that the actual and sole object of the painting is its material of figuration. For, after all, the things depicted do not appear as three-dimensional bodies, and neither personal feeling nor metaphysical conscious-being can, strictly speaking, be called an object. These elements participate in the material of figuration, as do Picasso's need to communicate, on the one hand, and his artistic powers, on the other. But this participation is of a special kind: all these elements of contents enter the material of figuration and become visible through it, but do not achieve form *in* it.[7] Rather, the material of figuration comes between them, being neither an expressionistic means of

7. [This discussion is probably related to a conception held by Walter Benjamin.]

representation nor an autonomous artistic form, and it veils the contents as it discloses them; it is a neuter, so to speak, which holds the various elements together but at the same time keeps them apart from each other. The material is not the synthesis of all contradictions, as was the marble of the pediment sculptures at Olympia;[8] it is not a finite means through which one glimpses the infinite substance, as in Romanesque and Gothic stained glass. It is an object by itself—hard, impervious, full of a "jerky rhythm of frequent stops, abrupt shifts, and new moments of frozen immobility" (Walter Benjamin). It is a *contrived* object, growing out of an abyss, containing the abyss in itself but never bridging it; it is an object born of manifold functions, to which it gives no reality but only a reified semblance of reality. That is why this material of figuration not only does not suggest the sensory qualities of touch, taste, and smell, but also lacks what Poussin called *délectation*. What Poussin doubtless had in mind was that the material should appeal to the senses, the sensual quality to the aesthetic feeling, and the last to the intellect in such a way that material and idea present themselves to the viewer as inseparable, so that he may perceive the essential unity of all his faculties and, by the same token, his creative freedom. Older artists had tried to supply this *délectation*, or at least its substitute, a sensual stimulus, to their material of figuration even when they portrayed evil, ugliness, and destruction. This was true of Baudelaire, the greatest of them all. Caricaturists, such as Daumier and Toulouse-Lautrec, fulfilled a historical task by showing how such a synthesis of negative content with formal *délectation* is possible.[9]

Picasso is their descendant, but he has had to be careful to avoid both excess in expression and lack of form. He tried not to repress the race of emotions toward their extreme and stood ready to go beyond the limits of art whenever feeling or its metaphysical counterpart—pure conscious-being—might so dictate. At the same time he was well aware that whatever is not expressed as energy, space, and time has no artistic existence. In other words, his need for communication was always in a titanic struggle with his creative powers because his reactions to experience were always so intense that they threatened to find an outlet in direct bodily action rather than in art. He found temporary peace in the objective materiality of the material of figuration, but only at the cost of the painting's autonomy. It never acquires a life of its own; the material of figuration never does attain freedom, never pulsates in rhythm with the world, because it is the product of a conscious and unconscious act rather than spontaneously developing form which *becomes* a second nature.

From whatever angle we approach the constitution of the material of figuration we discover two factors belonging to two fundamentally different levels of reality: black and white, which express pure conscious-being as the one and general ultimate principle, and

8. [The author discusses this in his unpublished ms. "Classical Man in Greek Art."]

9. [The typescript reads "unmöglich" (impossible), but we believe the author to mean the opposite.]

line, which expresses specific, individually experienced emotion. The real world—both the world of objects (nature) and that of history (society)—lies somewhere between. Unlike abstract or surrealist painters, Picasso made the titanic effort to preserve both worlds and to record as much as possible of them. His artistic emotions were always physical, not merely intellectual, and he knew that without relating emotions to bodies, space, time, and energy, art is not possible in the first place. This is why Picasso's predicament is so grave: confronted with a subject of history, he cannot portray the events in their immediate facticity. The question then arises: If the subject matter of this painting is not the bombing of Guernica (which certainly was the occasion for it), what is it?

I shall choose a few from among the many very different interpretations of *Guernica* to illustrate my thesis that form and content have not attained unity in this work and hence that its content is necessarily ambiguous.

According to Herbert Read, the content of the painting is symbolic and its symbolism manifest and clear:

The light of day and night reveals a scene of horror and destruction; the eviscerated horse, the writhing bodies of men and women, betray the passage of the infuriated bull, who turns triumphantly in the background, tense with lust and stupid power; whilst from a window Truth, whose features are the tragic mask in all its classical purity, extends her lamp over the carnage. The great canvas is flooded with pity and terror, but over it all is imposed that nameless grace which arises from their cathartic equilibrium.

Not only Guernica, but Spain; not only Spain, but Europe, are symbolized in this allegory. It is the modern Calvary, the agony in the bomb-shattered ruins of human tenderness and faith. It is a religious picture . . .[10]

Against this interpretation it must be said that Truth with her night lamp brings too little light. Authentic tragedy is absent because there can be no question of pity and terror unless fate is *within* us as well as exterior to us, so that an individual's resistance to it is actually possible. Picasso, however, portrays passive submission. Accordingly, there is no catharsis here, but at most comfort and hope for those who can accept Picasso's unpolitical solution for political events—i.e., those who are completely out of touch with their time. It seems to me that the bull does not cause the fire, which Picasso clearly indicates. The bull is not even its symbolic cause—more properly, not its allegorical cause, for we must not lose the distinction between symbol and allegory, fundamental to any theory of art.

Herbert Read's allusion to bullfighting has found echoes among American interpreters (Harriet Janis, Vernon Clark, and others). But as long as we retain anything of the essence of the bullfight, it strikes me as a most inadequate allegory. Bullfighting is a

10. "Picasso's 'Guernica,' " in *A Coat of Many Colours* (London, 1945), p. 319.

contest, not a surprise attack like the Nazi bombing raid; it is a well-ordered struggle governed by strict rules, in which a certain balance is maintained between the human intelligence and the bull's physical strength, such that the outcome may be characterized as a "moment of truth." The bomb is the absolute opposite to such a "moment of truth"; it masks the powerlessness of a power which seeks to conquer without struggle or sacrifice, because the will to fight has degenerated through loss of genuine ideals and those who resort to bombs must destroy their own nation sooner than the foreign one. Furthermore, it is possible to interpret the bullfight as the freeing of a society from its brute forces, blind instincts, etc.—a kind of sacrificing of the lower instincts through the intelligence and vigilance of the matador. The bombing raid, on the contrary, is an attack by blind instinct, by the unredeemed urges of stupidity and brutality.

Using the allegory of the bullfight, one arrives finally at the point of seeing in the bull—the only animal unaffected in the painting—an allegory of Franco, as if Picasso were not a convinced Loyalist who despised Franco. One cannot solve this problem by an interpretation of the bull's face, which—taken out of context—depends on the whim of the interpreter. Where Herbert Read sees "lust and stupid power," Christian Zervos speaks of "a life throbbing with promise," of "a feeling of permanence, of imperishable strength," of the "sureness of its glance which convinces us that nothing essential is lost," of "an animal face . . . with eyes freed from the confusions which entangle thought, the culmination of power liberated from death and perfect, possession of time and fate, whence a new day will burst forth."[11] Vernon Clark gets entangled in an obvious contradiction when he says that "the bull, villain of the piece, is the only figure in the mural that has any dignity—the only figure whose strength is solidly grounded, both in abstract structure and pictorial detail, and in which the two elements are united toward a single end." But instead of concluding that the bull is not "a symbol of Franco and fascist brutality," he bases all his further inferences on this fallacy: "In the bull ring, we remember, the horse is the comic relief, the symbol of the decrepit, the broken down, the ridiculously outworn. Yet it is with such symbols as this that Picasso identifies the things that died at Guernica—with such symbols as a warrior whose decapitation reveals the hollow body of a mannequin."[12]

To avoid such implications, which are in flagrant contradiction with Picasso's convinced Loyalism, Harriet Janis invented the following variant: "It is drama that is forced off schedule by the escape of the bull into the streets. There a surprise attack has been made, not only upon the torero but upon the onlookers as well. In the conflict, neither the horse, the rider, nor the audience has had a proper chance to defend itself against the

11. Christian Zervos, "Histoire d'un tableau de Picasso," *Cahiers d'art* (Paris), XII (1937), no. 4/5, pp. 105–10.

12. Vernon Clark, "Picasso and the Guernica Mural," *Science and Society* (New York), V (1941), p. 76.

unleashed furies of the bull. The end is tragedy. The horse (possibly as Spain) has been wounded twice, gored by the bull and stabbed by the spear of the rider as he fell. The horseman (possibly as the young Republic) . . ."[13]

It remains the secret of Harriet Janis how the bull could have set the house on fire, what makes tragedy of a massacre, why Picasso, an ardent Spanish Republican, permitted Spain—the young Republic—to be murdered (even allegorically), why the enraged bull has not harmed the mother, or why, finally, Picasso does not show us the bull in all his destructive fury, but with it all behind him. The allegory of the bullfight is nonsense, even though Picasso does give some grounds for it by choosing the bull, horse, and rider as leading actors. In fact, this misinterpretation must have arisen from a false association between Hemingway's *For Whom the Bell Tolls* and Picasso's painting, an association which intellectuals, thanks to their "culture," could not escape.

Juan Larrea, in his book *Guernica*,[14] took a different approach, starting from Picasso's observation that the horse had in the past symbolized for him a woman whose failure to reciprocate his love inspired feelings of revenge. According to Larrea, Picasso felt the same way about Nationalist Spain; hence he represented it as a horse and worked his "pictorial magic" at its expense, seeking to destroy it.[15] A stream of blasphemy, he goes on, pours from this Franco-horse, directed against the Holy Ghost, which is symbolized by the dove. The man trampled by the horse is, according to this interpretation, a defender of the Republic, and his arms, outstretched as in crucifixion, brand Franco's Catholicism as anti-Christian; turning to magic, Picasso brings in the hoof as a counterbalance, "a talisman of good luck, a very successful substitute for the triumphant raised fist of the initial sketches." The bull, then, stands for the Spanish people, full of contempt for the horse, "in whose destruction it is apparently not anxious to intervene." The mother with child is "the motherhood of Mother Spain" and "the childhood of Spain," while Picasso has left open the question of whether the child is dead or merely unconscious. The bull, by protecting them, protects Spain's present and future. By placing the bull next to the mother, "with her mouth almost touching that of the bull (the Spanish people) and sharing, as it were, her breath with the animal's," Picasso makes the mother stand for Madrid. Thus, Larrea reasons, the bull, by means of pictorial magic applied by "Picasso [the] militiaman, wielding his brush as the others did their guns," has prevented the conquest of the capital which Franco and his Fascist allies had kept under siege for months. The woman with the lamp is the Spanish Republic, figured as a female warrior against obscurantism, which is personified by "the horse in its death-struggle." According to

13. Sidney and Harriet Janis, "Picasso's 'Guernica'—
A Film Analysis with Commentary," *Pacific Art Review*
(San Francisco), I (1941–42), no. 3/4, p. 22.

14. (Paris, 1945); tr. A. H. Krappe (New York, 1947).
15. Ibid., p. 33.

Larrea "the essential feature of this intense drama is . . . the struggle of light against darkness." The two figures at the right have only the parts of extras.[16]

All this, however, is only the starting point for Larrea's interpretation, revealing no more than the surface of Picasso's mind, as it were. Beneath lie unconscious surrealistic depths which Larrea set out to decipher. At this unconscious level *Guernica* symbolizes the end of the world. The bull sees and knows—as the light in his eyes proves—something which is hidden and which Larrea calls apocalyptic wisdom: "I am the Alpha and the Omega, the beginning and the end." The bull's tongue is "the Creative or Generative Word in the absolute sense . . . the *Logos spermaticos*" (in contrast to the horse's neighing against the Holy Ghost). And this "creative entity of the divine Word . . . has been historically incarnated in the Spanish people." Thus the bull, the woman, the child, and the dove shown on the left side of the painting constitute a "compressed ideogram symbolizing the Word, on the one side and by way of a background figure, the divine Bull in the form of the Father and the *Logos spermaticos*. Below is the Son, and on one side the Holy Ghost—that is, Western divinity in its trinitarian form, plus the Mother, transforming the Trinity into a Quaternity."[17]

Here, surely, is the moment for Homeric laughter, although Larrea, a poet, carries his fantastic interpretation a good deal further. Quite certainly, Picasso has no more sneaked in the refugee poet's provincial Basque Christianity than his New World internationalism or the hoof superstition, while Larrea should not have overlooked the fact that it has seven nails, a point which might have supplied him with a theme for endless speculation—*Guernica* as a symbol of the world's creation. A more serious question is whether Picasso really believed himself to be a magician capable of slaying Franco with his brush, in occult harmony with the forces of world history. Such a view seems to have been confirmed by Zervos, who said: "The possibility for a man to extend his power as far as he wants, to master energies of incalculable scope, which he can set in motion at the chosen moment . . . is in no way bound up with normal conditions; it derives absolutely from his own supernatural power."[18] This would suggest that Picasso identified himself with the bull—whatever the latter may stand for—and that he felt responsible for the defeat[19] of the Spanish Republicans because, in his recourse to powers of magic, he had somewhere made a fundamental error—failure to realize that genuine magic can be effective only if followed up by real action, the real action of a coherent social group, not the aesthetic action of an egotist in his studio.

Let us leave the magic issue for the moment. Larrea's contribution to our understanding of the painting might lie in his equation of the horse with Franco, suggested to

16. Ibid., pp. 36–39.
17. Ibid., pp. 59–61.
18. P. 111.

19. [*Guernica* was completed by mid June, 1937. The Republic was not defeated, however, until the surrender of Madrid, March 28, 1939.]

him by Picasso's equation of a horse with a hostile woman. Now, this would give us a wholly personal kind of allegory, or, as Larrea put it, "an understanding of this metaphor will be possible only for those persons who know the explanation given by the artist as to his symbolism."[20] Whether symbol, allegory, or metaphor, all must remain a very low sort of mystification as long as they do not either derive from the life of the society that believes in them and whose artists share this belief, or else represent a cultural tradition so that an artist who employs them can appeal to a certain class and expect to be understood. Now, even the latter alternative is scarcely applicable here. The horse is commonly regarded as a noble, spirited animal, man's companion in some of his most dangerous undertakings; in earlier epochs, when man had not yet learned to ride, he believed that the horse carried the powers of the dead to the fields of the ancestors. Even in the bullfight the part played by the horse has only recently taken on a meaner character. Picasso's personal allegory and personal magic may of course owe something to it. But the important consideration here is not only the fact that individual allegories, perhaps valid in easel paintings for aesthetes, are out of place in a historical painting intended to influence the masses. Even if Picasso had resorted to the long-forgotten banderole, the fact would remain that individual allegories can appear only when form is divorced from content and some substitute for their missing unity must be found—i.e., on the borderline between art and literature. Were Picasso to provide an allegorical key to *Guernica*, it would still be true that what he produced is ineffectual as propaganda and dubious as a work of art.

Nonetheless, one is reluctant to accept the extreme diversity of the existing interpretations as final. In point of fact the diversity may be legitimate, provided that some common principle of analogy runs through all interpretations. We have no choice but to study form and content separately, to find out whether—if not unity, congruence, or coincidence—at least some approximation, parallelism, or correspondence obtains between them. For only in this way can we ascertain the method by which *Guernica* was created, and the reason for Picasso's choice of it. Let us, then, try to grasp the subject matter without undue resort to allegorical interpretation, keeping in mind the results of our formal analysis above—namely, that there is a gulf between the empirical emotion and the metaphysical conscious-being in this work and that Picasso tries to keep as many historical and representational elements as he can, granted the existence of this gulf.

We have already noted that, contrary to our reading habits, *Guernica* starts at the right. There we find the woman who is on fire, wildly extending her arms while the rest of her body seems to be sinking into a funnel-shaped form. The fire could only have been produced by the bombing; Picasso follows history here, showing the effect of the bombing and assuming that the viewer will know what caused the fire. But the painter also shows

20. P. 34.

the burning woman as an emotion which reaches its highest point through pain, its boiling point, as it were: the affect of completely helpless panic in the face of unexpected death, as sudden as it is certain.

At the left the counterpart of this panic terror is a kind of imperturbability. Here too we have the panic scream, a mother in despair over her dead child; but above her is the stoic ataraxia of the bull, whose head is turned around—the posture is known to us from paleolithic art, where the bull's head is given in profile, the horns in frontal view. The animal's open mouth is just above the mother's. Even were the tongues not stressed, we would suspect that some oral transfer of energies is taking place here. The bull, the active male standing over the receptive woman, is here an agent of fecundation of which the mother, in an agony of sorrow, is yet unaware. The suggestion is that of new life succeeding destruction. The bull as a metaphor of male strength is so ancient in human history that the image may be regarded as part of our cultural heritage. It may denote here the sexual energy of the Spanish people or simply that of life in general.

When we turn from the nonallegorical scene of helpless panic at the right, and the allegorical image of ataraxia at the left, to the large middle portion of the painting, what do we find? Surely we must here recognize the dying horse and the dying man beneath. How have these deaths come about? Was the man riding the horse and were both killed together by the same external cause? Or was there some sort of struggle between man and horse in which each mortally wounded the other? Or were they both struck down by the external cause while they were struggling? What suggests the struggle is the spearlike weapon that pierces the horse and a small wound which may have been a blow from the sword. What suggests an external cause of death is the third and largest wound in the shape of an up-ended lozenge. This last possibility seems the most plausible. In this case the warrior would stand for a soldier of Republican Spain and the horse would stand for Franco or Fascist Spain. Such an interpretation gains support from a sketch by Picasso showing Pegasus emerging from the horse's wound; thus the horse would be equated with Medusa, and would become a symbol of Franco. This is an odd mixture of the representational and the allegorical. The forces of the Spanish Civil War are present—but it is not their struggle with each other that is portrayed; rather, we see them overwhelmed by external forces and struggling against death. It is possible that the horse is uttering a curse (depicted in a form which appears as a weapon on the ceiling of Altamira[21]) and that the soldier senses the bull's magical transfer of power to the woman. If so, the form above the horse's head would have to be an allegory of the Nazi bomb, for

21. [Cf. the author's *Prehistoric Cave Paintings*, figs. 23, 24. At the time Raphael wrote, the shapes he is speaking of—so-called claviforms—were usually regarded as weapons—cf. ibid., fig. 35 and p. 5—but in more recent scholarship they are interpreted as symbols of the female sex or of fertility. Cf. S. Giedion, *The Eternal Present: The Beginnings of Art* (New York, 1962), pp. 190, 242, 257.]

all that an electric light bulb was drawn inside it at the last minute; the form itself seems to reproduce the Greek symbol of lightning. It is interesting to note that the large central area is the most ambiguous part of the painting, a fact all the more significant in that it depicts a struggle. If we disregard the objects represented and examine the feelings conveyed, the scene would most readily seem to denote the realm of the demonic, located between panic and ataraxia.

Besides the division of the painting into three parts we therefore find a threefold development of the subject matter. On the first, or representational, level the development is from the most brutal murder, through struggle, to a renewal of life. On the second, or emotional, level we go from the passive panic of despair, through the consciously demonic, to ataraxia. On the third level, that of the creative method, the formal development leads from purely representational portrayal to a mixture of representation and allegory and then to pure allegory. Here there arises a question crucial for our understanding. Does the emphasis lie in the large middle section, in which the struggle has ended but not the agony, or does it lie in the left section, in the resolution of the conflict by the bull?

The answer may lie in careful interpretation of the woman with the lamp. Whereas the woman at the bottom right provides a physical transition from the right to the center —her escape from panic into struggle—the woman with the lamp provides a more spiritual transition. She is not running but trying to see; the night lamp gives a poor light, however. Held as it is right next to the bomb, it expresses deep irony as well as social criticism: the world being destroyed is as obsolete as the night lamp and the wooden sword; the world in process of being born will not have to cope with dead tradition. We might go further and view the woman, as does Herbert Read, as the allegory of truth. Her arm is strong, her grasp firm, and her profile incisive; she suggests something positive, the power of reason and enlightenment. Earlier studies for the painting, where the bull was shown in its full width, indicate a more unmistakable connection between the allegories of truth and fecundity: the woman's arm was level with the bull's back and almost touched it. Is this "truth" throwing light upon the carnage or does it pick out the bull as ultimate hope and certainty? Because the bull has been reduced in size and relegated to the left, and because the horse's head has been moved up, the pure duality between the spiritual and the physical allegory, between truth and fecundity, comes more clearly to the fore. It is characteristic of the great part dualism plays in Picasso's world view.

The other figures and signs in the painting will now have to be reinterpreted accordingly. Take, for instance, the open-beaked bird trying to fly upward but apparently unable to do so. Has it succumbed to the horse's curse or is it deflecting the curse from the bull? Or, if the horse represents not Franco but an innocent victim of the bombing or an allegory of struggle to the death, does the bird transfer to another world the strength of the animal which continues to fight even in its death agony? Such action would be in keeping with the symbolic significance the bird of death had in works of paleolithic and archaic times. We might also ask: Is the table an altar of sacrifice? What is the meaning of the arrow, of the seven nails in the horse's hoof, and the seven flames (3 + 4) at the right, near the woman on fire? I shall not try to answer such questions of detail. Their purely formal intent may be to keep the viewer occupied with riddles. But the longer he remains under the painter's magic spell, the less likely is he to be moved to act; the artistic details obstruct and destroy the political effect.

A normal reaction to the above "interpretation" would be to quote Paul Valéry's ironic remark: "Monsieur, votre sens est excellent, je l'adopte" ("Sir, your guess is as good as any; I'll take it"). To produce yet another interpretation, all we need do is turn to the jagged form at the top; Picasso has drawn an electric light bulb inside the "bomb" to suggest how readily a beneficial invention may be transformed into a destructive force in the modern world; or—if you like—that good produces evil and vice versa; or better yet, that good and evil are simultaneously present in any set of facts. If every component of the painting were interpreted according to the principle of *both/and* [rather than *either/or*], we could make of the bull, besides an allegory of nature's inexhaustible vitality or mankind's unshakable moral force, a portrayal of Franco's (and all other "Führers' ") impassive sadism: the bull is untouched by the mother's anguish over her child and tells her cynically that the next coitus will produce new cannon fodder. Moreover, the horse might be interpreted, not only as Franco cursing, but as a defiant animal refusing to surrender even after the death of its rider. (In this case Picasso's hint to Larrea would show itself to be a deception, arising with necessity from the basic methodological axiom of interpretation itself, or else Larrea's conclusion would be an inescapable fallacy.) We would then have to assume that the painting's ambiguities are a necessary consequence of Picasso's axiomatic premise that the function of allegory is to give an appearance of unity to contradictory contents. The viewer would thus be compelled to suspend judgment, since he would not only be able to provide contradictory interpretations for every detail but would even be obliged to do so. But, with all this, allegory does not disappear; i.e., it does not cease to be a mere substitute for form. What we have left in the end is not artistic form, synthesizing meaning and vision—however numerous the meanings—but a split between the concrete and the universal which makes interpretation anybody's guess. Had Picasso succeeded in giving form to the emotional complex of terror, chaos, barbarism, destruction, helplessness in the face of blind social forces, no recourse to the artist's private mythology would have been necessary and the viewer would not have been obliged both to look for interpretations and to suspend judgment. As it is, the viewer is made the victim of an allegory which is not self-evident and must leave him

XX   POUSSIN. *Winter (The Flood)*. 1660–64. 46⅝×63 in.

XXI   GOYA. *The Third of May, 1808.* 1814. 8 ft. 8 in. × 11 ft. 3⅞ in.

unsatisfied: his emotions and his judgment are being torn apart and set one against the other, so that he is stultified rather than stimulated to creative action.

An important aspect of Picasso's artistic imagination is disclosed when we note that the development from panic to ataraxia corresponds to the two features of the material of figuration which were noted above. Panic as an extreme emotion, frozen into affect, is obviously expressed by line; however, the fact that the bull's sexual power stands for unchanging conscious-being must be regarded as an arbitrary use of allegory. Furthermore, the development of the emotions from panic through demonic struggle to ataraxia discloses only a relative continuity—relative because the ataraxia does not grow organically from the affects which precede it but is opposed to them as a *deus ex machina*. But even this relative continuity is in sharp contrast to the relatively great discontinuity between the objects and stages of the action. The two are conditioned by the inner rhythm of the emotion, by its jumps from one extreme to the other, by the dispersal of several currents of the same emotion into unlike objects or by the confluence of unlike emotional currents in the same object, by the transition from silent gestures to screams—by the need for a great many equal stresses. Any possibility of balance between emotion on the one hand and objects and events on the other is excluded by the nature of the emotion itself, which is extensive and extreme, not intensive and concentrated—it is mere affect. Under the pressure of these affects Picasso could record only those elements of bodies which are transformable into gesture, which he does not conceive of as growing out of the plenitude of individual or social existence, but rather as opposed to a pure conscious-being. The latter cannot respect the autonomy of the person and must replace it with the empirical individual self which can approach conscious-being only by means of exhibitionistic gestures. The same affects set limits to the portrayal of actual events, which can be conceived neither within the continuity of historical development nor as a unity of mood such as Poussin achieved in his *Winter, or The Flood* (Plate **XX**) or Goya in his *Third of May* (Plate **XXI**). Events, too, are broken up into isolated gestures which can only be repeated and varied and which are pushed to such extremes that they make no appeal to the viewer's capacity to act, to his enthusiasm, to his freedom. But without such an appeal no painting is historical or political.

The weakness of Picasso's artistic imagination is disclosed by the fact that he does not choose to make a sacrifice of the bull in order to enlist its magic powers; instead of sacrifice, which is a ceremonial social action, he merely invokes the pure force of nature, which transfers itself without ritual or ceremony from one creature to another (unless Picasso meant to endow the bull magically with all the vital energies of the Spanish people or of the world in general). In other words the bull, the only creature spared by the bombing, no longer plays the part society assigns it; it has become an autonomous being upon which society is dependent for its physical survival or rebirth. This relapse into a spurious magical transfer, which is supported neither by a faith in the unity of all natural beings and their affinity nor by the existence of an organized social force capable of translating magic into reality (and the genuine magic of the paleolithic age involves these two factors)—this use of atavistic relics detached from their ideological and chronological contexts is a spiritual rootlessness wholly in keeping with the Fascist barbarization of capitalist society, as expressed in the bombing raid. Furthermore, this naturalistic biologism, in its disguise as an allegory baroque in form and preprimitive (or, more accurately, unhistorical) in content, signifies that the artist considers himself a part of society only to the extent that he dominates it—not as a member of a community, performing limited though valuable functions. Knowing no such community, Picasso imposes his allegory in an absolutist manner on that part of society which needs it because it can only talk and talk and cannot act, and therefore thinks it understands Picasso, though actually it misunderstands him. He appeals to an insignificantly small group of literati who inhabit an imaginary world, a world that cannot find artistic realization because its inhabitants, instead of confronting reality, idolize dreams. Finally—and this is the crux—Picasso responds to a historical and political fact in naturalistic biological terms. This twist has since been repeated often enough (e.g., by Camus in *The Plague*), but it does not reflect a Copernican twist forward. Rather, it is a Fascist twist backward. It treats man solely as a being of nature; it relieves him of the responsibility for not making his own history. The same principle underlies the Nazi theory of racial superiority and the thousand-year *Reich*; the only difference between the Nazi beliefs and a belief in the sexual power of the Spanish people is one of degree; long before Picasso painted *Guernica* Nazi poets such as Gottfried Benn[22] had bridged the difference by means of a biological aesthetics. In both cases the cause is the same: the artist does not understand political history—whether individual facts, its development, its nature, or its motivating forces, which are not natural but social in character.

We have deliberately stressed this unfair analogy to lay bare the ideological absurdity of Picasso's allegory. It might be objected that in *Guernica* the biological factor is completely overshadowed by the significance of the bull as symbol or totem of the Spanish people. As totem animal it assures the survival of the tribe; more than that, it also is a projection of the nation's soul, of its unity conceived of as independent of the sum of its members. But what even more fundamentally separates Picasso from the Nazis is the presence of a second allegory: the appeal to reason, totally lacking in Nazi ideology.

22. [Gottfried Benn (1886–1956), German poet and writer, embraced Nazism in 1933, but soon recognized his error, fell silent, and was ostracized by the regime after 1936. After the war he admitted his error publicly. A selection of his work was published in translation as *Primal Vision*, ed. E. B. Ashton (New York and London, 1958).]

However, Reason, Enlightenment, and Truth are bourgeois abstractions without specific content; they parallel the famous trinity of *Liberté, Egalité, Fraternité*, whose capital letters served to camouflage the fact that they were positive values only for the upper classes but empty promises for the lower classes. All the petty bourgeois revolutions of the nineteenth century were both made and crushed under the banner of these big words. The fact that in the Spanish Civil War they were merely an empty, negative formula was proved by the chatter about nonintervention current before Picasso painted *Guernica*. Although the appeal to Reason goes far beyond Nazi ideology, it provides no concrete solution—real or allegorical—that could point the way to the defeat of Fascism.

Picasso was doubtless sincerely Republican, but subconsciously he was at the time caught up in a petty bourgeois, and hence reactionary, ideology. Here we glimpse one of the reasons for the split between line and color and between empirical emotion and metaphysical conscious-being as well as for the use of signs and allegories as a means to bridge the gap. Picasso as a social animal—and this is the most fundamental aspect of man—actually inhabited two worlds which met in the social stratum to which he belonged. He was personally unable to choose between them. In this historical painting Picasso met the limits of his artistic powers because he had stunted his self-education as a human being (apart from his training as a specialist of painting) and had not yet worked his way from self-alienation to self-realization. Thus this painting, which was inspired by a historical event, could not turn out to be a true historical painting but only a hybrid offspring of the "goddess" Reason and the "god" bull—a hybrid which could be realized artistically only in the form of an allegory. Picasso's ideology made it impossible to solve either the political or the artistic problem because this ideology did not elevate the historically conditioned to the suprahistorical and universally human, but dragged it down to the petty bourgeois which had already shown itself to be antihistorical and antihuman.

Our conclusion remains valid when we accept ambiguity and suspension of judgment as solution for the allegories. For this simultaneity of opposites necessarily implies a relativism which can be indulged only by a social stratum not actively engaged in shaping history. In today's society this stratum is the petty bourgeoisie, whose various components are held together by their seeming neutrality in the face of the hostilities between the history-shaping powers. The petty bourgeois mistakes this relativistic attitude for tolerance, holding it superior to the either/or dogmatism indispensable to the struggling parties; in reality, however, this tolerance is merely indifference and bound to fall into one or the other warring camp—more accurately, bound to shift back and forth between them—in the face of the compulsion to take action. This is reflected in *Guernica* by the contradiction between the dramatic eloquence of the work and the skepticism implied in it, as well as by the fact that the extreme character of the emotions makes suspension of judgment with respect to the allegory impossible.

Our analysis of the content of *Guernica* has disclosed that its fundamental theme is not contemporary history or natural environment but the artist's own feelings, which he has transformed into specific affects. For this reason, only an analysis of this transformation can illuminate the relation between form and content—i.e., the artist's method.

We have already mentioned that Picasso does not build his feelings into a unified state of feeling, conceiving its many components as mere differentiations of an underlying unity. Such a vivid, sensory emotional atmosphere is possible only when subject and object, feeling and action, coincide and interpenetrate, and this in turn is possible only when the oppositions have been conceived of as self-positing conflicts, i.e., when it is by their own internal movement that they achieve synthesis. The cold brutality that characterizes both destruction and continuation of life in this work might be viewed as providing a kind of negative emotional atmosphere, but the repetition of identical expressive movements and of identical accents speaks against such a view; this cold brutality lacks all possibility of an inner development (from exposition through unfolding to completion), without which the emotional atmosphere could not be aesthetic but is naturalistic and sentimental. Since Picasso's own emotions were not attached to objects or to existence but merely expressive of his subjective reactions and attitudes, he may have tried to avoid the inherent danger of sentimentalism by pushing feeling to the extremest pitch, i.e., by transforming it into affect. Affect is distinguished from passion by its compulsiveness being stronger than the resistance to it. Now, to Picasso the most intense charge of emotional energy is that which attains its goal without any resistance and by the shortest route. Beyond that point it can only be annihilated. This conception implies a specific relationship of the affective energy to movement and to its objective vehicle—man. In Picasso each affect has its own isolated movement; no affect ever strives toward any other. Hence there are constant beginnings and stops, resulting in an addition of particles whose only connection lies in the fact that mere variants of the same affect have been employed. Each movement in part turns back upon itself, the end reverting to the beginning with a compulsiveness in which the inertia implicit in each charge of energy asserts itself. In so far as the movement does not turn back upon itself, it points to an open, "spurious" infinity because it has no counterpart in man's inwardness, in his self-determined, autonomous individuality. In other words, the human vehicle of the affective movement is conceived as a mere means serving to attach the movement to a body. In consequence man cannot resist it, cannot transform its extension into intensity. Instead of encompassing man in his entirety, the movement reduces him to a single gesture—but not one in which he objectifies his inwardness; rather, the gesture results from a charge of energy that assails, overpowers, and subjects man; he is not the cause but the product of the affective movement, victim of an alien determination beyond all possibility of self-determined resistance. This is why Picasso's affects are never tragic, although the impression of an objective power transcending the individual is constantly produced. What is lacking is any affirmation of this fateful power by the individual, a personal assimilation of the suprapersonal. Picasso's concept of man is too narrow to express such a parallelogram of the forces of fate and character; what we find is not the idea of man, or man in the likeness of God or the autonomous person, or even man as an average—but simply everyman, the screaming suffering human animal. Picasso reduces this human animal to a motor-sensory fiber that lacks the synapses conducting to thought and consciousness— only the bull possesses these!—and of which he shows only the end point as an explosion of the energy charge. The affective movement is not tragic but titanic, and this titanic effort is never blocked by a counteraffect, never obliged to fight; it simply is repeated until it terminates itself, at the same time being terminated from outside. At its climax it is confronted with the indefinable and it ends in the shriek of anguish and impotence of dehumanized man before the ineffable, the inaccessible. The viewer cannot add anything to the affective movement, he can only gaze upon it, completely numbed, until the initial shock gradually wears off, because the affect is partly too vague, partly overdetermined, i.e., because it does not develop from the particular to the universal. Therefore Picasso is also unable to portray affect as it unfolds; he can only show the final stage, only the extreme point, and this extreme point has been given the same emphasis throughout, the same extreme charge of energy. As a result, authentic time is excluded—whether as existential time, since man is reduced to the motor-sensory, or as time for systematic formation, since the explosion of the charge of energy is all we are given. There is no crescendo, no diminuendo, only the simultaneity of beginning and end, however great the distance in space may be. The movement is merely external, merely the path of the greatest possible charge of energy over the shortest possible route—hence involving the shortest possible time. It is intended to produce shock, and is the more effective the more quickly it horrifies and paralyzes the viewer.

This charge and explosion of energy that destroys movement and time may seem at first to characterize the individual affect only. We have noted that there is a transformation across the picture width from unconscious panic to conscious imperturbability, from complete helplessness in the face of historical events to the Stoic ideal of ataraxia. Expressed in more formal terms, the development is from the wild confusion of the three women to the impassive calm of the bull. In terms of content there are three different affects here, with different functions, successive both in time and space; but they are not three stages of a single affect. Picasso tried to relate them meaningfully, but they do not grow out of one another. They are not phases of a single entelechy developing spontaneously; rather, they run along a path through time and space which is dictated by the artist, dependent upon his whim even when he introduces the *deus ex machina*. Instead of a continuously developing entelechy we find discontinuous eruptions and catastrophes; a more serious fact is that these discontinuities in time and space are not internally de-termined, but depend upon the artist's will. The transition from the destruction of life to faith in its indestructibility does not arise out of the central struggle, for all the note taken of a will to resist, but rather out of the artist's attempt to produce a twofold happy ending by allegorical means. At no point does the painting cease to be contrived. The visual element, in consequence, gives way to an emotion which does not develop into a unified situation but is built up into a sum of affects and effects, the meaning of which must be deciphered instead of revealing itself.

The fact that Picasso begins with the space-time realization of an affect—i.e., the discharge of an emotion at its maximum intensity—implies a rejection of pure and empty geometric space, all perspectives, and the relations of bodies to background. Long before *Guernica* he had replaced these with the energy field, the main features of which are as follows. Most important, despite movements in and out of depth, bodies and space are not treated separately by giving priority to either, and both are equally dependent on energy. Second, the movement of a body through space into depth is not distinguish-able from the movement of a body around its own axis; in other words, while the viewer looks into depth, he also sees the objects from all sides; hence different views of one and the same body can be shown at the same time. Third, the solid body does not deprive space of its transparency, and the eye perceives several strata of space simultaneously. However, this transparency of space never takes on the character of transcendence (as it did in early Christian catacomb painting and in medieval stained glass); space is finite. Fourth, space is not measured as an extension of depth into infinity but by the contraction of planes whose intensity is greatest when their extension—i.e., the intervals between them—becomes infinitely small; in other words, space is no longer apprehended in terms of maximum distance, but rather in terms of a least possible distance, provided it be linked to the greatest tension between clearly distinct planes. Fifth, space does not result from different directions and dimensions which meet in one point, as in a system of co-ordinates, and have equal importance for structuring space; since the various planes are arranged according to the principle of the most intensive contraction, depth tends to eliminate time, while the dimensions of height and width are left to deal with movement and time (elsewhere better brought into static balance than in *Guernica*). Sixth, the artist is not confined to a single method of figuring space; he may employ several methods at once and even include fragments of linear perspective. These are the chief principles which were developed by Picasso and Braque over a forty-year period. They add up to a new method of figuring space, but they are rooted in a tradition far older than the methods based upon laws of linear or aerial perspective.[23]

23. [The author explains this in an unpublished essay, "Braques Raumgestaltungen."]

As for the manner in which these principles are applied in *Guernica,* the following details may be noted. Picasso uses various means. The window opens a view into a world outside the pictorial space and is clearly surrounded by a fire that could not have been caused by a bull no matter how enraged, but only by bombs. The lines which converge in the table play with linear perspective, but its one vanishing point is not answered by anything from the right side of the painting. Thus, perspective—contradicting its nature —produces an effect of asymmetry. One of Picasso's principal devices is to connect movement in depth with the rotation of bodies on their own axes—or, more precisely, with suddenly arrested moments of such rotation resulting in simultaneous views of the same body from several vantage points. We see this especially in the heads. The bull's head, for example, is shown in profile, while the horns are in frontal view; elsewhere we find both eyes visible although the face is seen in profile. The customary interpretation is that Picasso simply juxtaposes various views, each of them static, and any implication of movement in such bodies must be attributed to the artist alone. But in my opinion it would be more exact to speak of two simultaneous movements, one which involves the entire field of energy in movements both forward and backward and one which rotates the body centrifugally on its own axis; then these movements would be stopped abruptly, and their impetus converted from full movement into a body at rest. With this sudden arrest successive views become simultaneous views; the result is a new kind of interpenetration between bodies and space.

This conversion of a twofold dynamic into a static state would then be closely linked to the super-imposition of numerous layers of space. This makes it possible to show the movement from back to front and from front to back simultaneously, and consequently to cancel out this twofold movement as an event in time while preserving the tension between the opposite directions of the same dimension. Picasso is clearly fascinated by the idea of static simultaneity, in which all the complex factors of intense dynamics are transcended and retained[24] in an optimal tension within a state of rest. Picasso's fundamental problem in figuring space is to render fully the dynamics of the natural and human world as a static system of tensions. He realizes this with the help of color—by keeping black, white, and gray apart, so that they can never model one another as shadow (i.e., the color planes cannot become self-sufficient units in space), and by forcing the colors (as smooth surfaces charged with energy) into interrelationships of contraction whose tension contains both the abandoned dynamics and the aimed-at statics. Since his blacks, whites, and grays never lose their identities, they force the reduction of visible depth to zero and the elimination of time in the process of figuring depth. The converse is also true: because Picasso transforms dynamic elements into a system of static tensions he must keep

24. [The author says, " 'aufgehoben,' d.h. überwunden und erhalten," indicating by the quotation marks and the added explanation that he is echoing Hegel.]

his colors uniform, and hence is obliged to express movement by line or else in another dimension, width rather than depth.

This brings us back to the contrast previously discussed between metaphysical conscious-being and empirical emotion. The gulf between them is manifested in Picasso's figuration of space, of which figuration of depth is only one aspect. To begin with, space is not built up according to the classical geometric model of a system of co-ordinates with a central point of reference for all dimensions and directions. If we were to look for such a central point of reference in *Guernica*, we would have to imagine it lying in the vaguest area of the picture, somewhere in the body of the horse. The use of color in this area—overlapping stippled planes—is the only exception with respect to the characterization of the colors given above. Here density of color and tension between planes (as well as formal definition) are abandoned. We find instead an indefinite something, at once present and absent, which, despite the stippling—or because of it—produces the effect of a void which irritates rather than appeals to our senses. Because this complex of planes is surrounded by strong accents, stormy movements, and shrill cries, it attracts our attention and expresses, as it were, a protest against the system of spatial co-ordinates. Thus, despite the compositional scheme, the space is not architectonic but diffuse.

A second indication that the fundamental contrasts are only superficially related is the peculiar relationship between continuity and discontinuity. To the eye the energy field is finite and built up by the accretion of discontinuous complexes. Yet the field is everywhere present, nowhere interrupted, even where there is a marked separation between planes. This presupposes an underlying continuum: but where is it to be seen? It has been covered up by the wealth of detail. At the same time the fundamental continuity is not abolished by the discontinuities between energy groups. (This contrasts strikingly with the early classical pediment at Olympia, for example, where the background separates the individual figures and where there can be no question of any underlying continuum, any field of energy, but only of plastic groups against an empty space.)

The same fundamental contrasts surely account for the fact that we remain uncertain whether the action takes place indoors or out. It would be possible to argue the case either way. This uncertainty is in keeping with Picasso's intention of portraying not the representational but the emotional reality, and the latter not alone but in relation to the plenitude and silence of absolute conscious-being. Moreover, since the emotions expressed are brutal, destructive ones, a clearly three-dimensional space would come into conflict with the theme and its treatment. This is also why the emotional atmosphere is not uniform: the gap, the gulf between empirical emotion and metaphysical conscious-being, can only result in extreme affects (screams, fear, frozen horror). Picasso is interested not in a unified (physical or psychic) space, but in rendering diverse reactions to the gulf that yawns between emotional movement in space and nonspatial, metaphysical conscious-being.

In so far as there is development in depth in this work, we find it in the passage from the dead soldier to the black areas behind the objects. This means that although three-dimensionality has been abolished, it has been replaced not with an open infinity (to be interpreted in cosmic terms) but with a terminal black plane of resistance which eludes all determination. (We have already discussed its metaphysical character.) Between these two diverging modes of reality are located the stippled planes which make up the body of the horse. No sort of inner development is involved (entelechy, progress from the possible to the actual, emanation, etc.) but merely transition, external mediation. Therefore the order of the three factors can vary and the black can appear now in the most proximate plane, now in the most distant plane, without weakening the contrast. The black is, as it were, a soundless echo from the world of metaphysical conscious-being, the very silence of which intensifies the energy charge of the empirical emotion, raising the cries of agony to the earsplitting crash of a collapsing world. It is in this fashion—acoustically—that the yawning gap is filled.

Having discussed the content, we shall now proceed to an analysis of the formal aspects of the painting. As we have already remarked, the movement is from right to left, the reverse of the usual, requiring the eye to travel from the end of the picture to the beginning before it can move from beginning to end. As it goes from left to right the eye is sent from shock to shock, and because it cannot understand them, it skips from one to the next. This forces the artist to place one of the strongest charges of energy at the end of the eye's first journey; as a result, the effect of the progression from exposition through development to consummation and resolution is impaired when the eye reads the picture from right to left. This right-to-left movement, which follows the content and meaning of the picture, begins simultaneously at top and bottom, i.e., at two separate places (which detaches the dimension of height more or less from that of width, as the latter was detached from the dimension of depth, as we have seen). Both upper and lower courses lead toward the same goal, level with the horse's head. The lower course proceeds along the diagonal and stops somewhat short of this point; the upper one, following the inclined horizontal, reaches it and is led on by the horse's head. Here a wide gap, however, all but arrests the leftward drive; it is resumed on the other side only by the direction of the otherwise static bull's head. The artist has prepared this transition from fortissimo to quietude partly by progressively shortening the laps of the movement and partly by widening the intervals between them.

The course at the bottom does not have this character of a slowing down but continuous movement; it is combined of two movements meeting from opposite directions; one from the left runs level on the ground while the other from the right rises along the diagonal; both produce a kind of paradoxical divergence and create a hiatus that is punctuated by the vertical thrust of one of the horse's legs. Observing that the end of the upper course is joined to the beginning of the lower by the slanting line that connects the bull's head with the woman's body, we find a movement running alongside the edges of the picture but twice interrupted: left of center (top) and right of center (bottom). The two gaps are connected by the sloping lines of the horse's neck; the horse's head is pushed out of the triangle formed by a relatively calm area between the movements on top and bottom. The dynamic movement and the static forms, symmetrically placed, of the external composition are not related internally; even their external relationship (such as it is) is reduced to a minimum. Picasso has not here, as elsewhere, attempted to balance unequal masses, either on the broken vertical axis or on the horse's neck, the slant of which links the two main scansions of the movement. This is not to say that the painting is out of balance; but the balance is a static, terminal state, and its origin in an alternating movement between two unequal masses is concealed from the eye and from consciousness. All that is static seems as though rigidly crystallized, while all that is dynamic wheels around it, albeit not evenly or uninterruptedly. The discontinuities of movement and the dissociations between dimensions isolate every particle of movement from the whirling over-all movement and make any of the particles seem frozen, too; their arrangement, on the other hand, may be said to possess dynamic value, precisely because it goes beyond the particular movements, however abrupt. In this twofold adjustment between the dynamic and static elements—their separation notwithstanding—we cannot help recognizing Picasso's will to portray the spiritual chaos of the bombers and of a world dependent on bombs, in terms of such order as is indispensable to a work of art. As long as Picasso stays within the formal element his purpose is clear and unambiguous. Difficulty and ambiguity begin when he tries to give the formal process a concrete content and to invent for the latter a new extra-artistic, philosophical, or allegorical solution.

We still have to consider the dimension of height. The treatment varies in character as we move across the picture: we can distinguish five groups. At the sides the upward movement is simpler, more homogeneous, and considerably more rapid than it is at the center: the distance between bottom and top is traversed without resistance or interruptions. The treatments at the two sides are the reverse of each other: the right (beginning) is open at the top and the left (end) is closed at the top. The former implies the "spurious" infinity and the latter a questioning and answering, self-containment, repose. In the middle area the dimension of height is strongly articulated into several levels: the man on the ground, the body of the horse, its head, the allegory of the bomb. Since there are also differences in depth, the movement gets slower as it goes up, and we are given the impression that the distance from bottom to top is longer than it is at the sides. This articulation of height within the central triangle by means of objects is further contrasted with that along either side of the triangle, where the tempo is faster because it runs along an incline. The right side of the triangle lies on the picture surface, while the left moves into depth. With respect to this formal movement there can be no question of development even at its most superficial in terms of different accents. The eye receives no orientation regarding the articulation inside the triangle. The eye may start at the top or at the bottom, move from cause to effect or vice versa; it may linger in the empty areas of the horse's body and from there shuttle up and down between cause and effect. In each case the effects are clear in representational terms but the cause (electric light bulb, sun, lightning, bomb) is so uncertain that it may be doubted that there is a cause at all. If one exists, it has the same degree of reality as the effect—in contrast to the horse's body, which seems to have almost no reality at all. But even taking our point of departure there, we can only leap to the lowest or to the highest degree of reality; there is no development, either from the potential to the actual or from the undeveloped to the developed—in short, there is only intensification and repetition.

If we adopt a still more formal point of view, we can see that one horizontal open form (the tubular arms of the fallen soldier) reappears at the top as a narrower, closed form (the bomb). From the outstretched form at the bottom nothing emerges save a shriek but, although the mouth is wide open, it does not carry (in contrast to the horse's open mouth, although its neighing does not reach its destination either). On the other hand, from the closed form at the top twenty-four ($13 + 11$) black and thirteen or fourteen reddish-white jags radiate, giving the small form a strong accent which may justify interpreting it as a bomb. Between the fallen soldier at the bottom and this "bomb," both of which are well defined, no third form occurs; the area between them is undefined and scarcely accounts, in visual terms, for the transformation of the one form into the other. Thus, although with respect to subject matter, form, and method we find changes and various degrees of reality, we find no inner development from cause to effect, whether as emanation, deduction, or whatever. In contrast to the abruptness of local movements and explosions of affect there is a bare minimum of over-all movement, a mere division into levels which differ from each other chiefly in the degree of reality. The use of only one mode of reality is compensated for by a strong charge of energy, the tension between unreconciled oppositions within it, and the multiple explosions issuing from both.

The two areas still to be analyzed are those between the side rectangles and the central triangle. Each forms roughly a triangular plane, symmetrical in relation to the other but filled up very unsymmetrically. At the right there is the arm of the woman with the lamp, which we have already described as an allegory of (critical) Reason or Truth, and which consists formally of a number of overlapping transparent layers. At the left, however, there is a simple, nearly empty space which includes the table and the bird.

The latter carries off either an ineffectual curse or the horse's or soldier's surviving strength (according to how we interpret the horse). The two areas are of considerable significance in terms of the subject matter; the significance is enhanced by the difference of the forms filling the equisized spaces and by the different ways by which the areas are approached from the bottom. In the right one of these two "interludes" we find at the bottom the woman whose panic-stricken flight is arrested by the sight of the new carnage at the center. Her head is thrown back, and above it we find the larger, more self-possessed head of Truth, whose arm continues the movement at the top (with a slight downward inclination), the movement toward the goal—the horse's head and the uncertain allegory (lamp, sun, lightning, bomb)—which the woman in flight can merely see but not reach. To this extent Truth's head and arm (two breasts are shown in addition) would stand for the allegorical consummation of all the woman in flight is instinctively searching for despite her panic. Knowledge achieves that which is denied purely animal existence. With this development in terms of content the formal development accords only in a very superficial sense: the fleeing woman's back-thrown head compels the eye to notice first the underside of Truth's head, and then from its top to move on to the arm thrust forward out of the narrow window with such forcefulness and formal resource. What unites these figures formally is the identical goal toward which they aspire in their separate but mutually supporting ways. Moreover, Truth's arm is related to the outstretched arms of the fallen soldier, partly by the great similarity between the two forms, the similar firmness of their realization and of their strong grasping, and partly by the sloping line of the horse's neck, which in conjunction with the horizontals might be represented in the following diagram:

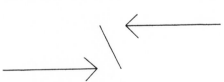

Thus physical death is linked with the life of the spirit, the present with the future.

As for the interlude to the left, it is not quite clear whether the dark-gray empty space lies in the horizontal dimension or whether it also performs a function in the development of the dimension of height, for which it would then represent the fifth group. It is impossible to discover any formal continuity for it; the horse's tail, especially, seems rather to exclude it. However, we could point to the sudden contrast between fullness (at the bottom) and emptiness (at the top), to the abrupt change from the soldier's shriek to silence. It is in this silence that the attempted flight of the bird, which would seem to take away death and all that goes with it, occurs. This silence and emptiness would then prepare us for the action of the bull—not a killer but a fecundator, coming at the close of a life-and-death struggle, allegorically on the side of life, perhaps not merely in the sense of assuring its survival but also in the sense of preparing a better life, better because after all Reason has co-operated. In this view the second "interlude" would use a still stronger sudden transition for structuring the development of height than does the first. Common to both is aspiration toward a goal situated in some undefined future, whereas in the center area the prevailing relationship is causality.

Summing up, we may thus say that in each of the three dimensions we have found movements and changes and that these involve different things in each. In the depth dimension there was the antithesis between corporeal existence and noncorporeal being; in the width dimension it was the opposition between panic and ataraxia as well as the separation between the dynamic and the static; and in the height dimension there was the contrast of existence, cause, and goal. But nowhere could we interpret these changes and movements as an inner development, whatever methodological form we tried to ascribe to it. And yet Picasso did not portray a dynamic event with exclusively static artistic means; for even in the external composition and the symmetrical arrangement of the parts there are not only asymmetries but also dynamic details. What we find is that Picasso lifted the historical event out of historical time, associating it with a conception of time which we must now analyze.

Taking historical time as our own time, then, time is nothing but content, what the impressionists meant by the given hour of a given season. But when they conceived cosmic time as perception time they were already going beyond the a priori concept of absolute or empty time, time thought of as a neutral container. Once each sensation was considered to have its own time, time became conditioned, once more a posteriori. But the fact that time is conditioned does not prove that it is *merely* content; time as content and time as the form of this content are not the same thing; form does not follow from content mechanically. Art reflects every kind of external time (historical as well as cosmic, however different otherwise) in class and individual consciousness, that is, several subjective kinds of time correspond to one and the same objective time. Time as artistic form is always an equation between the one objective (historical) time and the many sociologically and individually determined interpretative kinds of time. But to begin with, these latter are still content—a content, however, that directly codetermines the form of time—creative time. How does Picasso conceive objective time, interpretative time, and creative time, and how are these interrelated?

Many things are going on simultaneously at different places in *Guernica*, but there is neither simultaneity of perception, encompassing the whole from one vantage point, nor consecutiveness in the unity of action. The events are isolated in groups, and for each group again there is neither simultaneity of perception nor continuity of succession. Objective time is shattered, atomized, or—more accurately—reshaped as a conglomerate of isolated time elements. These elements are structured alike as follows:

(1) What is represented is never action as it takes place but action that has already taken place. This is in contrast to the "causal moment" as Leonardo, for instance, represented it in *The Last Supper* and to the "fruitful moment"[25] when past and future cast their reflection into the present.

(2) To Picasso the last moment of the accomplished action is not the moment when a cause has exhausted all its effects, but the moment of maximum effect as represented by the most intense charge of energy. Other portrayals of maximum charges of energy occur, for example, in the best paleolithic cave paintings and Egyptian sculptures, where they had an objective, suprapersonal character, whereas in Picasso they derive from a personal emotion.

(3) When a maximum charge of energy has been attained, it may be perpetuated either through existential intensification of the object (paleolithic art), by the magic action upon the infinite of the things represented (Egypt), or by the group's belief in magic signs (neolithic age); or else the accumulated charge can be exploded and destroyed (Picasso). The time required to accumulate the energy is never shown (in this Picasso does not differ from paleolithic painting, Egyptian sculpture, or neolithic signs). However, in Picasso the time required for the discharge seems to depend on the following factors:

(a) Extension in time and space are in inverse ratio, i.e., the impression is created that relatively large distances are traversed in a relatively short time.

(b) The charge of energy encounters no resistance and is as powerful at any one place as any other; its course is one explosion. This is possible only because it is not bound to the inner time of its vehicle and especially not to the existential time of man; it merely flits through him. What this means can best be seen through a comparison with Egyptian art,[26] where the charge of energy is not anchored in man's inner time either, but where the human body is used as its vessel, holding together the entire accumulated energy as a full present time and expending it only at a single place, the eye, in such a way that it never diminishes.

(c) The path of the discharge is bifurcated, one part flowing back to its starting point and one ending suddenly at its peak. Thus the discharge carries its own resistance within itself; but in addition it encounters, when its time is spent, metaphysical conscious-being, which has never been subject to time (or to movement). In other words, the explosion takes place at the borderline between the empirical and the mystical moment. Thereby Picasso transforms historical events into mere moments of energy discharge whose completely developed meaninglessness (in the explosion) is confronted by timelessness inviolate, supertemporality, whose meaning and being are indestructible.

25. Lessing, *Laokoon*, section III.   26. [The author discusses this in an unpublished essay, "Der Schreiber."]

Objective time being transformed into a conglomerate of time elements (without simultaneity or continuous succession), and each of these elements into the explosion time of a subjective emotion, the question arises: How are these elements interrelated? To begin with, from a purely superficial point of view, each of the explosions of affect is *directed*. The directions may serve as links (usually along a diagonal line), or as divisions (through the contrast between verticals and horizontals), or as both simultaneously (by means of parallels). All these directional factors connect time with space and transform affects of personal origin into effects which lead the viewer to search for an objective cause. Thus the cause is not the primary, conditioning, and dominating factor, as it is in Leonardo's *Last Supper*, but rather the very last thing, the goal, and it is found only as a reified cause. In addition, a connection is paradoxically provided by the leap of discontinuity. We have discussed this in detail with reference to how the affect of panic turns into the affectlessness of ataraxia. Here we shall merely add that just as affect does not lead to tragedy, so such a turning does not lead to authentic catharsis. What we have here is fatalism—tragedy's worst enemy—whether formulated as a bull or as "life goes on." On the basis of its directionality and discontinuity, affect-time can be represented now as a path, now as a leap, now as a thrust. The collision of various time elements makes duration impossible: the atomized time elements smash up. All these representational forms of time remain in the closest connection with pictorial space or, more accurately, with the energy field. For what we have here is not a hollow vessel existing prior to time, nor can it be said that space is a product of time. Both depend on the same cause—energy, and in realizing the latter they are sometimes dependent on each other, sometimes not. They are two different entities but together they constitute the form of the same energy.

After this analysis of the spatiotemporal figuration of energy it will become clear why Picasso had to resort to allegory as a substitute for internal unity. We have said that Picasso does not show the stages of events or of affects but only the last stage, the moment of explosion. Such a supercharge of energy must exceed not only the artist's ordinary energy but also the energies and powers of his society and epoch and then be given artistic form. In earlier epochs this was done successfully on the basis of two premises: the artist, as magician, had all the powers of society at his disposal, i.e., he was inspired by the aspirations of his group and could believe that his magic was sufficient not only to slay an animal, for example, but also to secure the resurrection of a dead man. The second premise was that magic took its object as seriously as possible, as the alter ego both of the sorcerer and of the social group he represented, whether the object of magical action was a political adversary, an animal, or a dead man, all of whom belonged to a single social universe. This is why the slain animal could be propitiated, the powers of the conquered adversary appropriated in a ritual repast, and the dead brought back to life in the female's womb, i.e., in the clan's posterity.[27] And, most important of all, the physical and ideological forces of the social group were always there to translate the magic into actual or imagined reality. These premises also apply, *mutatis mutandis*, to totemism.

Obviously none of these conditions exists today. Society despises the artist and the artist despises society. Art today has no social function and the beggars' rewards given to artists serve merely to camouflage the fact that no life remains in this atavism. The adversary, particularly the political one, is occasionally feared, often ridiculed, but most often branded as a criminal. Under these circumstances the artist can achieve the charge of energy in question only on two conditions: that he be endowed with an uncommon temperament that overcompensates his social uselessness by a Caesarean consciousness of his superiority, and that he degrade the adversary. As a result, the adversary is represented by a negative allegory, while the artist is seemingly exalted to a positive one. If the horse stands for Franco, Larrea is probably right in saying that Picasso worked his "pictorial magic" upon it: of its three wounds the smallest was probably inflicted by the soldier, the larger one by the bomb, the third (caused by the wooden spear) by Picasso himself. By the same token Picasso would have identified himself with the bull—who stands for vitality as such or that of the Spanish people. Now, bestiality can never be adequately allegorized by an animal, for even the most cruel animal merely gratifies its instinctual needs, whereas conscious bestiality presupposes making the lowest instincts metaphysical absolutes, something only man can do. Of all animals within our cultural tradition, few are as far removed from bestiality as is the horse; even the contempt with which the horse is killed in the course of the bullfight and then thrown to the knacker has a different source. On the other hand, the bull has long been regarded as a symbol of male sexuality and hence of fecundating power. As such it lacks clear and superior consciousness, and its function depends on submission and sacrifice.

Thus Picasso, in trying to practice personal magic, was led to use metaphor with respect to both the horse and the bull. Needless to say, the use of magic against a personal allegory is a sophisticated invention, an unworkable delusion, in short, sheer nonsense in terms of art. (The same is true of personal mythology.) We may note that the bodies of the two animals are scarcely realized: the bull's is left in shadow, the horse's eviscerated, and all expressive values are concentrated in the heads. This is always the case when clarity of artistic figuration must give way to psychological statement, the latter being as arbitrary and ambiguous as the former is necessary. Finally, the two animals are not related formally, separated as they are by a large dark area with only the mysterious bird inside it. Instead they are juxtaposed as two moral extremes; the horse being an allegory of everything negative, immoral, despised, hated, everything that ought not to be, and the bull an allegory of everything positive, biologically infinite, worthy of reverence. But

27. [The author discusses this fully in an unpublished essay, "Wiedergeburtsmagie in der Altsteinzeit."]

if the two extremes are to be interpreted according to the axiom "both/and" [rather than "either/or"], that is, if both allegories are ambiguous, the result is a suspension of judgment which is accessible only to the intellect, not to artistic intuition or aesthetic feeling. If Picasso were to be detected as the magician in the painting, it would be most plausible to identify him with the woman trying to throw light on this scene of bombardment. In reality, the painting militiaman did not kill Franco with his pictorial magic nor save the Spanish people from death by starvation. He merely reacted to a physical explosion with an intellectual explosion, thus putting himself on the same level as his adversary, as if under his command. The spirit explodes only when it suffers more than it understands, when it lacks the knowledge and wisdom necessary to place itself on a level that cannot be reached by the will of the adversary, because it is precisely the level on which he will be defeated. Picasso himself must have realized this later when, faced with the implications of the atomic and hydrogen bombs, he abandoned his attempt to shape world history by means of art and tried to participate as a man, if not as an artist, in the historical reality.

We have shown that in Picasso's creative process a well-defined conception of time intervenes between the point of departure in emotion and the result in a spatial energy field: the gulf between the empirical moment of exploding energy and the mystical moment of eternal truth—the gray, timeworn truth that life cannot be annihilated, not even by bombs, but goes on forever. Why has so unoriginal a theme necessitated such formal originality, such extremes of shrillness and violence, such discontinuities and deformations? Because Picasso was unable to deduce his particular subject matter (the bombing of Guernica) from the universals of his world view. He can give artistic form to the universal, but when it comes to the particular he must, if he is not to lapse into sentimentality, envelop his subject matter in a vagueness which is a contrived, not a structured profundity, which does not derive from the mystery of form but from an affectation of mysteriousness or skepticism.

It is the gulf between the empirical and the metaphysical worlds in all their manifestations, which no artistic method can bridge, that has driven Picasso to private allegory. Born of the split between the finite and the infinite, his allegory is itself finite in the formal sense: the horse denotes x, the bull y, and so on—i.e., it has the form of an equation with several unknowns, even though each of them may have double values, with opposite signs. It is of the nature of allegory that it cannot directly manifest its immanent tendency toward explicitness; hence, every allegory receives into itself many historically developed and individually transmuted cultural details. It becomes a riddle whose very mysteriousness gives it a semblance of profundity; and the more partial riddles it contains, the more infinite its meaning seems. But the need for a banderole giving the actual solution of the allegory reveals that actually the allegory is finite, that there can be only one correct solution, though an indefinite number of near solutions or guesses. Allegory thus cannot serve as a bridge between the finite and the infinite. This is what makes allegory fundamentally different from authentic symbolism. The symbol may contain many meanings, extending over the entire range of the human spirit, but such meanings are interrelated and their content deepens as we progress from dimension to dimension. The symbol, for all its visible finitude, points to the infinite: it is a sensory synthesis of the finite and the infinite and hence has a character of necessity. Allegory is merely a metaphor for the gulf between the two and hence always arbitrary.

This accounts for the fact that Picasso, in the course of the work on *Guernica,* not only changed the number and arrangement of his figures but also the allegories. An early preliminary sketch exists of the dying horse giving birth to Pegasus, as if out of Medusa, but later this idea was abandoned. The bird was shown dead at the right instead of alive at the left; there was a wheel, later removed; the arrow was added only at the last moment and its significance remains obscure; not even the mother with the child was brought into proximity with the bull until a later stage. Picasso seems to have groped his way to the system of allegories finally shown. It is visually simple enough, but full of riddles when we examine it in detail. Thus allegory serves as a substitute for symbolism, and the more meanings it seems to suggest, the less creative power it embodies artistically. Picasso's allegories are rooted neither in his own age nor in tradition, but in the isolated individual; he alone possesses the key to them. By resorting to a personal system of allegories he confesses his inability to portray the driving forces of modern society in a work which treats a specific historical event—and this alone is the meaning of a genuine historical painting. Picasso relegates human history to the unbridgeable gulf which exists for him between the empirical and the mystical, the particular and the universal, the finite and the infinite. All he did succeed in giving expression to was the infernal folly of the petty bourgeois spirit run amok.

We have tried to analyze the painting in terms of its material of figuration, and of the form, content, and allegories it contains. We shall now discuss it in the terms of its effect on the viewer, to cast further light, this time from the outside, as it were, on Picasso's artistic method. (The same method was not necessarily employed in Picasso's other works.)

To begin with sensory perception: the painting appeals to almost all our senses. Although the eye is primarily involved, there are passages in *Guernica* which are not perceivable optically, either because the artist's aim was to keep them out of range of the eye or because they stimulate motor rather than visual sensations. Other passages, which can be seen, cannot be touched, and some of these suggest the domain of the ineffable conscious-being, in which seeing is an intuition or vision of some primal metaphysical phenomenon. Still other places stimulate the sense of touch, as where two diverging planes meet to form a sharp edge, but they lead to visual or motor sensations. Most cases of motor sensation in this work are made explicit: the frantic flight, for example, the outstretched limbs, wide-opened mouths, etc. The bull's posture is the calmest attitude shown, but it is achieved only *after* the abrupt twisting backward of head and forequarters; it is furthermore associated with the flaglike tail, and as a result the viewer is compelled to connect the bull's mouth with its anus. However, though the figures perform all these movements to inspire corresponding sensations in the viewer, the over-all effect is to reduce the viewer to immobility. He is not stimulated to physical activity, to decision, let alone to conscious action. The positive aspect of the effect is not movement but stupor, and the latter is not produced by an optically perceivable chaos of movement but by the chaotic din which the painting seems to give off, so shocking the viewer that he can only assume a passive attitude toward the screaming affects of the canvas.

Picasso makes use not only of various sense perceptions (and their organs) but also of a variety of responses. While the eye is at one point obliged to pursue a lengthy course, at another it must make a leap, and at still another experience a head-on collision. This continual alternation between passivity and activity, between continuity and discontinuity, forces constant reorientation upon the viewer and demands that he be elastic and agile; at the same time Picasso obstructs him at points of collision—in short, he does everything to make active perception, absorption, empathy, contemplation, and enjoyment impossible. These constant changes are designed to prevent the act of perception from being an end in itself and to accelerate it as much as possible; even the frequent repetitions of approximately equal charges of energy serve the purpose of ruling out the repose of simultaneous perception and shortening the time of perception. If perception were encouraged to linger, an accumulation of the viewer's energies would weaken shock and induce aesthetic enjoyment as well as spontaneous activity, freeing him from the artist's control. The degree of shock is in direct ratio to the rapidity with which the viewer is reduced to stupor. Here the senses are stimulated only to be numbed. All this expresses the artist's tyrannical will to power, his attempt to dominate the viewer, whether by compulsive magic or by a kind of shadowboxing with the viewer's mind, consciousness, and freedom.

The primary effect Picasso has aimed at is shock. Two elements may be distinguished: surprise that so energetic a shock has been produced (for we do not see how the energy was accumulated) and that the shock, despite the intensity of the energy behind it, is so quickly ended (for we witness only its explosion). Nor is affect presented for its own sake: no more than the sensory perception is it permitted to last; were it so permitted, we might take sentimental pleasure even in this situation of terror. The aftereffects of any one explosion are not felt because, like waves, each is directly followed by another, so that all the aftereffects tending to secure the autonomy of the emotion are destroyed. Here, too, Picasso brutally assaults the viewer's sensibilities. He cuts short the development of emotion; he drives the viewer from affect to affect and ultimately drives him beyond all affect. The monotonous repetition of shocks shows that Picasso does not intend the shocks to be enjoyed for their own sake; he makes use of affect only to dissolve it into affectlessness. This purpose is served by the twofold development—across the painting, from panic via struggle to ataraxia and, from bottom to top, from the dead soldier to the rather exhibitionistic allegory of Reason. Both the physical and the spiritual allegory to some extent resolve horrified shock, but they do not produce catharsis in the viewer because the resolution has not arisen inevitably from the catastrophe and because the catastrophe itself is not a human one but inhuman, antihuman. The bomb was produced by a dehumanized society and its victims are portrayed as self-alienated. The former is rooted in the essence of our age, the latter in the limitations of Picasso as artist unable to transcend present history and only able to respond to its destructive forces in an allegory of hope for the future, comforting but not cathartic. Indeed, as we shall presently see, the allegorical solution in the end serves only to lull back to sleep the viewer who may have been aroused and shocked.

For neither the act of sensory perception nor the development of the explosive affects can be completed without Picasso's recourse to certain cultural and personal clichés—instead of stimulating thought, Picasso relies upon ready-made thoughts. Just as he has excluded *délectation* from sensory perception, he has excluded the process of thinking from thoughts. Instead of leading the viewer from the senses via feeling to active understanding, he assaults the senses with affects and imagines that the latter can be mastered by bits of cultural lore, received beliefs as to the powers of nature or reason. To split up the human faculties in this way is to build up suspense by making us inquire into the meaning and content of the allegory. *Délectation*, in a word, has been replaced with a riddle. The statement of the latter is so complex that the viewer must grope in the dark unless he is a specialist in solving such equations with many unknowns or until Picasso provides him with a banderole. Once we have solved the riddle or decided it has no solution, perception and emotional response have run their course. Truly great artists do the exact opposite: they suggest the solution as well as the problem, diverting the viewer from the literal content and focusing his attention on the artistic form. For their purpose is to enlarge the viewer's freedom, not to do violence to him; to provide affective catharsis, not to pose riddles. In other words, the unity of the effect in which Picasso's contrasting points of departure are merged—individual emotion and metaphysical conscious-being—is the shock inflicted upon the viewer's nervous system, a shock producing physical stupor and intellectual puzzlement—the question: What does it all mean? Since shock, in both aspects, is exhausted once the question is answered, we may conclude that the artist intended his meaning to be either ambiguous or undecipherable. The various shocks drive the viewer to ask questions; the questions drive him back to the picture, to be exposed to new shocks. Theoretically the viewer should be stimulated to make an infinite number of such jumps back and forth, but Picasso has failed to provide the artistic form for any such infinite contemplation.

Aesthetics, politics, and morality are replaced by a dogma whose value may be enhanced for true believers by its mysteriousness, but which remains valueless for non-believers who are not interested in what lies beyond art but only in art itself, or who respect real action in the real world more than the pseudo-intellectual activity of solving riddles, especially riddles that seem vague, antiquated, and petty bourgeois. This is a contrived painting and hence arbitrary and finite. This accounts for its fate, for the fact that the masses—and the anti-Fascist masses most particularly—were perplexed by it and quickly lost interest. The literati alone praised it in their turgid fashion because the magnitude of its conception, its boldness, and its inventiveness seemed to justify their own creative impotence. But all this does not change the fact that even Picasso, the greatest artist of our time, was unequal to the challenge of his age, belonging as he did to a class and intellectual climate which had outlived their usefulness. The artist in our modern bourgeois society is both a tragic and a comic figure, rooted in a society whose collapse he *must* desire yet unable to give artistic form to the emerging society he admires. He is condemned by both sides for opposite reasons.

It is perhaps not too rash to assume that Picasso would not object to the first part of the above statement. If he had still believed that painting can serve as a substitute for political action—not at all the same thing as using art to educate a people politically or as an auxiliary to politics (which can and must be done)—or that political problems can be solved by allegorical appeals to the *élan vital* of nature or to rational enlightenment, he would scarcely have joined the Communist party. His work on *Guernica* may have been one of the reasons why Picasso changed his political orientation, for it may have made him aware of the limitations of his former position, the other reasons being the events that followed on Franco's victory and led to the Second World War, which brought the Nazi conquerors to the streets of Paris and even into Picasso's studio. On the other hand, it is unlikely that he would agree with our assertion of *Guernica*'s artistic inadequacy (as distinguished from its propagandistic inadequacy), for then he could not stand by his statements that his art and his politics have nothing to do with each other or that *every* painting is political. (Even if it were, it still need not be Communist.) Whatever the reader may think of Marxism or Communism, both have always denied the possibility of divorcing practice (politics) from theory (art). This is particularly true of art, for the whole function of art is to give sensory form to the unity of practice and theory.[28] All Picasso could say in his own defense would be that the artist can give form only to an

28. [Cf. the author's *Zur Erkenntnistheorie der konkreten Dialektik*.]

existing society, not to one still in process of emerging, and that he can therefore give two things: a social criticism of bourgeois society in a bourgeois style and propagandistic support to the Communist party in its struggle to overthrow bourgeois society. From this it appears that Picasso is an inadequate Communist for lack of knowledge (which is naturally his own affair), and that he has not understood the limits of the method which led him to *Guernica*. The latter is a matter of public concern even if art in our disintegrating society is only a luxury product for snobs or an escape for psychopaths.

The method employed in *Guernica* must be regarded as inadequate not because the allegories used by Picasso admit of several contradictory solutions but because he was *compelled* to resort to allegory in the first place. Even if he were one day to give us the banderole with the only correct solution, the fact would remain that the form of this work is not implied in its content. Even if it might be considered too rigorous to place such a work beyond the pale of art, it must be granted that a work of which this can be said is at a lower artistic level than a work in which form and content are indissoluble. For only when such unity is achieved—and it is the specialty of the artist to invent the method by which it can be achieved—does the work transcend historical conditions and individual reactions and attain to suprahistorical, universal human validity. That was what Goethe meant when he said: "Do not talk, artist, create." There is a fundamental difference between the indirect language of allegory and the realization of a conception, idea, or aesthetic feeling in a self-sufficient artistic reality. Both methods are to some extent indirect, in the sense that the artist must go beyond the event or emotion that actually inspired him. But allegorical language actually conceals directness and literalness of approach, the obsession of the artist with what he wants to communicate, and as a result the work created by such a method remains imprisoned in the arbitrary and particular and is only *seemingly* universal; whereas the authentic artistic method raises the particular to the universal, the historical to the suprahistorical, the relative to the absolute, by embodying infinite meaning in concrete and finite appearance. The allegorical method renders the artist's dialogue with himself, and the artist who employs it is trying to tell the world about the discoveries in his self without really revealing them, without really objectifying them. Truly artistic method is a dialogue between the self and the world (or the cosmos), and results in a reality independent of both the artist and the world; whereas allegory creates only new obsessions, unfreedom, and dogma, true art liberates the artist from the prison of self, from his obsession with a particular idea, and creates freedom. The reasons for which Picasso was compelled to resort to signs and allegories should now be clear enough: his utter political helplessness in the face of the historical situation which he set out to record; his titanic effort to confront a particular historical event with an allegedly eternal truth; his desire to give hope and comfort and to provide a happy ending, to compensate for the terror, destruction, and inhumanity of the event. Picasso did not see what Goya had already seen, namely, that the course of history can be changed only by historical means and only if men shape their own history instead of acting as the automatons of an earthly power or an allegedly eternal idea. We must, however, stress the fact that Picasso's *Guernica* expresses a conflict between his great sensibility and need for communication, on the one hand, and his artistic powers on the other. Even if we set aside the elements of allegory, we must recognize that this work stigmatizes the destructiveness of a disintegrating society with a power no other artist has equaled.

VI. THE STRUGGLE TO UNDERSTAND ART

To see I was born,
To watch I was called . . .

GOETHE, *Faust*, Part II

What greater gain in life can man e'er know
   Than when God-Nature will to him explain
How into Spirit steadfastness may flow,
   How steadfast, too, the Spirit-Born remain.

GOETHE, "Lines on Seeing Schiller's Skull"

A reader of the previous essays in this book may be tempted to ask: "Why so much bother about art? What good is art today—now that part of Europe has become an economic province of the United States and another part a political province of Moscow?" The idealistic textbooks are full of answers to such questions, answers such as "Man does not live by bread alone," or Schiller's helpless and haughty statement: "We must indeed, if we are to solve that political problem in practice, follow the path of aesthetics, since it is through Beauty that we arrive at Freedom."[1] Such glittering generalities, however, are of little help in dealing with specific objections to art, such as are raised today in many different quarters. Stated as simply as possible, these objections are:

1) In the machine age art is atavistic.

2) Under capitalism art, an ideological superstructure, serves as an opiate of the people.

3) In our epoch, which marks the decline of the European spirit, art and the study of art are no longer possible.

The first objection is based on the premise that modern man controls the world by means of science and technology and that art has outlived its usefulness. This fact is allegedly proved by the present crisis in art. Modern artists, we are told, are people who are out of touch with the times; they shut themselves away in their studios to produce their trifles instead of taking their inspiration from the miracles of technology. Reversing the Biblical saying, their flesh may indeed be willing, but their spirit is weak.

To refute this objection we must first of all point out that technology means different things according to the point of view we adopt—the inventor's, the consumer's, or the cultural intermediary's. To the inventor technology is a productive act, whose nature need not be discussed here in detail. If we assume that the productive forces of society are as limited as those of nature, and keep within their limits, then any changes must affect all areas of production. No one will deny that ever since the eighteenth century religion and art have been retreating before the advances of science and technology. The nineteenth and the twentieth centuries have not lacked artistic talent, but they have

---

1. *On the Aesthetic Education of Man*, Second Letter; tr. Reginald Snell (London and New York, 1954), p. 27.

lacked a world view common to society as a whole. Visual art, instead of being unified in architecture, has been split up into an independent painting and an independent sculpture. However, the new economy has created new needs, and an unparalleled technology has provided the means for modern architecture. The only question is whether our spiritual foundations are solid and adaptable enough to make possible artistic as well as functional structures.

Le Corbusier summed up this uncertain situation in the phrase: "Construction or Revolution." This is a false alternative. Building may help delay an unripe revolution or glorify a revolution already made, but the idea that it can replace a revolution is a specialist's delusion.

The thesis that art in the machine age is an atavistic survival is based on two fatalistic assumptions: first, that each epoch is characterized by a *single* developmental tendency; second, that it is pointless—indeed, harmful—to fight for or against the given tendency. But history is neither a natural process governed by unchanging laws nor the realization of God's design for mankind. It is a human struggle: the struggle of human society to transform the treasures of nature and the creations of genius into a people's culture; it is the struggle of modern man with his tradition, in order to create the future. In this struggle man is not entirely free, but he certainly has the opportunity to free himself from obsolete conditions and to produce new ones more favorable to the development of his potentialities. This opportunity can be realized because each cultural epoch is dominated, not by a single tendency, but by several which contend among themselves. And man does realize it when he consciously picks out the most progressive element in his tradition, the element most pregnant with the future, boldly develops it (without giving up the wealth of diverse forms of culture, whose competition does not weaken but enhances the whole culture), and integrates the new attainment in the essence of man as a whole.

In this effort man is hindered by technology not as far as it is an act of invention, but by the uses to which it may be put—the purposes it may be made to serve, the powers behind it. It is not technology as such that obstructs and weakens the artist's creative powers, but the circumstance that society fails to control technology and is instead controlled by it. Although technology has helped increase productive forces, no economic, social, or political consequences have been drawn from this fact, whether with respect to distribution of products, property relations, or political organization. Unintelligent use of technology and its products brings an imbalance to the historical life of society and creates a conflict between the live and the dead, progressive and reactionary forces. As a result, centrifugal forces gain strength over forces of cohesion and man's will to shape the world is paralyzed.

This paralysis becomes more acute with the crisis of the cultural intermediary—

that is, the failure of precisely those social groups whose task it is (or should be) to pass on the works of genius to the whole of the people. The people, forsaken by the clergy, the academic world, journalists, are fed trashy films and radio programs, and their worship goes to film stars or sports heroes. The last remnants of spiritual life are threatened with extinction. But we cannot take a fatalistic attitude toward this situation. History does not make man, but man makes history, within the stated limits. However strong a given historical tendency may be, man can and has the duty to resist it when it runs counter to his creative powers. There is no fate which decrees that we must be victims of technology or that art must be shelved as an anachronism; the "fate" is merely misuse of technology by the ruling class to suppress the people's power to make its own history. To a certain extent it is up to every individual, by his participation in social and political life, to decide whether art shall or shall not become obsolete. The understanding of art helps raise this decision to its highest level. As a vessel formed by the creative forces which it preserves, the work of art keeps alive and enhances every urge to come to terms with the world.

The second objection is based on a specific theoretical view of economic life, on the doctrine founded by the great critic of modern capitalism. The main question Marx set out to answer was: How does it come about that man is the slave of the commodities he himself produces, and how can man free himself—become human again? His answer is: Human society is the basic fact, and its basic activity, continuously repeated, is the production of its means of subsistence and the propagation of the race. There is only one science (for understanding human society), and that is history, and the first object of this science is to formulate the laws governing the process of production and its development over the generations. The ideologies of law, government, art, morality, and religion are superstructures which grow upon this real objective activity. Marx was far from denying the importance of these superstructures in the historical process. Once they have come into existence, the state and law, morality, etc., react on the productive process; they are instruments of power in the hands of the exploiting class, and to the exploited they serve as opiates. On the basis of this insight Marx made the notorious statement: "religion is the *opium* of the people"[2]—a statement which vulgar Marxists are trying to extend to art.

This is not the place to analyze Karl Marx's theory of art.[3] I should like, however, to refer to a passage at the end of *A Contribution to the Critique of Political Economy* in which he brilliantly formulated the main, but still unsolved, problem of his own—and every— theory of art. He says:

But the difficulty is not in grasping the idea that Greek art and epos are bound up with certain forms of social development. It rather lies in understanding why they still constitute with us a source

2. *Contribution to the Critique of Hegel's Philosophy of Right,* Introduction.

3. [See the author's *Proudhon, Marx, Picasso: Trois études sur la sociologie de l'art.*]

of aesthetic enjoyment and in certain respects prevail as the standard and model beyond attainment. A man can not become a child again. . . . But does he not enjoy the artless ways of the child and must he not strive to reproduce its truth on a higher plane? Is not the character of every epoch revived perfectly true to nature in child nature? Why should the social childhood of mankind, where it had obtained its most beautiful development, not exert an eternal charm as an age that will never return? There are ill-bred children and precocious children. Many of the ancient nations belong to the latter class. The Greeks were normal children. The charm their art has for us does not conflict with the primitive character of the social order from which it had sprung. It is rather the product of the latter, and is rather due to the fact that the unripe social conditions under which the art arose and under which alone it could appear can never return.[4]

It is perhaps no accident that Marx's manuscript breaks off at this point, for he had come to a problem which he could not solve. How can art, that is, an ideological super-structure in a specific type of economy, continue to be effective after this type of economy has ceased to exist? How can the ideological superstructure be timeless if the foundation has a finite history? Marx's answer has nothing whatever to do either with historical materialism or with Communism as a guide for changing the world. It sounds petty bourgeois, almost indistinguishable from Burckhardt's answer in his history of Greek culture, save that the latter used the term "adolescence" rather than "childhood." If such a thing as eternal charm exists despite determination by historical, economic, and social conditions, then there must also be eternal sources that correspond. And if so, history cannot be the only science and the economy its primary object. The only alternative would be to provide an accurate analysis of the spiritual process that links up historical conditions with these "eternal charms"—more accurately, with the values created by men, transcending the limits of a given epoch but not the limits of historical time in general. The phrase "eternal charm"—which is doubly untenable, both as "eternal" and as "charm"—shows how far Marx was from having solved the problem he raised so astutely. We repeat, the problem remains unsolved.

And there are good reasons for this. If we apply to the thesis that art is an ideological superstructure, its own presupposition, i.e., that of historical materialism, we find that his-torical materialism itself is only an ideological superstructure of a specific economic order—the capitalistic order in which all productive forces are concentrated in the economic sector. A transitional epoch always implies uncertainty: Marx's struggle to understand his own epoch testifies to this. In such a period two attitudes are possible. One is to take advantage of the emergent forces of the new order with a view to undermining it, to affirm it in order to drive it beyond itself: this is the active, militant, revolutionary attitude. The other clings to the past, is retrospective and romantic, bewails or acknowledges the decline, as-serts that the will to live is gone—in short, it is the passive attitude. Where economic, social, and political questions were at stake Marx took the first attitude; in questions of art

4. Tr. N. I. Stone (Chicago, 1904), pp. 311*f.*

he took neither. He reflected the actual changes of his time, which is to say that he made economics the foundation of thought which it had become in fact. He did not lose sight of the further problem, but as he could not see the solution, he left it unsolved. Had he been able to show that an active attitude toward art also exists, he would have brought the understanding of art up to the level of his revolutionary position.

Whatever the deficiencies of Marx's theoretical attitude toward art may have been, he was perfectly aware that after the economic, social, and political revolution the most difficult revolution would still remain to be made—the cultural one. Nowhere did he ever exclude art, as he excluded religion, on the ground that there would be no place for it in a classless society. The pseudo-Marxists who put art on the same footing with religion do not see that religion sets limits to man's creative capacities, diverts him from the things of this world, and reconciles class antagonisms by obviously imaginary and frequently hypocritical theories of love, whereas art is an ever-renewed creative act, the active dialogue between spirit and matter; the work of art holds man's creative powers in a crystalline suspension from which it can again be transformed into living energies. Consequently, art by its very nature is no opiate; it is a weapon. Art may have narcotic effects, but only if used for specific reactionary purposes; and from this we may infer only that attempts are made to blunt it for the very reason that it is feared as a weapon.

The third objection to our concern with art and to our effort to understand it—an objection to art itself—does not come from technology or from historical materialism, but from the idealist theory according to which man is characterized by the intensity and diversity of his visions, dreams, ideals, and utopias, by the fact that he necessarily and continually opposes that which is not to that which is. Paul Valéry, the idealist artist of our day par excellence, has analyzed "the crisis of the mind" in the face of the damage caused by the First World War. Like the intellectual Hamlet he is, he inquired into its causes. And the answer he gave was:

What gives this critical condition of the mind its depth and gravity is the patient's condition . . .

So if I disregard all detail and confine myself to a quick impression, to that *natural whole* given by a moment's perception, I see . . . *nothing*! Nothing . . . and yet an infinitely potential nothing.

The physicists tell us that if the eye could survive in an oven fired to the point of incandescence, it would see . . . nothing. There would be no unequal intensities of light left to mark off points in space. That formidable contained energy would produce invisibility, indistinct equality. Now, equality of that kind is nothing else than a perfect state of *disorder*.

And what made that disorder in the mind of Europe? The free coexistence, in all her cultivated minds, of the most dissimilar ideas, the most contradictory principles of life and learning. That is characteristic of a *modern* epoch. . . .

Well then! Europe in 1914 had perhaps reached the limit of modernism in this sense. Every mind of any scope was a crossroads for all shades of opinion; every thinker was an international exposition of thought. There were works of the mind in which the wealth of contrasts and contradictory tendencies was like the insane displays of light in the capitals of those days: eyes were fatigued, scorched. . . . How much material wealth, how much labor and planning it took, how many centuries were ransacked, how many heterogeneous lives were combined, to make possible such a carnival, and to set it up as the supreme wisdom and the triumph of humanity?

In a book of that era—and not one of the most mediocre—we should have no trouble in finding: the influence of the Russian ballet, a touch of Pascal's gloom, numerous impressions of the Goncourt type, something of Nietzsche, something of Rimbaud, certain effects due to a familiarity with painters, and sometimes the tone of a scientific publication . . . the whole flavored with an indefinably British quality difficult to assess! . . . Let us notice, by the way, that within each of the components of this mixture other *bodies* could well be found. . . .

Hamlet hardly knows what to make of so many skulls. But suppose he forgets them! Will he still be himself? . . . His terribly lucid mind contemplates the passage from war to peace: darker, more dangerous than the passage from peace to war; all peoples are troubled by it. . . ."What about Me," he says, "what is to become of Me, the European intellect? . . . And what is peace? . . . *Peace is perhaps that state of things in which the natural hostility between men is manifested in creation, rather than destruction as in war.* Peace is a time of creative rivalry and the battle of production; but am I not tired of producing? . . . Have I not exhausted my desire for radical experiment, indulged too much in cunning compounds? . . . Should I not perhaps lay aside my hard duties and transcendent ambitions? . . . Perhaps follow the trend and do like Polonius who is now director of a great newspaper; like Laertes, who is something in aviation; like Rosencrantz, who is doing God knows what under a Russian name?

"Farewell, ghosts! The world no longer needs you—or me. By giving the name of progress to its own tendency to a fatal precision, the world is seeking to add to the benefits of life the advantages of death. A certain confusion still reigns; but in a little while all will be made clear, and we shall witness at last the miracle of an animal society, the perfect and ultimate anthill."[5]

European man, in whose mind the ideas, arts, and cultures of all nations and ages flow together as into a common market place; European man, culturally rotten to the core, has become incapable of spiritual production: such is Paul Valéry's view. It is a fact that since 1870 the dogma of the supreme or exclusive value of classical antiquity and the Renaissance has collapsed. Not only Gothic and baroque art, but also the arts of China, Japan, India, Asia Minor, Egypt, the African Negro tribes, the North American Indians, Mexico, South America, and the South Seas, are felt to be closer to us today than the art of the Renaissance; and when we think today of a revival of antiquity, we do not imagine it in any way like the ways Winckelmann, Goethe, or Burckhardt imagined it. This is not the place to discuss the role of these new elements in modern art. It is certain that they are not the cause of European spiritual disintegration but only a by-product of it. For the theory of art these new developments have been very fruitful. The multitude of phenomena compels us to recognize the relative character of subjects and styles; we

5. "The Crisis of the Mind" (originally pub. 1919), in *History and Politics*, tr. Denise Folliot and Jackson Mathews (New York and London, 1962), pp. 26–30.

have had to realize that many elements of art formerly regarded as essential were, in fact, secondary; we have also realized that the element common to all styles and subjects, the essence of art itself, is a specific variety of the creative instinct, active in nature and society, in philosophy and social morality. We know today how much mediocrity and trash our parents carried in their humanistic schoolbags. We know today that the great peaks of world art—the Buddhas of Borobudur, the Chinese Wild Geese[6] in the East Asia museum in Berlin, the young queen of Sheba on the so-called Royal Portal of Chartres, certain works of Mexico, Polynesia, and of paleolithic times—are of a quality rarely attained even by the Greeks. This discovery of the essence of art has sharpened our capacity for evaluation to an unprecedented degree—at the cost of a reverence for the mediocrity and trash that our parents and grandparents loved so dearly.

We shall confine ourselves to a brief remark on Valéry's cultural pessimism. When this idealist, this intellectual Hamlet, foresees that out of the ruins of war will arise "the miracle of an animal society" rather than the phoenix of a new community, we can only say: poor Hamlet. His fallacy is an elementary one: because bourgeois humanism is collapsing, he concludes that the world has come to an end. The inroads of foreign art may be symptomatic of the weakness and disintegration of the European middle classes; but this disintegration is the condition of a new upsurge. If we are successful in assimilating the alien cultures, we shall emerge from the struggle with a new, broader spirituality. But to this end it is, of course, not enough to be an intellectual Hamlet. Rather, we must have "the revolutionary devil" under our skin, as Bakunin used to say.

However different the various objections to a concern for art may sound, all of them have a perverse pessimism in common. That they are untenable becomes clear when we view art as a productive act which dissolves frozen, reified elements and gives permanent form to this process by combining opposites into unity. Art, to the extent that it creates true insights into nature and society, is one of the highest forms of the creative forces that dominate nature, society and the mind, and every work of art contains within it spiritual energies, the release of which can increase our own productive capacity. Our sense of human dignity is enhanced when we employ the energies released by our creative analysis of art for the cultivation of nature, for the development of personality, and for shaping a more just society.

Nevertheless, does such a thing as a "creative analysis of art" really exist? Can the layman ever experience the artist's inspiration, his own experience during the act of creation? But this is not important. The artist's experience before, during, and after the creative act, to the extent that it remains merely experience, is his private concern; it can be relevant to the viewer only if it has achieved artistic form—i.e., to the extent that

6. [A pair of hanging scrolls, formerly attributed to Mu-ch'i; ink on paper, late 13th century; Staatliche Museen, Berlin-Charlottenburg (East Asian section, Inv. No. 3569).]

the artist's experience is not *directly* expressed in the work. After all, the merest dilettante has almost the same experiences as the greatest artist: he too knows the lightning of revelation and the embrace of the Muse, ecstasies and depressions, zealous pedantry and the workings of the subconscious, moments of passion and moments of estrangement. An artist who attempts to justify his work solely on the basis of the genuineness, intensity, and importance of his experience can no more interest us than an artist who insists upon how "close" his work is to nature. In the foregoing essays we have given detailed examples of what we mean by an active analysis of art. Here we may sum up its main features:

1) Analysis must, like art itself, lead from the created work to the process of creation.
2) Analysis must reveal artistic creation as directed toward:
   a) an individual idea (conception) in which subjective-conditional and objective-absolute elements are combined;
   b) totality;
   c) necessity.
3) It must replace the world of things with a hierarchy of values.

What is the meaning of this statement: "Art and the study of art lead from the work to the process of creation?"

All of us take a pragmatic attitude toward the world when we are pursuing particular ends. The object performs a specific task for us or we perform a task with its aid. Beyond this we do not become aware of the concreteness of things; they are unreal to us in terms of sensory perception whether they are artificial or natural or else still in process of development. This is not a reflective attitude, because it does not inquire into the reasons of things and does not see things in their full context. Although Christ taught us to feel our unity with God in every bit of food and drink; although the wisdom of ancient India commands us to eat in such a way that we are conscious of thereby nourishing the whole world, we isolate each thing according to its use, making it and ourselves "stones among stones," being caught up in the endless cycle of need—means—gratification.

The aesthetic attitude is very different. It is uninterested, i.e., it pursues no purpose except this: to absorb the world through our senses—or the one inner sense—and to become one with it. It is not important how the particular part of the world looks that releases our aesthetic vision. What is important is to see it whole, in such a way that we extinguish all our momentary, individual concerns as well as the facticity of things outside us. We may find ourselves in harmony or disharmony with the world, we may feel the sublimity of the cosmos in relation to our tragic finitude or the ridiculous pettiness of our individual selves. Such an experience gratifies and purges us because in it our conflicts, whether with ourselves or with the world, are resolved.

Neither of the two attitudes does justice to the work of art, because the work of art is reality enhanced, which engages the senses both as a whole and in every one of its details and is yet a symbol of nonsensory meanings which extend down to still deeper layers without ever ceasing to appeal to our senses. And this enhanced reality, which has so misleadingly been called "illusion," is not ready made but develops before our eyes and in our minds, not in the sense that we re-experience the subjective process of the artist who created it but in the sense that we witness an objective spiritual development, a growth from germ to completion. We see how form is constituted by a specific artistic method and how form follows necessarily upon form. That is what I meant when I said that art leads us from the work to the process of creation. The icy crust of mere presence has melted away and we experience the creative process itself in the new, enhanced reality which both appeals to our senses and suggests an infinite wealth of meanings.

Placed in the midst of such a creative process, we would lose our way if the work of art itself did not guide us, showing us where the creative movement originates and what are its aims. As I have already said, this movement is directed toward three goals.

Let us consider the first characteristic of the unity between the subjective-relative and the objective-absolute. In the visual arts, bodies express psychic realities. Some bodies are inanimate, as for example, fabrics, vases, and other objects; that is, bodies without intrinsic psychic characteristics. Others are animate and possess psychic features of one sort or another. But this distinction between the animate and inanimate, so important to science, is of no importance to the artist. For his task consists in correlating the bodies he finds around him with his own state of mind. He has to find for each specific psychic content the stance, shape, and surface which can fully and uniquely express it. Conversely, for a given stance, shape, and surface of an object he must find the one corresponding state of mind and through it alone give life to what he sees. How is this possible, since body and soul are so different in quality and structure? Obviously, the only answer can be that a higher unity subsumes both without destroying their own characteristics.

At this point we must discuss categories as opposed to things, whether physical or spiritual. Every thing has certain specific characteristics; for example, it is individual, i.e., separated, isolated from the universal, and defined as to its particular nature in terms of matter, space, and time. Now, we can apprehend neither the universal nor the particular in themselves, but only as they are reflected in specific categories of the mind — senses, intellect, emotional life. To our sensory perceptions the earth stands still; intellectually we know it moves. We may dislike a man either because of his general character or because of particular things he does, and yet our reason can understand why he is the way he is or why he acts as he does. Thus, to begin with, we apprehend only phenomena — the reflections of "things in themselves" in our minds; the things in themselves are not *directly* accessible to us. It is also highly doubtful whether we can directly apprehend the categories, for they in turn depend on the existence of things; the categories do not create the things but only help determine their intellectual, sensory, and emotional character.

Just as things would never enter our consciousness were it not for the categories, so categories would never take on the character of objective entities if there had been no things for them to reflect. But how is it possible that things and categories, which are so different from each other, form a unity in the first place? And who can guarantee that this unity tends toward a congruence of the opposites, and is not a distorted image of unity, since we cannot have direct knowledge of either the "form in itself" or the "thing in itself?" For our present purpose it is sufficient to assume that the things compose themselves into unity through categories and that subjective categories are merely refractions of these objective categories in the various faculties of our consciousness. Under this assumption, things and categories are only two phenomenal forms and developmental stages of a single reality—objectively present matter in its unity and totality.

The difference just referred to between phenomena and "things in themselves" applies not only to the relation between the external world and consciousness but also to the relation between the conscious and the unconscious within the inner world. The unconscious contents are those which have either never been molded by the categories or which have lost their categorial form for one reason or another. Accordingly, to bring something from the unconscious to the conscious is to give it a categorial form. Thus the unconscious consists simply of raw material, and the presence of large amounts of such material in a work of art points to creative weakness rather than strength. For, unlike the external world, which has not passed through the artist's psychic apparatus but possesses its own categories, the contents of the unconscious mind have indeed passed through the psychic apparatus, but without being molded by it. This absence of categorial form may endow the unconscious with the value of a new subject for artistic creation, but the unconscious of itself has no artistic or metaphysical value, it is merely a reservoir of subject matter.

This brings us to the fourth and last antithesis: between the conditional and the "absolute." By conditional we mean every phenomenon, be it corporeal-psychic, categorial-objective, or created out of the topography of our consciousness. And by absolute we mean the whole of the objective world, which can never as such become a phenomenon, although it is the ultimate foundation of all phenomena. Moreover, for historical reasons we call absolute those images, religious or metaphysical, that mankind has evolved during the various epochs to denote the uncontrolled part of the world, which—it was always granted—never could be adequately described or imagined even though it is present in every representation and perception.

We also mentioned above that artistic creation seeks to combine the conditional with the absolute in an individual idea. "Combine" here denotes every kind of unification, merging, conciliation, and resolution of oppositions—indeed, even the tendency to stress oppositions. All such connections or combinations lead to an "individual idea"—an

XXII*a* Dürer. *Saint John the Evangelist and Saint Peter*, panel of "The Four Apostles." 1526. 79⅞ × 29¼ in.

XXII*b* Saint Peter (jamb figure). ca. 1100–1150. Height of figure 59 in. South Portal, St.-Pierre, Moissac

XXIII*a*   REMBRANDT. *Joseph and Potiphar's Wife.*
1634. Etching, 3⅞ × 4½ in.

XXIII*b*   REMBRANDT. *Joseph Accused by Potiphar's Wife.* 1654 (or 1655). 41⅝ × 38½ in.

XXIV REMBRANDT. *Joseph Accused by Potiphar's Wife.* 1655. 43¼×34¼ in.

idea in so far as both something sensory and perceptible and something typical, essential, and universally human is concerned; individual in so far as the idea is bound up with a people's mode of production in a specific epoch, its traditions, and the artist's own temperament, and can only originate and be realized under these specific conditions. The "individual idea" on the one hand reflects the aesthetic feeling induced in the artist by the situation of society at a given historical moment; on the other hand it is the starting point of the artistic motif, the definite form in which the idea is embodied and made sensual. The idea is the bridge between aesthetic feeling and motif. Artists' "individual ideas" may differ widely even at the same time and place, but each of them will invariably involve a tension of opposites and, ideally, a self-positing conflict, the realization of which determines the two directions of artistic creation we shall now discuss.

We referred above to one of these as "totality," applying the name to very different groups of facts. There is first the totality of the corporeal-psychic self. It is physical and encompasses volume, articulation, structure, and surface. It is psychic in that it includes man's cognitive faculties (body, senses, thinking, reason) and the successive stages of cognition (apprehension, absorption, and concretization).

In addition there is relational totality: relations to nature, ranging from accidental contacts with individual things to continuous subordination to cosmic laws; relations to people, ranging from friendship and love to familial and occupational companionship and the broader forms of societal and national or international life; and lastly, to cultural works created by church, art, science, philosophy, and other cultural domains.

So far we have only envisaged totality as external; we have not glimpsed the inner wholeness of the individual. We must now add spiritual totality—the facts of the mind. I shall distinguish three groups. The first refers to being and nonbeing. What we have in mind is not the fact of death as an end but the immanence of nonbeing at every moment of existence; we are always shuttling back and forth between these poles and this unbroken process of becoming and dissolving is always accompanied by the consciousness that we circle around the unfathomable and the unrealizable. The second group comprises the stages and forms of consciousness: the unconscious, the conscious, and the supraconscious, all the complex relationships between freedom and unfreedom. The third group includes the positing of value, the idea of perfect form, together with the will to actualize every potentiality. Every individual must be raised to the level of humanity, the relations between individuals to universal community; thinking must attain to law, piety to holiness, artistic creation to living form, etc.

Artistic creation involves the totality of dispositions, functions, relations, facts, and values—all of these in harmonious interaction: body and soul, inwardness and outwardness, the individual and the community, the self and the cosmos, tradition and revolution, instinct and freedom, life and death, becoming and being, the self and fate, struggle and structure, the Dionysian and the Apollonian, law and accident, structure and surface, contemplation and action, education and achievement, sensuality and spirit, doubt and faith, love and duty, ugliness and perfection, the finite and the infinite. Neither one of any pair of these terms should exclude the other nor should any pair exclude any other—they must all be brought together into a higher unity. Here, too, an example will be helpful: let us compare one of Dürer's apostles with one of the Romanesque apostles at Moissac (Plate **XXII**). Here we can see the difference between the human being who seeks a harmonious development of his whole personality and the human being who exhibits an excessively one-sided attitude to the world. At first sight the early medieval figure may seem the more striking, but on longer reflection it will be Dürer's apostle, who embodies individuality with uniqueness and universality, who will claim our lasting admiration.

"Necessity" is the second aim of artistic creation in combining the conditional and the absolute. This necessity appears in four ways: in the self-sufficiency of the work; in its inner unity; in the laws of its structure; and in its potential effect.

Self-sufficiency denotes, in negative terms, the work's independence of the artist's subjectivity even though—or precisely because—the work is filled with his entire personality. It also denotes independence of subject matter even though—or precisely because—the work expresses perfectly all its essential features. The work is not merely communication, concretization, personal utterance; it is not merely the repetition of inner states or the imitation of the outside world, but a structure (*Gestalt*) endowed with its own life—a life at another level than that of the psyche or that of things. This life is achieved by a method that creates and secures the fusion of law with phenomenon, of universal with particular, of structure with surface and, hence, the work's isolation from the outside world and independence of the inner world.

The inner unity of the work is what makes self-sufficiency possible. According to Goethe, what makes an artist is a "heart overflowing with a single feeling." But this unity of aesthetic feeling becomes form only to the extent that it is articulated into a complex of conflicts and tensions. Only on the basis of the tensions at work in it is the aesthetic feeling embodied in a motif and the latter so developed that every detail is a variation, determined by specific laws, upon the basic feeling and the main motif. The variations taken together concretize the unity of mood prevailing in the picture.

The unity of mood becomes unity of form and is secured by the same laws that govern the motif and the details. Every detail or individual form is a variation on the main theme and every variation is assigned a specific place in the picture. As we move up the picture from the bottom, we follow the development from unconsciousness through struggle to the clarity of consciousness. As we move from left to right, we follow the development of the action, the expression of will, and the existential relations. As we move into depth, we follow the relations between the physical and the immaterial. The artist may arrange his spatial and spiritual co-ordinates according to other principles, but he must always achieve the closest possible unity among these three series. In addition, every individual form is causally determined by the forms that precede it and at the same time by the overall intent. In this way the work obeys the laws of logic and is at the same time an organic structure, so that the antinomy between system and life seems to be transcended.

However, it is not only the development of the formal relationships that is subject to law. Since art appeals above all to the senses and seeks to reveal meaning through them, the laws of structure are realized only when they establish necessity for the senses—i.e., in the homogeneity, material continuity, and animation of the surface. Only the perfection of the surface marks the consummation of the work. Leonardo da Vinci said: "Invention is free and the easiest thing in art. The most difficult and noblest thing is the perfect sensory realization. It is for the sake of this perfection that the complex science of painting exists." "The perfect sensory realization," as distinguished from the mere play of fantasy, consists in the definite becoming infinite and the indefinable becoming finite, "so that in looking at the painting we forget it is a painting."[7]

Self-sufficiency, unity, and structure determined by law are closely interrelated, determine and supplement one another, and together produce a specific effect. The potential effect, as opposed to the concrete, actual effect, we designated as the fourth and last characteristic of necessity in so far as it determines the direction of the creative act. In predominantly religious art, such as that of the Gothic cathedrals and the temples of India, there are innumerable details of which the eye can be no more than aware. Even in the smallest picture there are always details that escape the most attentive viewer. What matters is that the viewer be made a part of the work, i.e., that the artist not merely reproduce the result of his experience but present it in such a way that all the means employed produce the same result for another person. The artist does not only create for the other person but above all for the sake of man's relation to the "absolute" (objective totality) and the perfection of the total configuration. This can never be achieved in finite terms and yet the artist must never neglect the finite to the point where he does not care or is unable to reach other men. An overmetaphysical approach is as inartistic as too egocentric an approach.

Our point of departure was the idea that art itself supplies the reasons for our interest in it. We have tried to define art with the aid of three concepts which at the same time constitute the reasons for our practical interest in it. The first two characteristics were that art leads us from the created work to the creative process and that art directs creation along specific lines, namely, toward the combination of the conditional and the "absolute" in an individual idea, toward totality, and toward necessity. We formulated the

7. [Percy Bysshe] Shelley. [Quotation not traced.]

third characteristic as follows: The world of things is replaced by a world of values conscious of their relativity. And with this a new mode of being emerges from the artistic process.

Artistic creation, by its nature, does not ascribe independent significance to subject matter. To be sure, the Annunciation is not a bacchanale, certainly not a sensuous one with Pan, the satyrs, and the maenads, though perhaps we might think of it as a spiritual intoxication, even as the reveling of the heart as it enters into union with God. To be sure, a historic battle—the conquest of Constantinople by the Crusaders, let us say—is scarcely to be confused with a rotting apple set against fresh foliage. But do not both involve victor and vanquished, with that reciprocal intermingling of plus and minus signs which makes everything dependent on our point of view? It should be clear that what a theme conveys is not the same thing as its subject matter but depends upon the artist, the meaning he associates with a given content, the conception he imposes upon things. True, the same meaning can be embodied in different things, and each thing conveys something of its own nature. The artist cannot neglect this, but what matters in a work of art is not this specific "something" contributed by the subject matter but the intensity with which the over-all meaning is conveyed by the figuration and for the sake of which whatever might create discrepancy between meaning and content is eliminated.

Intensity of figuration is not display of the artist's strength; not vitality, which animates the outer world with the personal energies of the creative artist; not logical or emotional consistency, with which a limited problem is thought through or felt through to its ultimate consequences. What it does denote is the degree to which the very essence of art has been realized: the undoing of the world of things, the construction of the world of values, and hence the constitution of a new world. The originality of this constitution provides us with a general criterion by which we can measure intensity of figuration. Originality of constitution is not the urge to be different from others, to produce something entirely new; it is (in the etymological sense) the grasping of the origin, the roots of both ourselves and things.

We can further specify this general criterion by taking into account the conditions that we have recognized as constitutive of the work of art. Then, if we study the manner in which the "absolute" has been linked with the conditional—that is the degree to which the conditional has been dematerialized and the "absolute" realized—we shall find that the more a work is both immaterial and concrete—in other words, the more symbolic it is, the more unlimited its meanings—the greater it is as a work of art. Similarly, with respect to the character of totality we may say that the more comprehensive, that is, both more polarized and more harmonious, even, we may say, at once more determinate and more freely playful, the greater is a given work of art. Finally, with respect to the character of necessity, we may say that the greater the diversity in unity, the greater the tensions, the more logical the structure, the more self-sufficient, the greater the work.

The fact that differences in the intensity of figuration do exist and that they indicate the most important aspect of artistic creation can best be shown by an example. Consider the various treatments Rembrandt gave the theme of Joseph and Potiphar's wife. The first version, an early etching (Plate XXIII*a*), is distinguished from the second (the painting in Leningrad,[8] Plate XXIII*b*) by its very conception of the subject. The earlier work suggests erotic sexual play, the later one depicts the comic situation of a female trying to oppose the idea of justice. The third and latest version (the painting in Berlin, Plate XXIV) is again very different in the determinants of the creative process; it comes closest to perfection.

The various degrees in intensity of figuration form a hierarchy of values, that is, an order in which each figuration has a fixed place between two others, one higher, one lower. We cannot express these degrees arithmetically or even name them—strong proof of the lack of interest in a scientific theory of art. A hierarchy of values certainly exists, although it is difficult to formulate it and although there is no such thing as a supreme, absolute value, but only the unceasing attempt to come ever closer to the *idea* of a perfect value. Creative power is limited, not merely because it is bound to historically determined conditions or to an individual creator, but in itself; and this limit appears in each work of art the more distinctly, the more extensively and deeply it gives form to the controlled part of the world. The work is neither creation *ex nihilo* nor imitation of the creation of the world. On the margin of what man can do there appears that which he cannot or cannot yet do—but which lies at the root of all creativeness. All great creators have felt this and have most often expressed it in religious language. When Moses wished to look upon God's glory he was told: "Thou shalt see my back parts; but my face shall not be seen."[9] And Homer says: "And when a god wishes to remain unseen, what eye can observe his coming or his going?"[10] And so on through the ages, down to Goethe and Baudelaire. This impossibility of direct and total vision is not without consequences. The creator's pride is broken in its encounter with objective totality, with the "absolute" of his epoch, and in this encounter a renewal of creative force takes place. Were creativity possible without the "absolute," the first creation would be the last.

Thus, although a creative theory of art is possible, in the sense of reproducing the method of figuration employed in a given work, the tasks involved are not easy or naturally performed by everybody. Everyone is born with a capacity to understand art but

8. [Purchased by Andrew W. Mellon in 1937. Now in the National Gallery of Art, Washington, D.C.]

9. Exodus 33:23.

10. *Odyssey*, X, lines 573 *f.*; tr. E. V. Rieu (Harmondsworth and Baltimore, 1959), p. 170.

no one has ever been fully equal to its demands upon him; the artist himself, after the completion of a work, is compelled to attempt greater things. "Form is a secret to most people." By this, Goethe doubtless meant that the essence of form is hidden from most people. But we may interpret his saying in the sense that form contains a mysterious element that cannot be revealed. Helen, beauty incarnate and perfect form, can be brought back from the underworld only by him who has trodden the path to the Mothers, "to the untrodden, not to be trod," to "the deepest, furthest depths."[11] Any investigation of art must therefore recognize that its main purpose is "to have probed what is knowable and quietly to revere what is unknowable."[12] With this restriction in mind, I believe that there are two paths that actually lead us to the essence of art.

The first of these paths is to think away the work of art before us and, without taking our eyes away from it, to ask ourselves what we must do to reconstitute it—conceptually, of course. In the preceding essays we saw that there are four fundamental problems:

1) The constitution of the individual form in terms of material and space.

2) The constitution of the work as a whole externally (format, immanent structural lines, lines of orientation) and internally (mode of reality, individual idea, aesthetic feeling, motif, etc.).

3) The constitution of the relations between individual forms within the work (internal and external composition, logic of the structure, etc.).

4) The realization of the individual forms as well as of the configuration as a whole.

Each of the four stages represents the artistic method as concrete phenomenon.

The second path is to compare the degrees of intensity of figuration. This is the path the untrained observer takes naturally, only to go astray quite promptly by identifying "beautiful" or "ugly" with his own likes and dislikes, i.e., unreflective judgments with subjective reactions.[13] But if we examine carefully what value judgments are for, we find that they are intended to express this objective fact: any two works of art take up different positions in the hierarchy of values, which—as we have shown—is a reality lying beyond personal taste and independent of it.

To deny the existence of universally valid criteria in evaluating works of art is not only to eschew one of the most self-evident problems but also to destroy the world of values, since the true and the good lose their normative character once art is left to individual taste. However, we should consider the value aspect of art, which is the most fruitful, only at the end. To evaluate the work of art we must be free of all personal feelings about the subject matter, must be able to view the latter impersonally, treating all subjects as equally legitimate and equally relative, and to renounce all expectations of perfection in

11. *Faust*, Part II, lines 6222*f.* and 6284; tr. Shawcross, pp. 240, 242.

12. *Goethe: Wisdom and Experience*, selected by Ludwig

Curtius, tr. and ed. Hermann J. Weigand (New York, 1949), p. 94.

13. [See the author's *Von Monet zu Picasso*.]

the absolute sense. We have shown above that there are, within these limits, criteria universally valid because they are identical with the essence of art. Their application to individual works may be called the normative method.

In addition to these two methods an auxiliary method of especial pedagogical value may be used. It consists in studying the work of the artistic imagination. Strictly speaking, it is as difficult as observing a tree in the act of growing. All that is accessible to us is stages in the completion of the work, never the process of work itself. But the former enable us to lift a corner of the veil. For when we have ascertained the stimulus or group of stimuli which inspired the work and compared them with the work in its early or late stages, we can deduce from the differences what has been added (or has remained constant, when the stimulus was another work of art)—and this then belongs to the essence of art. We can further confirm our conjectures when we see how the artist worked, again and again, beginning with the first sketch, which was a direct copy of his conception, until he arrived at a version which satisfied him.

A further albeit somewhat dubious method consists in comparing the works produced by the same artist at different stages of his life. While we must be sure to consider the age factor and differences in the intensity of figuration at different ages, we may assume that an artist who has matured comes closer to the essence of art and reveals it more fully. In this view the artist's whole career may be seen as a lifelong process of working on one and the same subject; the earlier versions will not be so close to perfection as the later, and on the basis of the successive works this difference can be discovered and formulated.

The creative theory of art, however, requires more than the reproduction of the artistic process by the viewer; it also requires that the spiritual energies released by the work of art be used to further the viewer's own creative powers.

We have said that art leads us from the work to the process of creation. This reversion, outside the theory of art, will eventually generate universal doubt about the world as given, the natural as well as the social. Instead of accepting things as they are, of taking them for granted, we learn, thanks to art, to measure them by the standard of perfection. The greater the unavoidable gulf between the ideal and the real, the more inescapable is the question: Why is the existing world the way it is? How has the world come to be what it is? *De omnibus rebus dubitandum est! Quid certum?* "We must doubt all things! What is sure?" (Descartes).[14] It is the nature of the creative mind to dissolve seemingly solid things and to transform the world as it is into a world in process of becoming and creating. This is how we are liberated from the multiplicity of things and come to realize what it is that all conditional things ultimately possess in common. Thus, instead of being creatures isolated among other isolated creatures we become part of the power that creates all things; thus the path to the "Mothers" is cleared before us. First we are freed from

14. *Meditationes de prima philosophia*, Second Meditation.

accidental, individual determinations and rendered capable of pure contemplation; next we are freed from pure contemplation and rendered capable of re-creating creation; and finally we are freed from re-creating and rendered capable of ourselves creating. Did art not exist to show us the path to creative activity we would never come back from the journey, as Faust did with Helen—the symbol of perfection—but be forever lost.

We said earlier that there are three directions—more accurately, three signs pointing in the same direction—which art offers us: the individual idea, in which are combined the conditional and the absolute, totality, and necessity. Creative activity thus directed can extend to the self and the shaping of the self; from there it may spread to social relationships and the shaping of society and, finally, to the realm of nature, including the forces of human labor, and the shaping of economic life.

Let us reflect on the implications of the term "shaping of the self." To be able to shape ourselves we must begin with the realization that we are not wholly products of nature; we must come to know ourselves. This is the beginning—though a difficult and highly responsible beginning. Since we cannot know ourselves directly, but only through our actions, it remains more than doubtful whether our idea of ourselves accords with our real motives. But we must strive unremittingly to achieve this congruence. For only self-knowledge can lead to self-determination, and false self-determination would ruin our lives and be the most immoral action we could commit.

In determining ourselves we consciously assert that which we have recognized as our natural disposition, our essential nature, i.e., the mode in which we can embody the whole and the absolute. We can realize self-determination only when we keep constantly in mind that the individual element in it is an idea, i.e., is made concrete in supreme perfection over the *whole* of our being and in unity with all other men. No individual—whether self or nation—has the right to break up this bond with the idea by presuming his individuality to be the idea itself. Actually, individuality is a fact of nature, whereas the idea is a spiritual challenge, an endless task. We fulfill it to the extent that we link our self-determination with the two other attributes of artistic creation—totality and necessity.

We have totality when our self-determination extends to all our faculties, when we are entirely permeated with it, neither one-sidedly intellectuals nor wholly creatures of instinct, neither solipsistically enclosed within our own heads nor passive and unconscious. We may not let the body wither for the sake of the soul, nor the spirit for the sake of material pleasures. We may not let ourselves become dependent on things, lest we lose thereby our freedom, and we must not abuse our capacity for play, thereby losing our sense of values. Rather, self-determination must include everything—selfishness and idealism, intoxication and sobriety, body and soul, freedom and dependence—if we are to develop into harmonious, integrated, world-encompassing human beings who, like Ulysses, would be neither god nor beast.

Totality in the shaping of the self implies, further, involvement of the self within all relationships, particularly the human and the cultural. Here lies a source of grave, perhaps unresolvable conflicts: the individual who strives for full self-determination aspires to wholeness, yet in his relationship with other individuals and with groups he finds that only parts of him are usable and therefore prized over the others, that they are given tasks whose execution and rights whose assertion conflict with his goal of total self-determination. Nevertheless, we must not evade such conflicts. In the face of each demand, of each right, we must ask ourselves: Can we meet it? May we use it? In every instance we must be governed by the general principle that before we can or should *act*, we must *be*. Otherwise, what we do is either mechanical or dogmatic, and nothing could be further from the lesson of art.

When the individual striving for self-determination confronts the demands of the actual world, he discovers that self-determination does not shut him off from the world, does not drive him to eccentricity and ineffectuality, but opens him to the world and the world to him, makes him capable of influencing it and of being influenced by it. In this we may recognize the working of necessity, or at least the material in the formation of which the necessity of self-determination becomes evident as we assert ourselves and humble ourselves and at the same time recognize the just claims of the existent. The kind of self-determination that is necessary is one which asserts itself against all temptations and difficulties, which can bear any cross, even self-denial. The kind of self-determination that is necessary is capable of estimating its own limits and of being content to remain within them; it leads to inner unity and community of purpose; shapes the self at the same time as it shapes the world, and in such a way that only those cultural forms are attacked for which we have new ones, basically different from the old and more adequate. Anything else would be to destroy the unity and continuity of human development, to defeat our own purpose. Such a self-defeat would be a moral defeat because it would rest upon a false self-determination.

Much the same may be said of the possible utilization of the spiritual energies latent in the work of art for the shaping of social life. We distinguish between organized and personal relationships among men. The personal relationships have immediate psychological and cultural roots; the organized relationships usually have a material basis— they have evolved from personal relationships which historically have lost their immediacy. Now, art places personal relationships above the others and provides us with ideal models of them. It depicts such relationships with a purity and consistency that we rarely achieve in real life, being only too much a prey to social pressures. Art frees us from enslavement to words, concepts, and false moral values by showing us that life knows differentiations that cannot be reduced to concepts as well as situations which cannot be judged by accepted moral standards.

Our attitude toward organized human relationships is also influenced by correct understanding and application of the spiritual energies stored up in the work of art.

Because art leads us from the work to the process of creation, it induces us to question the bureaucratic machinery in all its abstractness and to test its actual performance. Thereby art keeps alive our critical spirit with respect to the organized forms of relationships, and it does so not in terms of material necessity but in terms of our creative powers.

The individual must realize the limits of his creative powers. Every man contributes to the shaping of human relationships according to his individual capacities and, conversely, we must demand of the political body (state, etc.) that each individual be allowed to develop his creative powers to the maximum. This is the ultimate criterion of society's value.

We shall briefly discuss what art teaches us with respect to the shaping of organized human relationships. We shall confine ourselves to the concrete example of the state. First of all, we must recognize and realize the individual idea implied in historical development. Since this presupposes a specific relationship between the conditional and the absolute, all conditional political concepts such as economy, power, rulers, the nation, etc., mean nothing apart from their connection with the absolute which, in historical terms, can mean only the next higher stage of development. It is a utopian fallacy to speak of *the* individual idea of *the* state. There are as many types of state as there are historical forms of self-determination. To be sure, not all of them satisfy the principles of totality and necessity.

We say that the requirement of totality in the shaping of social life is met when *all* members of a given social group take active part. Furthermore, every social body must be capable of integration with larger social bodies. No social body has the right to proclaim itself supreme; neither church nor state is absolute sovereign. Finally, the individual must be treated not as a mere function, as "human raw material," but as an integral human being. These three factors can be summed up in one: the shaping of social life meets the requirement of totality when it has come as close as it can to identify with the idea of mankind—mankind meant here not quantitatively but qualitatively: the social body must attain a totality analogous to that of the individual self.

The social shaping of the state meets the requirement of necessity when, first, there is an internal balance among all the creative powers contributing to it, i.e., when there is justice. "Justice" does not imply that everyone has the same rights and duties but, as Plato long ago recognized in his criticism of ancient democracy, that everyone must contribute his share and receive his due, without prejudice of birth and with equal opportunities for all. Further, necessity is expressed as self-sufficiency, i.e., the capacity to live by one's own resources without infringing on the rights of others by force. Let us recall that every social body—from the most intimate to the most widely organized—is only a link in the chain of cultural values. Therefore no single social body, such as the state, or even the mere idea of a social body, may be identified with the whole range of values. The latter rests upon the free development of each link and its order reflects the comprehensiveness and intensity of each link. Anarchy would inevitably ensue if, on the basis of some theoretical fiat, we permitted one cultural form to oppress another. Any state which under any circumstances whatever persecutes science, art, philosophy, or religion by any sort of arbitrary measures is an immoral state and an impotent one, whose recourse to brute force camouflages its weaknesses.

We have said that art supplants the objective order of things and perceptions by a hierarchy of values conscious of their relativity. It changes our whole attitude toward life —not merely our understanding of it but also our evaluation of it, in fact, all our perspective. For now the "what" has lost its importance: profession and property, talents and noble feelings, however fine, good will and pure faith, are no longer the essential reality. The true and the good become less important than creative intensity, than power of realization. We may demonstrate all Plato's ideas to be false—and indeed, we could show that there is no such thing as absolute truth—and yet we should still have to recognize Plato as one of the greatest European philosophers, i.e., that he has come closer to the idea of perfect form than others. Or we may regard Napoleon, as many Frenchmen do, as an unscrupulous criminal, and yet only one man since and very few men before him achieved a creative action so nearly perfect, total, and necessary. The mobilization of energy must always be at the service of perfection, but without fanaticism. For art teaches us that every man who has realized his creative powers has done something he and he alone could do; at the same time, however, every personal fulfillment falls short of perfection. To the man who can recognize in every advance the Medusa head of the law of conservation of problems and creative energies, art shows the idea of perfect yet relative value. The closer we can get to it, the more distinctly looms "the absolute" (the objective totality). And the more conscious we are of the latter, the more intensively can we devote ourselves to the process of shaping, without sacrifice of self. We create not because we are one thing more than another, but because we are a reality that encompasses and ennobles the existent. Creation does not take us out of the world but helps us to stand back from it—the more so the more fully involved in it we are. We become simultaneously more real and more unreal—symbols, beacon lights. In this sense our awareness of relativity bolsters our aspiration to perfection. Meister Eckhart, in an entirely different context, put it this way: "To *keep busy* is to be involved with things superficially; to *do* something is to be informed by reason, and involved wholeheartedly. Only men who *do* are in the midst of things without being submerged by them. In the very thick of things, they yet stand at the very outermost circle of heaven, close to eternity."[15]

15. Sermon on a text from Luke 10:38. [Cf. Meister Eckhart, *Deutsche Predigten und Traktate*, tr. Josef Quint (Munich, 1955), No. 28. Max Raphael quoted from *Meister Eckhart's Schriften*, tr. Hermann Buettner (Jena, 1934), which is now considered obsolete.]

Creative instinct manifests itself with greater freedom in art than in any other domain. A creative, active study of art is therefore indispensable to awaken creative powers, to assert them against the dead weight of tradition, and to mobilize them in the struggle for a social order in which everyone will have the fullest opportunity to develop his creative capacities. The details of this social order cannot be anticipated without falling into utopian dreams. We can and we must be satisfied with the awareness that art helps us to achieve the truly just order. The decisive battles, however, will be fought at another level.

Sources of Chapter Mottoes

I

The quotations are from Joachim Gasquet, *Cézanne* (Paris, 1926), pp. 130*ff.*, 91*f.*, and 195 respectively.

III

FAUST: Was bin ich denn, wenn es nicht möglich ist
    Der Menschheit Krone zu erringen,
    Nach der sich alle Sinne dringen?
MEPHISTOPHELES: Du bist am Ende—was du bist.
    Setz' dir Perrücken auf von Millionen Locken,
    Setz' deinen Fuss auf ellenhohe Socken,
    Du bleibst doch immer was du bist.
Lines 1803–9; tr. John Shawcross (London, 1959), p. 65.

IV

Spinoza, *Ethics*, V. prop. XXXII.

V

Picasso: Quoted by Juan Larrea in *Guernica* (Paris, 1945); tr. A. H. Krappe (New York, 1947), p. 52.
Benjamin: *Ursprung des deutschen Trauerspiels* (Berlin, 1928), p. 176; rev. ed. (Frankfurt a M, 1963), p. 197.
Payne: *Mao Tse Tung: Ruler of Red China* (New York, 1950), p. 230.

VI

GOETHE: Zum Sehen geboren,
    Zum Schauen bestellt . . .
Lines 11288*f.*; tr. Shawcross (see above), p. 421.

Was kann der Mensch im Leben mehr gewinnen,
Als dass sich Gottnatur ihm offenbare:
Wie sie das Feste lässt zu Geist verrinnen,
Wie sie das Geisterzeugte fest bewahre.
Goethe: *Schiller's Reliquien*; tr. Edgar Bowring, *The Poems of Goethe* (London, 1853).

APPENDIX: Toward an Empirical Theory of Art

EDITORIAL NOTE

In 1941, Max Raphael began to draft a systematic exposition of his theory of art. Although it is evident from the main text of the present volume that the system subsequently was further refined, pertinent sections of the draft are here included, edited into a continuous form in order to clarify the author's terminology. The omitted material consists of analytic demonstrations, most of which, vastly expanded, reappear in the chapters of *The Demands of Art*.

PREFACE

This work sets itself the task of making art an object of scientific cognition.

Is it a chimerical undertaking to subject the irrational act of inspiration to Reason?

I might point out that the intellectually more courageous generations of the Middle Ages did not hesitate to dissect the mysteries of divine revelation. I might also point out that inspiration is nothing but an illusion on the part of the most barren class in modern society, an illusion which rests upon the distinction that arose in the nineteenth century between socially mechanized production of material goods and individual craft production of spiritual goods. It is a petty bourgeois fiction which has degraded art to a substitute for religion. I shall not waste the reader's time showing why the various theories of aesthetics and the many histories, psychologies, and sociologies of art have not even begun to come to grips with their alleged object of investigation. Also, the reader need not be reminded that before infinitesimal calculus was discovered, even nature could not be studied mathematically. What I propose here is to develop a theory of art that I call empirical because it is based on a study of works of art from all periods and nations. I am convinced that mathematics, which has traveled a long way since Euclid, will someday provide us with the means of formulating the results of such a study in mathematical terms.

Does this mean that, taking the exact sciences as my model, I propose to rationalize art?

Yes and no.

The intellect is only one of the human faculties, it is concerned with only one aspect of an object—whether in art or nature. But we also have subjective experiences of both nature and art which have no place in an empirical theory of art, although they undeniably contribute to our knowledge. More importantly, there is man's creative activity, and theory can investigate its laws; they are a particular instance of the universal laws that govern the mind's processes and are the object of the philosophical theory of knowledge.

I have no intention of relaxing the rigor of scientific method. I take it for what it is, or rather for what it has become in the course of its development and what it is yet to become. If there is still no exact theory of art, it is largely because the methods so far brought to bear suffered from self-imposed limitations. The most important of these involved the notion that every domain of knowledge must be built up from elementary units (the point in mathematics, the cell in biology, the sensation in academic psychology, etc.). According to this notion, the more complex entities must be constructed out of such elements with no reference to any concept of the whole. I believe that it is more in keeping with the facts of art to start with a more highly structured element whose components are variable and enter into many combinations, mutations, etc. That is to say, I should like to replace an abstract system of concepts, each designating a simple thing by a simple term, with a system of variable elements and variable functions. At the same time, I believe that it would not destroy but enlarge scientific method in the domain of art to pair the concept of particularity with the concept of totality—a totality which combines the same factors of form, content, and method at a higher level.

To be sure, art has aspects that demand a different approach. I have no intention of neglecting them. Because in art the universal manifests itself *in* the particular, it is no longer sufficient to "subsume" the particular under the universal. Furthermore, because art transforms historical realities into symbols and thus leads to a hierarchy of values, we cannot study it without reference to values, nor can we draw a sharp line between history and existence (as can be done in the natural and social sciences). To resolve this last problem, I envisage a theory of art consisting of three parts—phenomenology, history, and criticism.[1] Needless to say, these parts are interdependent, although—or even because—history is not entirely dissolved in art, nor art in history. To cope with the universal and particular, I introduce, in addition to the constitutive categories of element, totality, and relation, a new category, that of realization. Here again we speak not of an isolated category, but one implied in each of the others.

The first part of this essay, dealing with the basic descriptive concepts, includes chapters on individual form, over-all form or configuration, composition, and realization.[2] These are to be defined solely through the ways they are built up and developed in works of art, using as illustrations well-known masterpieces, yet extending the insights gained to lesser works and other epochs. In this way I hope to demonstrate the theoretical validity of my approach.

Only when all three parts of my theory have been elaborated—history and criticism as well as phenomenology—can the empirical theory of art be supplemented and completed by a mathematical theory of art. This will be the task of a generation yet to come—the task of a social class that will have lost all fear of Reason, that will no longer pay tribute to superstition and irrationality, and will have recognized the dialectical method as man's worthiest response to the enigma of existence.

M. R.

Aboard the SS Mouzinho, *Lisbon–New York, June 17, 1941*

1. [The author's manuscript is headed by a table of contents which shows that he intended to devote a separate part to each of these subjects, to be followed by a fourth part on the general theory of artistic creation. Internal evidence indicates that the manuscript breaks off before the author reached the end of the part devoted to phenomenology (Part I, "Basic Concepts of Description").]

2. [The author did not divide his draft into chapters. Chapter heads reflecting his plan have been supplied by the editors. Chapter IV, "Realization," was not written.]

PART ONE: Basic Concepts of Description

There are several types of description.

The first considers the object as given, and analyzes whatever qualities and quantities are directly accessible to sense perception. It cannot go beyond the classification of objects on the basis of external similarities (Linnaeus).

The second considers the object not merely as given, but the active, creative powers inherent in it; not merely the manifold part, but the essential unity. It understands (and communicates) what is directly accessible to the inner sense, to intuition, the essential insight.

The third goes beyond the immediacy of both the outer and the inner sense; it *thinks* the object, or, more accurately, it abstracts from its given aspects and builds it up from its elements and their inherent active properties, first conceptually and then experimentally (mathematics, physics, modern biology).

The first kind of description results in a catalogue of parts with no intellectual unification, it enumerates everything without explaining anything, it knows all and understands nothing. The second attempts to conjure up understanding by means of a kind of pseudoscientific mysticism, and violates the Newtonian principle of *hypotheses non fingo* by concocting hypotheses that explain everything. The third kind of description supplies the real explanation of the object: from empirically observed regularities in the object's own development and in its relations with other objects, it makes inferences as to its elements, their interrelations and their totality, and confirms these inferences by constituting and reconstructing the object. This is possible only if sufficient account is taken of sense perception as determined by intuition, and of intuition as determined by sense perception. Not until the two lower, imperfect types of description have made us thoroughly familiar with the nature and characteristics of the object, with its regularly occurring features and the ways in which it affects us, can truly scientific description begin its constitutive work. The basic categories in this process are the same in all domains, but their concrete manifestations differ in each.

In art these categories are: individual form, over-all form or configuration [*Werkgestalt*], composition, and realization. None of these terms designates a simple entity capable of exact definition but rather a stage in a process—a stage in which a number of concrete factors have combined in a unique way, and which has become relatively independent. However, each stage has been produced and exists only in the closest connection with the other three stages, and can be "defined" only in and through the process of reconstructing it.

I. INDIVIDUAL FORM

Individual form viewed as the first stage of the process of artistic creation has three aspects —form as immediate presence or actual form [*Daseinsform*], significant form [*Bedeutungsform*], and effective form [*Wirkungsform*]. The substratum of individual form consists of the materials used, the means of representation, sense perceptions, and modeling.

All artistic creation begins with the representation of a content (idea, world view) in a specific material (wood, stone, iron, bronze, glass, mosaic, etc.). The material is either present in nature (stone) and needs only readying, or is man-made from raw materials found in nature (glass, reinforced concrete). The artist chooses from the available abundance of materials only one or a few. In this he is guided by those qualities of the material which make it suitable for expressing in a work of art the spirit of an age, i.e., the ideas of the ruling class in a given epoch—qualities such as resistance (hardness, softness), pliancy, heaviness or lightness, transparency, color, smoothness, porosity, absorption or reflection of light, etc. But the artist is confronted not only by a number of qualities among which he can choose and which he can combine in the most various ways, but also by a certain indeterminateness of each. Whether he stresses the heaviness or lightness of a given material, its smoothness or roughness—whether, more generally, he adjusts himself to the requirements of the material or violates them (for instance, by compelling stone to produce the impression of pliancy or by sublimating and eliminating its materiality as such)—all this depends, up to a certain point, on his will, which is, however, determined to a far greater extent socially than individually. The spirit of an age cannot always be clearly expressed in a specific material; on the other hand, the material in which the spirit of an age seeks to externalize itself allows for a certain margin of free play —this margin, incidentally, is greater in the case of natural materials than when the materials are man-made.

Much the same may be said of techniques. Consequently, a technique is not merely an instrumental procedure of the hand, but also a method of the mind. Body and soul are very closely interrelated; for all that, between the extremes of an artist whose mind is all hand (Frans Hals) and one whose hand seems entirely sublimated in mind (Rembrandt), endlessly varied intermediate degrees are possible. Technique without mind is mere virtuoso play; mind without technique is impotent stammering: both lie outside art.

In art the natural or man-made material takes on new qualities—it is transformed into the material of figuration [*Gestaltungsstoff*]. Every material has a natural or artificial intrinsic value, but to serve the purposes of artistic figuration it must incorporate and express the material characters of the things and ideas (or feelings) represented. To create the new and homogeneous type of materiality of artistic form, the artist must use his material in all of its three aspects. The actual material characters of the objects to be represented must be disregarded, and substances as different as water, air, or stone must be rendered in the same material (e.g., paint), but their natural qualities must be imitated and differentiated to some extent. The degrees of such imitation may vary considerably, but it is artistically inadmissible to make imitation an end in itself, to aim deliberately at illusion. On the other hand, exclusion of any suggestion of an object and its physical, material qualities results in mere ornament.

The translation of the material qualities into the working material—either structured (stone, wood) or unstructured (pigment)—is further complicated by the circumstance that in art objects are not represented for their own sake, but as vehicles of feelings and meanings whose origins are personal, social, and religious. As such they have an immaterial existence; but when represented in the working material they acquire a material character. In their turn, the objects with which they are associated and which serve best to represent them acquire a certain nonmaterial character. This spiritual kind of substance may be sensuous, emotional, intellectual, or religious, transcendental, pantheistic. The working material has now been transformed into the artistic material, which embodies objects and meanings in close, indissoluble unity.

This transformation can be effected in various ways. Early Egyptian sculpture stresses the intrinsic qualities of stone (resistance, heaviness, rigidity, etc.) and links them directly with a meaning (often transcendent), whereas the material qualities of human figures (skin, etc.) are largely ignored. Some Gothic sculptures largely destroy the intrinsic qualities of stone in order to render the immaterial, spiritual, mystical element as directly as possible. In many Greek sculptures the surface of the object represented is differentiated, its material characteristics are brought to life, and are thus treated as equal or superior to the intrinsic qualities of both the stone and the feelings expressed.

But whether we are dealing with co-ordination, subordination, opposition, or interpenetration, in every case, even at this stage of constituting the material quality, a method is needed which concretizes the existing possibilities and transforms multiplicity into unity. Very different artistic materials can be made of the same raw material; but the function of the method becomes more apparent when several materials are used. Thus, in baroque architecture the combination of stone, plaster, and painting, and their different uses from floor to ceiling serve to give visible expression to the process of dematerialization, spiritualization so characteristic of Counter-Reformation art. Similarly, the abundance of materials used in baroque altars relativizes each individual material, and thereby spiritualizes materiality as such. Consequently the artist is not concerned with materials for their own sake—no material is inherently right—he is concerned only with methodically interrelating the three different types of materiality.

The next step in the creative process is the constitution of the means of representation. In the visual arts they are color, light/shadow, and line. Each of these elements can be varied endlessly. Here the term "color" does not refer to pigment but to the elementary colors and their combinations.

The means of representation may remain constant while the materials (stone, wood, bronze, glass, pigment) vary. Common to both is that they supply the material from which the work of art is formed and realized, just as the tree is formed from wood and the human body from flesh and bone, or cells. The difference between the two is that from the artist's point of view the material is inert and passive, whereas the means of representation are active, full of living possibilities. The tension between the material substance (discussed above) and the immaterial substance (of which more below) is of the greatest importance. Attempts have been made to deny it by ascribing direct expressive value to colors. But experience has shown that while at best an individual color has a certain tendency to a specific expression, this tendency is realized in different ways by different persons, including artists. Consequently, whenever the means of representation are divorced from the working material and the objective material qualities are not given their due, the result is not a less grossly material, more spiritual, more sublime, purer artistic material, but one that is vaguer, more indefinite, less complete. The artist must interrelate the two types of material, and thus create the definitive artistic material of his work.

Before going into this, however, we must consider the inner richness of the means of representation themselves.

In dealing with color we have, to begin with, the scale represented in the rainbow— red, orange, yellow, green, blue, and violet—which consists of simple and compound hues. The artist may use them in their pure form as local colors, and strengthen or weaken their intensity by relating them to the so-called achromatic colors, black and white, which he treats both as colors and as extreme degrees of light. This gives rise to neutralized groups of colors opposed to the local colors—one group that is more or less dark (gray, brown), and another more or less light (pink, flesh, straw-yellow, pale green, sky-blue). The weakening of specific intensity can be pushed so far that the color is merely a degree within the light-and-dark scale. But even the rainbow hues possess different spatial values, i.e., one color in relation to another may recede, come forward, or remain station-ary. This function can be supported by the warmth or coolness of the color, by its brilliance or dullness, by its quantity, which may vary from a dot to a spot or larger area. When colors follow one another in the same order as in the spectrum, their interplay acquires a dynamically continuous character; otherwise they have a discontinuous, abrupt character. Use of complementary colors (red and green, blue and yellow) results in an unstable equilibrium (analogous to the balance resulting from use of the golden section).

The scale of lights and shadows discloses a similar variety of elements, functions, and possible combinations. This scale ranges from extreme brightness to complete darkness; the intermediate degrees may be diminished brightness or increased darkness. Furthermore, light may be porous or nonporous, brilliant or dull, warm or cold, soft or hard, intense or mild, glowing or reflected, chromatic or achromatic. Various combinations of these factors produce different spatial (receding, forward-moving, static) and expressive functions. In both cases the functions may be strengthened by the quantitative factor (which may increase from a point of light to a large luminous area) and by the type of combination involved. The latter may consist in contrast (bright on dark, dark on bright), uninterrupted transition, or shift from middle tones to either extreme, and so on.

The countless qualities inherent in any single means of representation, even in isolation, are always linked to space. This is particularly true of line. It may be straight or curved, it may tend from the straight to the curved and vice versa, or the two types of line may be contrasted, in tension with each other, or interpenetrating. A line may break off abruptly or extend to great length, it may be strong or weak, it may change from definite to indefinite. It may be directionless and static, combine several directions, or continue in one direction slowly or rapidly. It may remain in one plane or perform a spatial function. It may serve as boundary to a form or have its own ornamental value.

Color, light, and line are first of all qualities which our senses apprehend in the outside world. In "nature" they occur in undifferentiated unity, i.e., color, light, and line do not appear in isolation; our senses respond to certain properties of the outside world by a mixture of the three, which only the intellect breaks up. The content of this mixture is determined on the one hand by the things themselves, and on the other by our consciousness, by our attitude, and by the degree of our attention. Correspondingly, this determination is arbitrary and variable. To replace contingency by necessity, man breaks up the undifferentiated unity into its components. This enables him to contrast them with one another, and to develop each of them into a specific function. Line defines volume, light emits vibrations, color yields qualities. These distinctions are entirely relative, for there is no such thing as a means of representation a priori, outside the creative act. Light can be used to define volume, and line to represent light vibrations. In addition, the variations of all three means of representation are governed by the same categories of intensity, quantity, etc., and this facilitates their correlation when they are determined and concretized in accordance with an idea or central feeling. These stages of breaking up, differentiation, and the corresponding concretization transform the matter of sensation into means of representation.

Our analysis has shown that each means of representation, besides a variety of qualities (and functions), also allows for a variety of possible arrangements, i.e., methods. These are now employed for the purpose of interrelating the means of representation and transforming them into means of figuration. In this process the tasks to be performed by each means of representation are taken into account and their differences are preserved but at the same time integrated into a higher unity. The extent to which a specific value is preserved or integrated depends on the method employed. In Rembrandt's paintings the dominant element is light oscillating between infinitely small differences, but his whole development as an artist is marked by his effort to absorb color into this mystical light so that color blazes up determinate from a general indeterminateness, and to render volume without tracing its boundaries, but solely by the subtle play of lights. On the other hand, in early Gothic stained-glass painting color is dominant, and correlated with it is a boundary line in another material, whereas light is suggested by brighter or darker areas within a given color. Whether the various means of representation blend, are contrasted in pairs, harmoniously co-ordinated, or whether two of them are subordinated to a third—in every case we are dealing with a specific method of unification. Absolutization of any one means of representation discloses a preponderance of biological or ideological interests over specifically artistic ones.

This occurs less frequently, however, than is asserted by some art historians who, with their mania for alternatives, insist that a style must be either linear or painterly. If line predominates through Ingres, color is always compatible with it; and those who call Degas primarily a draftsman can have no eye for his colors. It is fundamentally erroneous to maintain that light is employed at the expense of color, color at the expense of line, and so on. On the contrary, only through their reciprocal tension does each unfold its specific value, thus permitting each means of representation to yield its full inherent potentialities. Color, line, and light have different functions in the act of figuration, but they are all equally important for the constitution of the material that makes up the substance of artistic form.

The two processes we have studied separately—(1) given material into working material into material of figuration, and (2) sensory quality into means of representation into means of figuration—are actually simultaneous and closely interrelated; together they result in the constitution of what might be called the matter of art. The relative share of either may vary, but the variations are subject to the requirement that the immaterial component must serve to animate the material one, and the latter must serve as substratum to the former. Failure to meet this requirement results in pseudo-art, a painted world view devoid of artistic vitality (Hodler, Böcklin, Puvis de Chavannes, most abstract artists). In Romanesque architecture (hall churches, domed churches, basilicas) the two components are contrasted: whether light converges inward or flows out into the infinite, it is independent of the structure and the working material (or the material of figuration) employed: the immaterial paths of the light composition divert the attention of those entering the church from the rational structure. In Gothic architecture (Chartres, for instance), the two components are fused: the light refracted by the stained-glass windows is itself the material of construction, so that the stone becomes largely dematerialized. Thus a median gravity is produced, a median degree of light, a subdued color, an atmosphere that is both material and immaterial, but in which light plays the leading part, so that the alternation of columns and pillars, which has lost its structural meaning, serves to differentiate the refracted light and to animate the vibrations of the atmosphere.

Even within a single technique, e.g., painting, there are as many types of artistic material as there are methods of artistic figuration—indeed, as many as there are artists. The material is not something extraneous, accidental, noninherent, but something necessary, essential, for nothing has artistic existence without being manifested in artistic material. "That artist will be the most excellent in his genre whose inventiveness and imagination are, so to speak, directly fused with the material in which he has to work."[3]

Originally our various senses were one single sense, which was gradually differentiated under the continuous pressure of the outside world. Some of our senses (smell, taste) have not, so far, served as direct vehicles for art. The verbal arts and music depend on auditive sensations; in the visual arts all contents and forms depend on optical, tactile, and motor sensations—the first are dominant in painting, the second in sculpture, the third in architecture.

When we see things at a distance, our sensations are primarily optical; when we see them from close by we become aware of tactile sensations, and when we move toward them, of motor sensations—being more or less intense according to whether the transition is abrupt or gradual. We become aware of optical-motor sensations of another kind when we look at a painting that portrays not a given place at a fixed moment (e.g., many impressionist works) but one whose content compels our glance to move across the picture which may be lit from opposite directions (east-west, north-south) on each side, thus claiming to show the light of a whole day (many old paintings, e.g., Poussin). Some works

---

3. [J. W. Goethe, "Material der bildenden Kunst," in *Der Teutsche Merkur* (October 1788); *Gedenkausgabe der* *Werke, Briefe und Gespräche*, Vol. 13 (Zurich, 1954), p. 60.]

even suggest sensations that cannot be evoked directly in the visual arts: some of Holbein's series of the Passion[4] suggest noises, Courbet's seascapes, the taste of salt, Monet's landscapes, the movement of the wind, etc.

The tactile sensory qualities are similarly differentiated according to whether we are dealing with concavity or convexity, horizontality or inclination, roundness or pointedness, roughness or smoothness, etc. We may also distinguish pure tactile qualities (grasping, touching) from tactile-motor qualities (stroking, fingering) and from tactile-optical qualities (distant view of a sculptural relief).

Particularly rich are the motor sensory qualities such as we experience when we walk around a solid body (a sculpture in the round or a small edifice such as the Petit Trianon) or an empty space (in a cloister where our imagination is additionally stimulated by the contrast between the covered arcade and the open garth); when we move on the same level along a straight line from church entrance to altar, or from the center of a circular room to the wall, or along a curve (in an apse to see the chapels) or on different levels (ascending, turning, descending on a single staircase or on one of two separate or convergent staircases). In addition, there are differences in the motion itself, including its suspension, which may be of short duration (when we approach a Doric temple) or prolonged indefinitely (when we contemplate the façade of a Gothic cathedral).

Optical, tactile, and motor sensations are interrelated in works of art that combine architecture, sculpture, and painting. Such works are achieved by various cultures at the height of their development. For example, the façade of a baroque church does not invite motion into depth; it is a high relief with strongly contrasting tactile-motor movements that lead to optical-motor sensations. But the moment we enter such a church we become aware of the third dimension. The motor sensations associated with walking, however, are immediately arrested and transformed into motor-optical sensations: the movement into depth gives way to the image of the altar on which our glance concentrates, while the motor sensations referring to circular and peripheral motion remain in tension to the image. There is also an impulse to raise one's glance upward, past architectural elements and sculptures, to the deceptive space of the ceiling which suggests infinity.

The place in history of such unities as the Gothic cathedral or the Doric temple proves that the richest artistic sensibility was achieved not in periods of pure sensualism, but in periods in which sense perceptions were most readily combined with the other human faculties of cognition—the body, the intellect, and Reason. Even pure sensualism is rarely confined to only one kind of sense perception; it seeks to achieve its own type of completeness by expressing all kinds of sensation by means of one sense organ, so that pure seeing may activate all other sense organs. Furthermore, the sensory qualities themselves are modified as they combine with other human faculties. The optical sensations charac-

4. [Eight oil paintings on themes of the Passion in the Basel Museum.]

teristic of Van Eyck—who aims at expressing the density and resistance of bodies (Courbet and Cézanne also do this occasionally)—differ from those of Ingres, who brings the abstract intellect into play, and from those of Rembrandt, who gives visible expression to a certain type of Reason. The possibilities of differentiation are very numerous: Reason has various contents, and the intellect is capable of various operations.

A sensory quality may be associated with several human faculties. In *The Virgin and Child with St. Anne* Leonardo da Vinci embodies an idealistic conception of Reason in sensory qualities, which are most fully expressed in the shoulder line. Certain early twelfth-century sculptors stress the corporeality of their supernatural figures. In Giorgione's *Concert Champêtre*, corporeality, sensibility, intellect, and a pantheistic Reason are harmoniously balanced.

The sense perceptions evoked by a work of art differ in many respects from natural perceptions. They are more authentic, more immediate, more numerous; they are not compounded of memories, emotions, and subjective purposes to the point of losing sight of their object; they are unified within an encompassing spatial whole where they move in all dimensions; they are clearly associated with spiritual meanings. Actual form becomes significant form. But it would be false to assume that this has been achieved solely by the greater keenness of the eye or by the working of the intellect. The history of seeing can never be the history of art, because in certain arts the eye plays only a subordinate role (e.g., in architecture), and because art makes use only of such sensory qualities as are invested with specific feelings or ideas (usually those of the ruling class). This is equally true of methods of seeing. Only because sense perceptions become relativized under the influence of other human faculties (all of them or as many as possible) are they freed from their own materiality as well as from the materiality of the other faculties; only because they thus transform their materiality into pure intensity can they be unambiguously correlated with the inner sense, with feeling. Art is not produced by an isolated faculty but by the intimate union of all faculties, and the faculty that plays the dominant role is feeling. It is this process of assimilation and integration that transforms sense perceptions into aesthetic feelings, which are, so to speak, the inner aspect of perceptions.

In aesthetic feelings it is not an individual emotion but rather feeling as a whole, in its undifferentiated unity, that refers to an external suprapersonal power, e.g., fate (tragedy and comedy), to the point of absolute indifference and balance (beauty), to God, or to a specific historical situation. Just as different as the metaphysical points of reference are the types of relationship achieved. This gives rise to categories of feeling, each comprising a number of different particular feelings and imprinting upon all of these the same general character of the sublime, the extreme, the passionate, the harmonious, or the religious. One and the same emotion (love, jealousy, ambition, etc.) may take on an entirely different character according to the category under which it is subsumed.

Thus we have two aspects of pure inwardness—the sensory and the categorial-spiritual. The tension between them determines the nature and development of aesthetic feeling. As the feeling is externalized, it loses its own materiality, it ceases to be unobjectivized sentimentality. By being related simultaneously to a suprapersonal universal power and to an individual sense-percept, the feelings become relatively independent of individual emotional experiences, i.e., become aesthetic. They can be embodied—in terms of the categories—in auditive or optical sense material. There are tragedies not only in the verbal arts (dramatic epic) but also in painting (Poussin's *Winter*, Plate XX), in sculpture, and even in architecture (Temple of Poseidon at Paestum[5]).

History teaches us that specific categories of feeling are expressed in different ways in different epochs. For instance, catharsis, which is the main component in ancient tragedy, is absent from the tragedies of Racine and Corneille. It is possible to distinguish three epochs of aesthetic feelings according to whether they are associated with a religious power, with a power which is partly transcendent and partly immanent in relation to man, or with the earthly totality which includes nature, the soul, and society. Romantic irony resulting from the confrontation between the infinite subject and a finite object (e.g., in Daumier's caricatures) reflects the decline of religion after the French Revolution, the fall of Napoleon, and the frequent changes of government in France, all of which accelerated the relativization of values as judged by an ideal imagined as unchanging.

Thus the aesthetic feeling, like everything else pertaining to art, has a historical and a normative aspect. Viewed historically, works of art very different in content may have in common a fundamental attitude toward the world, which is determined by the degree of freedom achieved at a given stage of human development; feeling produced by this attitude reflects the manner in which the needs of the ruling class under given historical conditions are satisfied.

Now, the artist separates this feeling from its rational base (reflecting the extent to which man controls his destiny) and confronts it with the irrational component of the historical attitude (reflecting the existence of an uncontrolled sector of the world). The conflict between the rational and irrational aspects modifies the feeling—the antithetical elements diverge, each becomes more pronounced, or else they draw closer to each other. The pleasure derived from the mere satisfaction of a need gives way to a more sophisticated pleasure which involves a higher degree of freedom from material wants. The transformation of the historically conditioned feeling from the feeling of satisfaction to the aesthetic feeling is gradual and goes through many stages—from the sad to the tragic, from the gay to the comical, from the pleasing to the beautiful, from the peaceful to the idyllic.

5. [Cf. Max Raphael, *Der dorische Tempel, dargestellt am Poseidontempel zu Paestum* (see Bibliography, 1930).]

These degrees in the evolution of aesthetic feeling show that it is neither purely stationary nor purely dynamic—it reflects a creative process, an interplay between subjectivity and objectivity resulting in a type of reality *sui generis*, with a character of necessity inherent in it.

What has not been transformed into aesthetic feeling—ideas or materials, beliefs or techniques, speculation or crafts—can never be the matter of genuine art, but only of an art-substitute, however valuable this substitute may be as such. When we speak of a "beautiful" natural object or of a "tragic" historical event, the terms "beautiful" and "tragic" have only a metaphorical meaning.

Aesthetic feelings may be entirely expressed in terms of sensory qualities, and conversely, sensory qualities may serve only as a means to express aesthetic feelings. This is not to say that aesthetic feelings and the senses are mutually exclusive; on the contrary, differentiation of the sensibility implies differentiation of aesthetic feelings and enriches it.

Apart from material and content, artistic form is always a spatial structure: it is an element, a vehicle of space, it animates and creates space. Generally speaking, it involves the combination of the two dimensions of the plane with the dimension of depth. In painting, the two-dimensional surface is given and depth must be achieved indirectly; in sculpture, the three-dimensional body is given and the plane must be introduced to achieve the relative independence of individual views. This final stage in the process of constituting the form involves two closely related operations—modeling of individual forms and structuring of the artistic space. Modeling and structuring are of course inseparable from the constitution of materials and contents.

Modeling of individual forms begins with positing a peak or ridge of some sort (for instance, the brightest light in Leonardo's paintings) and from there proceeds into depth. Internal units are formed by grouping together the triads of light, dark, and intermediate tones, or of local color, brightening, and darkening. This last group is particularly evident in the stained-glass windows of Chartres, where the internal triadic unit is stressed by the outer boundary, determined by the size and form of each piece of glass with its lead frame. What is important here, however, is not this stressing of the outer boundary, but the fact that lateral, upper, and lower boundaries lie in different planes, for this alone determines the structural tension of the form. The distances between the boundary planes are less important than the degree of tension produced between them. If, as Cézanne had it, the form is modeled after one of the basic geometric shapes (sphere, cone, and cylinder), the tension between the planes is perceived more clearly and sharply. This is a compositional means in the constitution of individual forms.

Modeling of individual forms can be avoided either by keeping the means of representation homogeneous and uniform over broad areas or by breaking them up into parts so small (dots or commas) that they cannot be further differentiated. In the former case (e.g., Gauguin) we run the danger of introducing, side by side with decorative surfaces, a discontinuous and purely naturalistic perspective, for colors and tones have spatial functions, and pure uniformity cannot be achieved. In the latter case (impressionism) we obtain a space without bodies, a depth dimension without substance, a space without structure. Cézanne probably had in mind both cases when he said: "I shall never accept the absence of modeling and modulation, it makes no sense."[6] These are extreme cases.

If we wish to avoid such unilateral treatments, we are faced with the task of structuring the artistic space as a whole at the same time as the individual forms, so as to set the boundaries of the modeled forms in different planes. Structuring includes the following steps:

1. The space is articulated into its dimensions and these into their directions.
2. Into this static system of co-ordinates a displacement is introduced (e.g., the distinction in Greek sculpture between the supporting leg and the relaxed leg). This produces a tension between the energy of the displacement and the inertia of the static system. In this way the differentiated space becomes uniformly activated from a center.
3. The dimension of depth is broken up into a series of planes parallel to the picture plane, which are separated by equal or unequal intervals.
4. One of these planes is chosen as the axial plane; the others are situated behind it or in front of it. This produces a tension between the planes—a tension which holds them together and makes possible a degree of continuity. What matters here is not the magnitude of the intervals between the planes, but the degree of tension.
5. A similar differentiation and centralization is carried out by horizontal planes (for the width) and vertical planes (for the height). The resulting tensions make possible an internal limitation of the space. Its outward form is defined by boundary planes; the frontal and rear planes parallel to the picture surface are of especial importance.
6. Inclined and curved planes and lines introduced into the rectangular system strengthen the continuity.
7. If the planes parallel to the picture surface are set wide apart, the dimension of depth becomes predominant, i.e., the objects seem situated at different depths separated by intervals. To secure continuous development into depth the apparent dimensions of objects and the intensity of colors are decreased in accordance with laws which must be indicated.

6. [Quotation not traced.]

This breaking up of depth into planes which are separated by empty intermediate spaces must not be confused with perspective. Perspective is an attempt to organize depth rationally and scientifically, and hence it is as neutral in relation to art as, for instance, anatomy. It achieves a certain unity in the development of depth by referring to a vanishing point, but it closes the space outside the picture in the infinite distance and builds up the space from corporeal planes. Perspective becomes artistically significant only when it is combined with modeling and structuring. However, modeling and structuring are present even when there are no marked intervals between the planes, let alone perspective, for instance, in Persian rugs or early Gothic stained-glass windows.

Our description of the basic steps in the structuring of artistic form might give the impression of a rigid schema which can be applied uniformly to all subjects and to works of all epochs. But our description is abstract only because it covers a great variety of historical and methodical differences. Because modeling of individual forms is inseparable from the material and means of figuration, essential differences at once arise according to whether the artist models predominantly with pure colors or with tones. In the verbal arts, since the unifying form of auditive material is succession rather than juxtaposition, time comes to the fore instead of space, and what corresponds to modeling here is the punctual present, the point of transition between past and future. Precisely for this reason we must not repeat the mistake made by Lessing and already refuted by Goethe, which consists in absolutizing this difference and eliminating time from the visual arts or only from the structuring of their forms. In the visual arts time is expressed in, among other things, the number of planes parallel to the picture surface and the types of connection between them, in the ratio between concentration and diffusion of these as well as the vertical and horizontal planes, in the quantity of movement in the space-activating means, etc.; the way time is related to space markedly distinguishes the various types of structuring.

Other differences in the visual arts are produced by the degree of isolation of individual forms, by the differentiation of space into dimensions and directions, by the degrees of tension achieved between them, by the magnitude of distances between the planes, by the kinds of connection between them (continuous or discontinuous), etc. If we compare the function of the motif of the supporting leg and the relaxed leg in Greek sculpture with the part it played in the renaissances of the thirteenth, fifteenth, and sixteenth centuries, we find that at the turn of the fifth and sixth centuries B.C. this motif served to activate the space—a self-produced and self-sustained activation, a self-positing and self-renewing tension between spatial dimensions, directions, and movement. In the Middle Ages the motif marked the degree of man's freedom in relation to the stone block and to the transcendent powers, and still later, in the sixteenth century, it was a factor in the computation of balance, the measure of fluidity as against rigid stability. These different functions of the same motif are at the basis of various types and various degrees of activation of space. Whereas qualities form a system of things, degrees form a hierarchy of values. The various methods employed in structuring artistic form thus have a twofold significance, one descriptive, the other normative. Summing up, we may say that each of the elements of modeling and structuring listed above is inherently complex and allows for many types and variations. Without a guiding idea (feeling), the artist, although he is historically determined and hence subject to limitations, would be lost in a labyrinth of possibilities; but the guiding idea can be realized only with the help of a method of choosing and combining the most suitable elements of modeling. There are countless such methods.

It is precisely the crucial importance of modeling that accounts for its great variety. Every epoch has several characteristic types of modeling, and a single artist can develop several methods of his own, as Giotto did between 1304 when he painted the frescoes of the Arena Chapel and 1317 when he decorated the church of Santa Croce.

Up until now we have proceeded as if the artist's only purpose were to embody an immaterial complex content in a permanent visible form which exists in itself with its material, sensory, spatial, and temporal boundaries. But the form has also an existence "for others," it is not meant to exist only "in itself." This being the case, it would be as variable and contingent as any sense perception if the artist did not see to it that his work is perceived as he intends it to be. He does not merely reproduce the actual form, but creates an effective form. The means he uses are not limited to so-called optical corrections intended to eliminate or to emphasize certain distortions and foreshortenings (which reflect the ideology of a given epoch) that are effected by the eye in the completed work. He must take into account far more than that—the viewer, the size of his body, his eye level, his sense organs, and his psychic reactions must be drawn into the process of structuring the form.

To begin with, the image is set in an unequivocal relation to our body by certain clues—line of vision, meeting line, viewing distance, and guiding line (see Plate XXV). The first runs parallel to the level of our eyes and separates view from above from view from below. Its fundamental importance is illustrated by the height of the capital of the Doric temple. If the line of vision lies very high (e.g., Le Nain's *Peasant Family*, Plate XXVI), the glance is directed downward and suggests oppression, unfreedom; if it lies very low (as in many paintings by El Greco) it has an uplifting effect; when it is visibly and measurably displaced downward from the center of the picture (e.g., Leonardo's *Last Supper*) it suggests collapse. The meeting line runs parallel to the vertical axis of the human body between the eyes; its ratio to the horizontal and its absolute length measure the path from top to bottom; it furthers centering when present and diffusion when it is omitted. The viewing distance determines the optimal distance of the work from the viewer, the point from which the work is intended to be seen and the tempo with which the depth of the picture is disclosed.

In addition to these three lines which determine the sum of sensory stimuli in relation to our body—we may call them lines of orientation—there is a group of others which determine sense perceptions in reference to the physical shape of the artistic material. As soon as the latter has taken on an outward shape defined by a geometric figure (straight, curved, rectangular, cylindrical, etc.), its absolute measurements and the arithmetic ratios of its elements, a number of privileged points and lines are disclosed. In a rectangle, for instance, these are the horizontal and vertical axes, the diagonals, and the lines of the golden section. They have a tendency to specific expressive values: the axes emphasize the static elements, and hence the deviations from the static; the diagonals have a dynamic character, they converge and diverge; the golden section produces a balance between statics and dynamics, a unity in the multiplicity of division because the smaller part is to the larger as the larger is to the whole. This does not of course imply that these or similar lines could create art, but that they can be compatible or incompatible with the contents to be expressed, and that the artist must choose them in such a way as to avoid discordance and to achieve concordance and emphasis. Between the use of geometric lines with a minimal number of intersection points and the total disregard of such lines, which strengthens the impression of diffuseness, there are many intermediate degrees. The degrees are very numerous because the system of privileged geometric lines may entirely, partially, or not at all coincide with the system of orientation lines. The choice among all these possibilities is determined by the artist's method.

The artist can indicate his choice by a guiding line (see Plate XXV) along which the eye is intended to see the picture, and which directs the viewer in the system of privileged lines. The guiding line may coincide with one of the privileged lines or, independently of them, with the motif. Here too the artist is confronted with many possibilities, among which he must choose or invent the one most suitable to the content. Once again, the method is decisive.

The fact that the artist creates not merely actual form but effective form and that only the latter achieves a character of necessity is also apparent from the co-ordination of means of figuration with aesthetic feeling and its concretizations. Every color has a specific expressive tendency. Experiments with laymen and statements by artists have shown that this tendency is vague, and that its manifestations vary according to external circumstances, viewers, etc. This vagueness is lessened, however, when individual colors are differentiated in respect of warmth or coldness, intensity, etc., and further when they are combined with other individual colors—thus no purpose is served by ascribing constant supra-individual expressive values to individual colors. The interrelations of all these factors involved can vary from place to place even in a single work; what is crucial is that the artist must steer a middle course between relative expressive vagueness which leaves a margin for extraneous associations and overdetermination of these factors which eliminates the co-operation of the viewer. Only thus can he produce in the viewer his central idea (feeling) with all its implications.

Actual form is descriptive; effective form is suggestive, i.e., through it the artist, instead of trying to convey the contents and feelings to the viewer by fully describing them, provides him only with as many clues as he needs to produce these contents and feelings within himself. To achieve this the artist must act not upon individual sense organs but upon the whole man, i.e., he must make the viewer live in the work's own mode of reality. This is done, among other ways, by creating a distance between the viewer and the work. There are many intermediate degrees between attitudes of aristocratic aloofness and pantheistic fusion. What is common to all of them is that they introduce a new factor—the social, the universally human becomes a constitutive element of the form. But precisely because it is constitutive and not regulative ex post facto, actual form and effective form are not two different things but two aspects of one and the same act; they do not require two different methods. The artist must rather take the effect of the work on the viewer into account or, going one step further, compel the viewer to produce in himself the full import of the work, to renew it again and again. Such compulsion is an essential component of the form-creating process. This is not to say that every work of art achieves this power; it is, however, a question of value, not of phenomenological description.

The extent of the viewer's participation in the work varies. In the case of works that do achieve effective form, we are impelled to view them over and over, re-creating them each time; the process may go on indefinitely. In the case of an inferior work, we feel no such urge. This is how the artist gives a finished work the quality of continuing life: he gives the finite the character of infinity, activating the viewer's own infinite aspirations, awakening them and keeping them awake by certain features present in the actual form itself: tensions between opposites and their resolution.

The actual, significant, and effective aspects of form may be variously interrelated. In Romanesque art, actual form preponderates; in Gothic art, significant form; in baroque art, effective form. In certain Doric temples all three aspects achieve perfect balance and unity (e.g., the Temple of Poseidon at Paestum). Van Gogh, El Greco, and others aim at effective form in the sense of impressiveness, at the expense of actual form. Cézanne aims at effective form in an educational sense, and hence stresses an actual form which includes the significant. Ingres gives us actual form as significant without paying much attention to the effective. Works by pseudo-artists (Böcklin, Hodler, Puvis de Chavannes, etc.) supply only accidental relationships between the three aspects, whereas in genuine works of art the relationships are inherently necessary.

II. TOTAL CONFIGURATION [*Werkgestalt*]

Analysis of form as a process involving multiple variables has shown the following:

1. We do not use the term form to signify abstract relationships such as proportions, symmetry, etc. that can be "applied," but to signify something material and concrete, something with a content and a structure. Such abstract relationships are merely external regulative factors in composition, whereas form is a constituted existent.

2. Every actual form is constituted as effective form.

3. There are various types and degrees of form.

4. The choice of material, means of representation, sensory qualities, and type of modeling, and how these are to be combined, is determined and conditioned by a given content. So far, all we know about content is that it becomes accessible to us in the course of constituting form.

5. What unifies this as yet unknown content and the nascent form, and endows them with autonomous existence, is the method governing the artist's choice and the kind of synthesis he achieves. The fundamental problem of an empirical theory of art is thus neither content *or* form nor content *and* form, but the method by which an artistic form is created for a given content.

Artists will surely have no objection to this formulation of the problem. Rodin said: "If you want to write a good book about me, just study one of my sculptures. All that matters is my method. A work that never came off will suit your purpose better than a good one, for it will show the limitations of my method. Should you be unable to discover my method from study of a single work, then you'll never write a decent book either about me or about art. Of course, art critics write about everything under the sun except art."[7] To Valéry's objection that "it is not easy for a philosopher to grasp that the artist passes almost without noticing from what is called 'form' to what is called 'content' and back again—how for example a type of sentence may occur to him before he has written it down and supplied it with a meaning, or how the idea of a form means to him no more than that the idea is demanding form,"[8] we might reply that from the point of view of method, transition from the one to the other is not only possible but perfectly comprehensible.

Theoreticians, as distinct from artists, might object that our formulation is too abstract, too idealistic. But apart from the fact that a high degree of abstraction is unavoidable in any science, however emotional and sensuous its subject matter, we run no danger of making empty statements, for what we are calling "method" is nothing but

---

7. [Quotation not traced.]   8. [Paul Valéry, "Léonard et les philosophes," *Œuvres I*, Pléiade (1957), p. 1244 *n*.]

the specific way a given content finds form (for others). Although it is a determining force, content is accessible to us only to the extent that the method is progressively concretized in being applied. Quite apart from this, every content has a long history which, in the case of modern works, can sometimes be reconstructed from biographical or historical data, but more often cannot. But this is a historian's problem. For purposes of description, the only relevant content is that which enters into the work directly from the artist's experience. It may embody less than his total experience, but it may also embody more, for only in the act of artistic creation does the content become fully conscious of itself.

If the content is an experience rooted in objective reality, an experience revealed and completed in the process of artistic creation, it cannot be treated as a fixed, ready-made existent, such as might be "recorded" or "imitated." Nor can it be analyzed in purely psychological terms as a temporal process. It can only be viewed at the point where it becomes conscious of itself through the artist giving it form. From the object man wrests its order and essence, but he does this necessarily through the instrumentality of his mind. This instrument is not a pure a priori form that imposes its laws on a formless, chaotic mass of sense data; more generally, mind is not pure form, but both form and content, i.e., it is something unique, subjective, historical, but at the same time constant and universal. Subject and object are not identical, nor are form and content; form and content are found both in the ego and in the non-ego. It is the essence of the process of artistic creation to bring form and content, objectivity and subjectivity, as close together as possible. (Absolute coincidence is unattainable; determining how far apart they are at any given moment is, of course, the function of criticism.)

It follows that method is not some extraneous bond between a ready-made but chaotic content and an a priori form void of content. Rather, method is the life of content in process of achieving form (objectively viewed) and the life of form in process of acquiring content (subjectively viewed). These two processes are simultaneously externalized in the course of artistic creation. Between the extremes of merely external juxtaposition and internal unification, there are many possible methods. Forms and contents differ not only in their natures, but also in the degree of closeness to which they are brought. In every case, the content reveals a structure of its own, i.e., a complex of physical, spiritual, intellectual, and emotional elements. Moreover, an infinite gradation of contents results from the fact that in the course of artistic creation a content is related to the totality of all possible contents. A whole world view may be embodied in one object, and, conversely, one object is chosen and shaped in order to embody it. The series of gradations from the physical to the metaphysical, from the emotional to the logical, is matched by a continuous chain of meanings which range from the subject of the work to its ideational content. Thus "form" turns out to be as rich in meaning as "content." The increasing complexity of content as we move along the chain of meanings is paralleled by the gradation of form from that of the bare category to full artistic configuration. As the synthesis of all opposites, the configuration—the work as a whole—discloses them in individual detail in process of synthesizing them. Phenomenological description of artistic methods enables us to ascertain every intervening stage between pure form and pure content.

In constructing form we have proceeded as though an individual form could be developed independently of the whole of which it is a part. In actual fact, however, individual form is produced at the same time as total form, the configuration: both are created in the closest interdependence, so that some features are common to both and may be discussed in connection with either. This holds true especially of the mode of reality of the work, which must not be confused with the mode of its life, i.e., with the method of the artist's procedure. The act of creating form, we have seen, has an objective and a subjective, a logical and a historical aspect, and the two may be combined and synthesized in various ways. In this act the artist transcends his own personality as well as his subject matter (derived from nature or history), and as a result the mode of reality of his work takes on autonomy in relation to the mode of reality of the outer and inner worlds, being and consciousness; the relative autonomy of the work is a synthesis of the two. This *sui generis* reality may be called "appearance" [in the sense of "illusion"] only with strong reservations; it becomes concrete in very different ways and to very different degrees, and falls between the extremes of the physical and spiritual, materialist and idealist planes of reality.

As an example of one type of method let us take Giotto's (Plates XI, XII). He shows us two worlds: a supraterrestrial world of lightness, freedom, bliss, and infinity, and a terrestrial world of gravity, dependence, sorrow, and finitude. A world of bodies in space, full of antitheses, is related to a spaceless world in which all polarities are abolished. The upper world encompasses the lower, but there is a gulf between them, and we can glimpse the upper world only from the edge of the lower. Despite this leap into transcendence, the two worlds are linked, and happenings in the one correspond to happenings in the other. One channel of communication is the revelation of supernatural phenomena, another the building of a world of entities and essences, which differs from both the sense-perceived and the religious worlds.

Giotto does away with direct connection between God and the physical/psychic realm: he inserts between them a kind of thinking that sets the world off against his consciousness as a reality of its own—a world in which all changes and accidents are reduced to their essential constants, their being and becoming. And with the kind of passion that turns upon itself, this thinking frees content from the stigma of being merely human by ascribing to it a metaphysical reality—i.e., a reality at once material and immaterial. Giotto creates metaphysical forms of pure intuition, the divine Ideas of sensory qualities, the substance and essence of sense perception, and thereby the expression of the immanent presence of God. The world of Giotto's figures is governed by the principle that a thing cannot simultaneously be and not be, which is asserted with Thomist zeal in the face of birth, death, and other physical changes, including the deformations caused by human sensuality and appetite. A one-sided intellectual principle has been raised to the rank of a metaphysical principle of being, the world has been transformed into immutable entities and substances.

Thus, Giotto represents the synthesis between the Christian world of revelation and an Aristotelian interpretation of the ancient world. Other contemporary methods, also historically determined, fused Christianity and Platonism, still others detached Aristotelianism from Christianity, to mention only a few. Although the thirteenth century was less individualistic, more systematic, and more collectivistic than the twelfth, it was none the less free from absolutist uniformity.

The medieval view of the world included three distinct levels which were linked with each other by the divine revelation and the doctrine of Incarnation, on the one hand, by the activity of the human reason on the other. The chief task of the mind in this era was to eliminate the contradictions between faith and knowledge, so as to safeguard transcendence and immanence alike. As feudalism declined, immanence gradually absorbed transcendence, and knowledge, faith—a process culminating eventually in the great rationalistic systems of Spinoza and Hegel. Rembrandt represents a stage in this great development toward a pantheistic world view. Rembrandt's method continuously concretizes a substance, combining antitheses in flux (materiality and immateriality, body and soul, spirit and space) in a self-contained structure suspended between two extremes.

Giotto tried to link together, by a metaphysics of intuited substance, the three worlds (senses, thought, and faith) in a hierarchically articulated unity and totality. By contrast, the impressionist Monet recognizes only one reality—that of the senses. And whereas in Giotto empirical perception was wholly absorbed in universal ideas, as though the world had never been apprehended directly by the senses, Monet addressed himself to the senses alone, and confined the process of assimilation to that which can be perceived by them. By then religion and metaphysics had lost their appeal, and only those intellectual functions were recognized which served directly to differentiate, elucidate, and integrate sense perceptions.

We have discussed the mode of reality and the mode of life of the configuration of the work; we shall now consider its inner and outer form. The elements in analysis of outer form are format and genre. The format is defined by its basic geometrical figure, its absolute magnitude, its quantitative relations, its boundaries, its center, and the privileged lines which depend on the basic figure.

The basic figure may be simple, such as the ground plan of the basilica (cross) or compound, like the arching rectangle of the stained-glass window, the frame of a baroque altar, baroque ceiling painting, etc. It may be bounded by straight lines which form right angles, more or less regular or static, or by a flowing curve bending one way or another (the *trumeau* in the portal of the cathedral of Moissac, Plate XXVII). Such figures reflect the peculiar features of a given historical epoch.

The absolute dimensions of the format are of great importance for the expression. The infinite aspiration of the Gothic cathedral, expressed in its monumentality, could never be developed in a work of small size. The Doric temples of Magna Graecia—if we except the Temple of Zeus in Agrigento—can be divided into two groups according to the ratios (length, width of the building, and height of columns): 60–24–8 (10) meters and 35–15–6 meters. Once Greek tragedies ceased to be trilogies, their content underwent an essential change. Inherent in every individual idea is the right or proper size for its realization, which the absolute dimensions of the format either realize or negate.

No less important are the relative measurements, for instance, the ratio between the two axes of an ellipse, according to whether it approaches the circle or the straight line. As the Gothic cathedral is given a broader base, the earthly dimension is strengthened at the expense of the spiritual one. As the rectangle approaches the square it acquires a certain indefiniteness—Manet employs such a format to express doubt. As to vertical and horizontal rectangles, we find the most pleasing balance between the static and the dynamic when the respective sides are in the ratio of the golden section.

Basic figure, absolute magnitude, and relative dimensions constitute the boundary which must be distinguished from the interior form of the configuration. The boundary determines certain privileged lines and points—for instance, the two axes and two foci for the ellipse, the horizontal and vertical axes, the diagonals and the divisions according to the golden section for the rectangle. The axes may be given varying prominence and meaning. One of the axes (e.g., the vertical) may be intersected by other axes, even when the horizontal axis is omitted entirely. The central vertical axis may be the motif or linked with the motif, e.g., in the *Belle Verrière* at Chartres (Plate XXVIII), Mary's symbolic inclination of the head receives full emphasis because it is the only strong deviation from the dominant vertical axis. Leonardo's *Last Supper* expresses the collapse of a community with the aid of a horizontal axis displaced visibly and measurably downward from the center.

When only one diagonal is used (not balanced by the other), it expresses movement. When both are present and point in the same direction, they result in a play of supports, located at the point where they intersect and diverge. This is their function, for instance, in the *trumeau* of the portal of the cathedral of Moissac (Plate XXVII).

In the rectangle middle axes and diagonals intersect at the center of the format which center is circumscribed by the lines perpendicular to the points of division according to the golden section. The characteristic feature of the golden section is that it not only divides (as in the case of the division into halves or thirds) but it also unites; differentiation and integration are effected in the same proportion ($2:3 = 3:5$ or $3:5 = 5:8$), so that unity and multiplicity are harmoniously combined. Furthermore, all definitely horizontal or vertical rectangles are one-sidedly dynamic, whereas those that approximate a square tend to be static or shapeless. Rectangles whose sides are in the ratio of the golden section, on the other hand, express a living, fluid balance between the static and the dynamic—an effortless union of opposites. The golden section was so important to Dürer, always in search of beauty, that he considered the improved method for computing it, which he learned from Paccioli, an epoch-making discovery. But the very harmoniousness it offers sets a limitation to its usefulness, for in art only that is pleasing which stems from the methodical unity of form and content. Some contents would be destroyed by use of the golden section or permit only a regulative, not a constitutive, use of it.

The three groups of lines have very different expressive values. The main axes form a static scaffolding, a system of centering wherein the dynamic diagonals may meet. The lines rooted in the golden section describe an area around the center of the basic figure. This area is delineated by dividing height and width in both directions according to the golden section and connecting the eight points of division. The resulting congruent rectangle is significant in relation to the amount of its content. If it is filled with objects (as in Corot's *Roman Landscape*, Plate XXV), the picture takes on a melancholy gravity; if, on the other hand, it is relatively unoccupied, the picture assumes a degree of spiritual freedom (e.g., Rembrandt's *Potiphar's Wife* in Berlin, Plate XXIV). All differences come together in unity at the center, which is, at the same time, the starting point from which we assess the pictorial reality against everything outside the picture.

The artist may adapt himself to these formal properties and treat them as objective requirements for the expression of specific psychic contents; he may also ignore them as requirements in order to assert his creative will. By referring them to a minimal number of central points, he gives the impression of a fixed, solid scaffolding, whereas by deliberately disregarding them, he can produce the impression of diffuseness, freedom, and naturalness. He may emphasize now one element, now another, or he can combine the elements at will and relate in different ways the system of geometric privileged lines suitable to his subject with the system of orientation lines. His choices and combinations are derived from his method and his subject.

The shape of the format—its outer boundaries—and its inner form may be in harmony or may clash with one another in many different ways. The outer boundaries may be unaccentuated, nonarticulated, or blurred (as in impressionist paintings, where the openness of the picture leads the eye beyond it into earthly infinity). The boundaries may be stressed in themselves, i.e., as a hairline division between an inside and an outside, so as to emphasize their discontinuity. This is the case with the glass wall of the Gothic cathedral where the exterior buttresses point inward and the cross vault inside presses outward. The invisibility of the connection between supporting and supported elements introduces a specifically Christian irrationality into the rationalism of the Gothic construction. The boundary may absolutely transcend the enclosed form and content, as in the geometric ornamentation of the stained-glass windows at Chartres which depict legends. The boundaries may be different from their content and yet their articulation may determine the inner form so that immanence and transcendence are simultaneously expressed—for instance, in Giotto, where the articulation consists of a special grid (Plate XIV), essentially distinct from any mere division of the pictorial surface into squares. Inner form may imply outer form so that a special pattern for the latter becomes superfluous (Poussin's *Seasons*, cf. Plate XX); or the outer form may take on independent value as expressive silhouette, leaving the inner form a relatively arbitrary filling (Cranach). Here, again, various methods are observable. The historically determined qualitative aspect is linked with the artistically determined normative aspect.

Among the external determinants of the total configuration, specific laws of genre are also important. Each genre has its specific characteristic as well as an element that applies to all the arts. Note that the visual arts and the verbal arts are classified according to different principles: the former include painting, sculpture, and architecture; the latter, epic, dramatic, and lyrical literature. And yet we find examples of epic painting, lyrical sculpture, plastic drama, and painterly epics. The two classifications obviously rest upon the properties of the material. Words may clash with each other, or come together softly or flow on quietly, and these distinctions—contrast, transition, and coordination—may be transferred to the materials of the visual arts. This is why we may speak of dramatic, lyrical, or epic painting, sculpture, architecture. The materials of the visual arts can be divided according to whichever sense perceptions predominate: distant images suggest purely optical impressions, close-up views suggest tactile impressions, and motor sensations lie between the two. The blurring of boundaries where parts overlap, sharp delimitation of fully occupied areas, movement from one element to the other, whether continuous or discontinuous, rapid or slow, over short or long stretches—all these can also be applied to auditory materials. Differences between the materials make possible two different principles of classification, but these do not exclude one another, and may even overlap.

The artist uses format and genre, the external determinants of the over-all configuration, merely as means, and their function is regulative rather than constitutive. For instance, when elements such as the geometrically privileged lines with their symmetries gain the upper hand (as is the case with Hodler), the result is a lifeless schema. In genuine works of art the over-all configuration fully actualizes the potentialities of the individual form from which it is inseparable; concrete determinateness of over-all configuration and individual forms is achieved only through their closest interaction and union. The whole has no reality without its parts, the parts have no function without the whole. The method implied in the individual forms must be fully unfolded and concretized in the over-all configuration: we can understand the latter by studying how the individual forms have been combined into a whole, and how each follows necessarily from the whole.

We speak of an organic or quasi-organic configuration when every individual form is determined by all the others and serves a specific purpose in relation to the whole (Poussin, Leonardo, Houdon, etc.). Such a configuration is self-contained, self-sufficient, speaks for itself—in order to understand it we need not refer to nature or to the artist's personal experiences. It is autonomous, more accurately, has become autonomous as a result of the process of artistic creation. There are, of course, many degrees between absolute autonomy and partial dependence upon the world of things, upon religious or metaphysical realities, subjective emotions, etc.

Nonautonomous configurations may be objective, subjective, or decorative according to whether they remain dependent on the world of objects, on the artist, or on the materials used.

The objective type is illustrated by Monet's paintings: for all their lyricism they remain bound up with the description of a localized atmosphere. In their contents the here-and-now takes precedence over the universal, the momentary over the enduring. Reason and the human body are alike eliminated as cognitive faculties; the intellect serves only to analyze and differentiate sharpened sense perception, and the feeling accompanying it is vague. This reduction is reflected in the omission of modeling: the individual forms shrink to tiny shapeless spots of color, and the pictorial structure is supplanted by a naturalistic aerial perspective. The work as a whole is reduced to a cutout, a narrow channel through which flows the universal atmosphere. Things and atmosphere, object and subject, are not in reciprocal tension, let alone reconciled; the unity achieved is undifferentiated, monistic. Although this monism constitutes artistic form, although the object is grounded in its punctuational unity, this grounding does not go beyond an initial stage, falls short of universal validity. Inasmuch as this type of configuration remains bound up with the world of things it may be called "imitative."

The subjective type of nonautonomous configuration, which may also be called "expressive," aims at rendering subjective intellectual and emotional contents as directly

XXV   COROT. *Isle of San Bartolomeo, Rome.* 1826–28. 10¼ × 16⅛ in.

Looking at the painting we find that Corot has concentrated the left-to-right movement of the viewer's head (path of the eye from margin to center to margin) on the railing of the bridge, thus fixing the line of vision. He has further concentrated the raising and sinking of the head on the meeting line which is located in the steeple as it rises beyond the roofs. Hence our viewing is related to a coordinate system that corresponds to our body; its static character is loosened by a more dynamic line, the guiding line: the curve formed by the two paths of light on the water going through the arches of the bridge. This line begins in the position of the viewer, and this position is determined by the optimal viewing distance.[9]

9. [From Max Raphael's manuscript "Corot: Kunst unter dem Liberalismus: Monographie eines Bildes."]

XXVI   Louis Le Nain. *Peasant Family.* ca. 1640. 44½ × 62½ in.

XXVII   South Portal, St.-Pierre, Moissac

XXVIII *Notre-Dame de la Belle-Verrière*. 12th century.
Stained glass window (upper part). Chartres Cathedral

XXIX Seurat. *Le Chahut.* 1889–90. 67 × 55½ in.

XXX*a*   TINTORETTO. *The Last Supper.* 1547. San Marcuola, Venice

XXX*b*   TINTORETTO. *The Last Supper.* 1555/60. San Trovaso, Venice

XXX*c*   TINTORETTO. *The Last Supper.* 1565/70. San Polo, Venice

XXXI*a*   TINTORETTO. *The Last Supper*. 1580. San Stefano, Venice

XXXI*b*   TINTORETTO. *The Last Supper*. 1594. San Giorgio Maggiore, Venice

XXXII*a* *Synagogue*
(cast; original in the museum of the Cathedral).
ca. 1220. Strasbourg Cathedral

XXXII*b* *Synagogue*. ca. 1230–40. Bamberg Cathedral

and as emphatically as possible, in violation of the inherent laws of things. Whether the contents are biological-voluntaristic (Van Gogh) or religious-mystical (El Greco)—whether we are dealing with Nietzsche or Dostoevski—makes little difference: in every case the contents reflect the isolated individual's attempt to discover the absolute, to grasp the eternal flux. Under the pressure of ever more intense feeling, oppositions and resistances are left out of account. Metaphysical need for expression supplants form with formula, substantial entities with deformations, the comprehensive view with the narrow view. Oppositions, instead of being reconciled, are pushed to the extreme of exacerbation. In sculpture these violations of art's limits are manifested when corporeality is reduced to a minimum, when the dimensions are inflated, when the finite is forcibly raised to the infinite. They are manifested in painting when the barriers between life and art, art and religion, the terrestrial and the supraterrestrial, are torn down, when mystical raptures or collective exaltations are more or less explicitly urged. Excessive preoccupation with the self leads to a state in which the self is obliterated by identifying itself with a divine (or satanic) power—with the Holy Ghost. The artist sees himself as a demiurge; but this very excess strips away meaningful content, richness, and autonomy from the individual form and from the over-all configuration. An individual dominated by an explosive motor energy that stems from "the absence of hesitations, reflections, from the extraordinary simplification of the given intellectual horizon,"[10] cannot create self-renewing life —life continually reborn from its own unresolvable conflicts—but must, in polar opposition to the life of the organism, accept the process of becoming as something given. All he can do is describe its surgings, its ups and downs. But "description" alone, even of the most sublime things, can only yield a fragmentary configuration. It leads to the substitution of formless symbolic meanings for genuine over-all configuration. A dynamism which unfolds spontaneously rather than in response to obstacles consumes itself.

Art is an interplay, an equation of three factors—the artist, the world, and the means of figuration. We have noted what happens when either nature or subjectivity is overemphasized. Comparable overemphasis upon the means of figuration results in the third type of nonautonomy: the decorative type. Here it is the mathematical character of planes and volumes, the substances of the material, the immanent geometric lines and abstract proportions that are stressed: such elements are treated as absolutes, determining form of themselves. So dogmatic an approach results in a sort of materialism or naturalism equivalent in effect to the materialism of imitation or the naturalism of subjective psychology. The unity of space is broken up into a mathematical part and a naturalistic part, the unity of body into an a priori and an a posteriori; modeling is abandoned, and tactile-motor impressions, in so far as they cannot be eliminated altogether, are left to

10. [William] James. [Quotation not traced.]

chance. The specific values of both experience and deliberate will to form are falsified, and reconciliation between them is made impossible. The universal takes on the semblance of monumentality, and the particular gives off the titillations of personal mythology (Giulio Romano, Gauguin, Puvis de Chavannes, Hodler).

Monet, Van Gogh, and Gauguin illustrate the three types of nonautonomous configuration. How vastly different autonomous or organic configuration is can best be illustrated by Cézanne. He combined color, line, and light not to describe reality but to develop the conflicts inherent in it; out of the materiality of experience—he re-creates the structure of the earth, the corporeality of things, the ways they are bound up with the immaterial atmosphere—he has created a conflict of energies that develops into an organic whole governed by its own laws.

In all the instances cited the artist strives to give his work inherent necessity and arrives at some sort of relationship between necessity and chance. But in the instances of nonautonomous configuration necessity is a function of contingency, whereas contingency is a function of necessity in autonomous configuration. The desire to achieve a necessity utterly beyond contingency may have haunted men more strongly when their circumstances of life were more hazardous. The urge, the temptation, must have been great to eliminate the split between subject and object in empirical existence—to reduce space to the plane, the boundary to the simple figure, the variety of compositional forms to repetition, the material to its simplest visible form: in short, to discover the unique, fixed, unchangeable mathematical sign of art, the ornament. When ornament is used as a constitutive element instead of being introduced at a specific place in the work, however, stylization must result and the virtues characteristic of ornament are abandoned.

In Seurat's *Le Chahut* (Plate **XXIX**) the form of the bows on the slippers recurs in every other object—the eyes, the mouths, the mustaches, the hair, the corsets, the folds of the skirts, etc. But this curving line does not possess the mathematical rigidity of a universal sign; instead, it has taken on a singular kind of abstruse vitality. It is not repeated exactly, but rather varied in a number of ways which are determined not by the intrinsic laws of the composition but by taste, by the naturalistic bodies, and by a physical-physiological law of complementary colors, believed at the time to have scientific validity. Genuine ornament is a condensation of a content, so strikingly real that it may be repeated indefinitely (even in a straight one-way direction) without causing boredom.

III. COMPOSITION

Individual form and over-all configuration are united by the compositional means, but the process involves several stages. The artist first constructs for the work a sort of spinal column whose function is twofold: (1) it combines individual forms in such a way that their totality clearly discloses the content, and (2) it serves as the fundamental entity to which all other forms relate by way of preparation or derivation. Thus the artist translates a content into a complex of forms, but this is not possible until the underlying idea (feeling) has been articulated, the subject developed into a meaningful content, and the iconographic motif transformed into the individual idea. This is why the motif cannot and should not be so exhaustively fixed that everything else would have to be grouped around it arbitrarily: for all its determinateness, it must contain the possibility of further development, i.e., it must itself appear as the result of the preceding process and determine the further stages. It must be an act, and as far as possible a self-renewing act. It might be asked whether artistic invention is not hampered by such requirements, considering that there are feelings that cannot be rendered at all or cannot be rendered as a complex of forms. Actually some feelings are so vague, so elusive, so diffuse, that they do not tolerate anatomizing, are not compatible with a spinal column of forms, although they can be translated into visual terms (Monet, Van Gogh, Claude Lorrain). Again, there are others which in being so transformed lose their purity or defy translation altogether (the purely spiritual and mystical feelings). But to the extent that the feelings of pure spirituality (faith) and pure sensuality are freed from their isolation and related to the other cognitive faculties or to other realities, there are ways of expressing them in a motif, though a long historical development may be needed before it can be found. Thus Rembrandt, in his drawing *Joseph Interprets Pharaoh's Dreams* (Plate XVIII), portrayed the miracle by making the space heavy at the top and light at the bottom, i.e., by reversing the law of gravitation in the play of light and shadow. Tintoretto (in his *Last Supper*, in the church of San Giorgio Maggiore, Venice, Plate XXXI*b*), rendered the transubstantiation by gradually dematerializing the heavy, fully rounded bodies in the foreground, arriving at a fully noncorporeal swirl of lights and shadows in which glowing sheaves of fire and the figures of angels hover over the mundane table setting.

The motif has two components, one general, the other particular.

The general component involves sublimation of an undifferentiated rigidity, a shift of interrelated masses such that fluid balance is produced between them. To paraphrase Hamlet: The world is out of joint; the artist's task is to set it right. Examples of this function of the motif are the supporting leg and the relaxed leg in Greek sculpture, and the Gothic capturing of the thrust of the pointed vault by buttresses and arches.

The particular component is a combination of lines and colors that determines a specific expressive value—for instance, the two wedgelike areas in Giotto's paintings (e.g., Plates XI, XII) between the leftward shift of an oval and the rightward shift of a diagonal. The rotating motion which is the motif in many of Degas' paintings (e.g., Plate X) (and inspired the form of Flaubert's *Education sentimentale*) seems to be associated with specific feelings (social pessimism, contempt for the bourgeoisie), which have sociological causes (the periodical crises in capitalist society, "the eternal return"). The geometric figure which the ensemble of forms may assume never exhausts the motif, for it cannot be separated from the methodical unity of the means of figuration without the artist's lapsing into abstract formalism.

The elements of the motif may be related to the privileged geometric or orientation lines in the most various ways, may entirely disregard them or largely coincide with them. In Tintoretto's *Last Supper* mentioned above dematerialization proceeds along a diagonal or, more accurately, in the interplay between this diagonal and the foreground plane. In the *Belle Verrière* at Chartres (Plate XXVIII) the slight inclination of Mary's head receives its accent from the dominant vertical axis. In Leonardo's *Last Supper* the vertical axis, by emphasizing the displacement downward of the horizontal axis, expresses the collapse of community ("Behold, the hand of him that betrayeth me is with me on the table"). But the differences between free and structure-bound motifs are secondary as compared with the combinations between the general and the particular aspects of the motif, the shifting and restoring of balance. One aspect may preponderate, the two may be juxtaposed, one may be derived from the other, and so on—there are as many possibilities as there are methods.

The difficulty an artist experiences in finding the simplest, clearest, and most adequate motif for his individual idea will not be underestimated if we keep in mind that he must discover the individual idea at the same time as he invents the motif. Moreover, his individual idea is the harder to arrive at, the more steeped in tradition his subject matter. It took Tintoretto (Plates XXX, XXXI) almost fifty years, i.e., his entire artistic life, to make the progression from the horizontal table around which Christ and the apostles are grouped in the *Last Supper* of 1547 (San Marcuola, Plate XXX*a*) to the version already mentioned of 1594 (San Giorgio Maggiore), in which he successfully renders the mystery of transubstantiation. Two intervening versions (San Trovaso 1555/60, and San Polo 1565/70, Plates XXX*b, c*) show Christ and some of the disciples making vehement motions either in depth or forward, around a table placed obliquely in the center and surrounded by empty space. What is new is the direct transition from the stillness of unfilled space to figures in motion, and from these to the foreshortened table around which they are grouped, the emotional turmoil placed between the void and the inert object, and the paradoxical attempt to center attention on what is not at the center, but off at one side and partly hidden. Only in 1580, at the age of sixty-two, when he painted the *Last Supper* in the church of San Stefano (Plate XXXI*a*), did it occur to the painter to place the table stretching obliquely into depth, more precisely, along a wall running off into infinity. The new arrangement, however, serves to maintain the unfilled space of earlier versions (the table no longer occupies the foreground) rather than to dematerialize the bodies. Not until the last year of his life did the artist do away with clear delimitations of space (Plate XXXI*b*). Unfilled space is now absorbed by filled space, and corporeality gradually dematerialized; the movements in it are mere functions of the lights and shadows that encompass the terrestrial and the supraterrestrial world alike: these lights and shadows move back and forth between the two. That it can take a whole lifetime to crown an artistic career by the creation of a motif should help us to understand that motifs differ not only in kind but also in quality, according to whether they are arbitrarily posited by the artist or self-posited (founded on an inner conflict). Which is to be the case depends on whether they express the dominant ideas of an epoch in their specificity, totality, and greatest depth, or merely give us a conventional image of them, a sectarian view. Of course, between the extremes of artificiality and spontaneity, between total absence of conflict and self-positing conflict, there are countless intermediate degrees.

Every example shows that the motif is bound up with an individual idea, and that both are produced simultaneously and in the closest dependence upon each other. The characteristics of the individual idea are:

1. It is simultaneously an idea and a feeling.
2. It contains the contrasts between the particular and the general, the individual and the universal, the original and the banal.
3. It is a progression toward ever deeper meanings.
4. It is the nodal point from which secondary ideas and feelings develop. These are the more numerous the broader and more fruitful the original contrast is and they dwindle as the contrast becomes weaker. Occasionally, for religious reasons (as in Egyptian sculpture), individuality is suppressed, while at other times universality is subordinated to the life of nature (as in impressionism). It may also happen that the feeling is insufficiently substantial, not differentiated enough. There are as many possibilities as there are methods.

Much the same may be said on the relation between idea and feeling. The individual idea endows the subject matter with deeper meaning, and gives aesthetic feeling greater determinateness—it dematerializes subject matter and concretizes the aesthetic feeling. Consider the peculiar way, iconographically speaking, the Christian subject of the *Defeated Synagogue* (alongside that of the *Victorious Church*) was treated in the south portal of the Strasbourg Cathedral (Plate XXXII*a*). In terms of aesthetic categories, it expresses the feeling of the tragic. In addition, it reflects the attitude of a woman to whom the conflict between beauty and chastity signified the fate of womanhood as such, and who experiences the loss of chastity as the loss of life itself. The same subject allows of very different conceptions, as we learn when we compare the Strasbourg statue with the contemporaneous *Synagogue* at the Bamberg Cathedral (Plate XXXII*b*).

We might also compare different treatments of the Last Supper. Like all great spiritual texts, the New Testament contains the expression of an unresolvable conflict: Christ has just proclaimed bread and wine to be identical with his flesh and his blood, and immediately adds that one of his disciples is to betray him. The connection between these two statements is not accidental but necessary because the disciples, being mortal and hence essentially imperfect, can receive the sacrament which they so urgently need only through betrayal. Tintoretto refers to the prediction of betrayal as implied by the mystery of transubstantiation. Ghirlandaio, on the other hand, pictures the Last Supper as a final melancholy gathering as the night is falling. Leonardo associates his individual idea explicitly with the betrayal. In his version, the apostles are moving either toward Christ or away from him, and some of them turn away from each other. These movements, which run wavelike through the picture, and the arrangement of the figures in groups of three have the effect of an ironic comment: attention is called to the inner confusion of these men, whose composure has been shattered by a few words from the one unmoved, unshaken Being upon whom they utterly depend. In thus contrasting the disciples' dependence, their need for a Mediator, their inner helplessness with the imperturbability of the God-Man whose inner peace and outer solitude are equally perfect, Leonardo linked the betrayal of Christ with the institution of the Last Supper, the event with the mystery. By realizing the event in its extremest terms, Leonardo disclosed its mythical dimension.

It might be objected that only at the time these artists lived and worked were such diverse conceptions of the Last Supper possible. Christianity had ceased to be universally binding, and its dogmas were undergoing historical modification. This objection overlooks the fact that the class structure of society always leaves room for different individual ideas which reflect the various material interests and the progressive or regressive tendencies of the respective classes. On the other hand, it should be observed that every artist has only a limited store of individual ideas, which he assigns to different subject matters (as Goethe did in *Werther, Tasso, Elective Affinities*, "Marienbad Elegy"). The individual idea is a progression toward ever deeper meanings, and either the outer layer (subject matter) remains constant while the deeper layers change or the other way round. No doubt there is such a thing as an optimal ratio between the narrowness of subject matter and breadth of the individual idea.

Bibliography of Max Raphael's Published Writings

Abbreviations: *DFR*   *Deutsch-Französische Rundschau* (Berlin-Grunewald)
                 DKD   *Deutsche Kunst und Dekoration* (Darmstadt)
                 Kbl   *Das Kunstblatt* (Berlin)

1913   *Von Monet zu Picasso: Grundzüge einer Ästhetik und Entwicklung der modernen Malerei.* Munich, Delphin-Verlag.

1914   "Zur gegenwärtigen Bedeutung der Schiller'schen Ästhetik," *DKD*, XXXIV:5 (August), 339–46.

"Der Tastsinn in der Kunst," *DKD*, XXXV:8 (November), 145–57.

1915   "Die Wertung des Kunstwerkes," *DKD*, XXXVI:2 (May), 84–99.

"Über die Arbeit des Künstlers," *DKD*, XXXVII:7 (October), 61–74.

"Über einige Grenzen der Malerei," *DKD*, XXXVII:9 (December), 203–10.

1916   "Die Ansprüche des modernen Kunstgewerbes," *Innendekoration*, XXVII (February), 63–77.

"Die deutsche Landschaft als malerisches Sujet," *DKD*, XXXVIII:1, 2 (April and May), 57–62; 131–41.

"Die Idee des Schöpferischen," *DKD*, XXXVIII:5 (August), 308–16.

1917   "Über den Expressionismus: offener Brief an Herrn Prof. Rich. Hamann," *Kbl*, I:4 (April), 122–26.

"Das Erlebnis Matisse," *Kbl*, I:5 (May), 145–54.

"Das moderne Museum," *Kbl*, I:8 (August), pp. 225–30.

"Das Problem der Darstellung," *Die Kunst für Alle* (Munich), XXXII:21/22 (August), 418–23.

"Purrmanns Atelierecke," *Kbl*, I:11 (November), 336–40.

1918   "Das Buch mit Abbildungen," *Dekorative Kunst* (Munich), XXVI (March), 176–85.

"Max Pechstein," *Kbl*, II:6 (June), 161–75.

1919   "Alexander Gerbig," *DKD*, XLIII:11 (February), 309–10.

         "Die Gestaltung des Menschen in der Malerei," *Kbl*, III:3 (March), 76–83.

1920   "Ernesto di Fiori," *Kbl*, IV:6 (June), 183 ff.

         "Wiegele und Tscharner," *Kbl*, IV:9 (September), 264–72.

1921   *Idee und Gestalt: Ein Führer zum Wesen der Kunst.* Munich, Delphin-Verlag.

1923   "Über Gustav Wolff," *Der Cicerone* (Leipzig), XV:16 (August), 742–47; also in *Jahrbuch der jungen Kunst* (Leipzig), IV, 190–97.

1924   "Über Johann von Tscharner," *Der Cicerone* (Leipzig), XVI:3 (February), 136–39; also in *Jahrbuch der jungen Kunst* (Leipzig), IV, 293–99.

1930   *Der dorische Tempel, dargestellt am Poseidontempel zu Paestum.* Augsburg, Dr. Benno Filser Verlag.

         "Das Werk von Le Corbusier," *Der Kreis* (Hamburg), VII:15 (May), 286–89.

1931   "Die neuromantische Auferstehung des Mittelalters und der kulturkämpferische Neuthomismus," *Neue Schweizer Rundschau* (Zurich), XXIV:4 (April).

         "Anmerkungen über den Prosastil von Paul Valéry," *DFR*, IV:7 (July), 553–63.

         "Die pyrrhoneische Skepsis," *Philosophische Hefte* (Berlin), III:1/2, 47–70.

1932   "Zur Kunsttheorie des dialektischen Materialismus," *Philosophische Hefte* (Berlin), III:3/4, 125–52.

         "C. G. Jung vergreift sich an Picasso," *Information* (Zurich), No. 6 (December), 4–7.

1933   "Ein Jahrhundert französischer Karikatur," *DFR*, VI:5 (May), 291–303.

         Proudhon, Marx, Picasso: Trois études sur la sociologie de l'art. Paris, Éditions-Excelsior.

         Introductory text (pp. 5–16, *Introduction à une architecture en béton armé*) to an illustrated brochure: *Groupe scolaire de l'Avenue Karl Marx á Villejuif, réalisé pour la Municipalité par André Lurçat, Architecte.* . . . [Paris,] Éditions de l'architecture d'aujourd'hui. No date.

1934   *Zur Erkenntnistheorie der konkreten Dialektik.* Paris, Éditions-Excelsior.

1937   "A Marxist Critique of Thomism," *Marxist Quarterly* (New York), I:2 (April–June), 285–92. Tr. of pp. 157–71 of *Zur Erkenntnistheorie . . .*, 1934.

1938   *La Théorie Marxiste de la connaissance.* Paris, Gallimard. Tr. of *Zur Erkenntnistheorie . . .*, 1934.

1945   *Prehistoric Cave Paintings.* Tr. Norbert Guterman. New York, Pantheon Books (Bollingen Series).

1946   *Marx y Picasso: Los pintores modernos a la luz del materialismo dialéctico, en un estudio sobre la sociología del arte.* Tr. R. Sajon. Buenos Aires, Ediciones Archipiélago. Tr. of two essays in *Proudhon, Marx, Picasso . . .* , 1933.

1947   *Prehistoric Pottery and Civilization in Egypt.* Tr. Norbert Guterman. New York, Pantheon Books (Bollingen Series).

1960   *Teorija Duhovnog Stvaranja Na Osnovi Marksizma.* Sarajevo, Veselin Maslesa. Tr. of *Zur Erkenntnistheorie . . .* , 1934.

1968   *The Demands of Art.* Tr. Norbert Guterman. Princeton University Press (Bollingen Series).

INDEXES

Index of Terms

This index, otherwise selective, concentrates on the author's critical terminology; a number printed in bold type indicates a page where a definition is provided. The symbol ∼ between page numbers means *passim*.

General Index